Dog Days Out

CONWAY
Bloomsbury Publishing Plc
50 Bedford Square, London, WC1B 3DP, UK
29 Earlsfort Terrace, Dublin 2, Ireland

BLOOMSBURY, CONWAY and the
Conway logo are trademarks of
Bloomsbury Publishing Plc

First published in Great Britain 2024

books before they go to print, changes
to such information can occur during the
production and lifetime of a publication.
Therefore, we also advise that you check
with businesses or venues for the latest
information before setting out.

Bloomsbury Publishing Plc does not
have any control over, or responsibility for,
any third-party websites referred to or in
this book. All internet addresses given in
this book were correct at the time of going
to press. The author and publisher regret
any inconvenience caused if addresses
have changed or sites have ceased to
exist, but can accept no responsibility
for any such changes

This book is a guide for when spending
some time outdoors. Undertaking any
activity outdoors carries with it some risks
that cannot be entirely eliminated. For
example, you might get lost on a route or
caught in bad weather. Before you spend
time outdoors, we therefore advise that
you always take the necessary precautions,
such as checking weather forecasts and
ensuring that you have all the equipment
you need. Any walking routes that are
described in this book should not be relied
upon as a sole means of navigation, so we
recommend that you refer to an Ordnance
Survey map or authoritative equivalent.

This book may also reference businesses
and venues. Whilst every effort is made
by the author and the publisher to
ensure the accuracy of the business and
venue information contained in our

A catalogue record for this book is
available from the British Library

Library of Congress Cataloguing-in-
Publication data has been applied for

ISBN: PB: 978-1-8448-6650-2;
ePub: 978-1-8448-6649-6;
ePDF: 978-1-8448-6652-6

10 9 8 7 6 5 4 3 2 1

Typeset in Aestetico
Designed by Austin Taylor
Printed and bound in Thailand by
Sirivatana Interprint

MIX
Paper from
responsible sources
FSC® C103447
FSC
www.fsc.org

To find out more about our authors and
books visit www.bloomsbury.com and
sign up for our newsletters

Dog Days Out

365 THINGS TO DO WITH YOUR DOG IN THE UK AND IRELAND

LOTTIE GROSS

CONWAY

LONDON · OXFORD · NEW YORK · NEW DELHI · SYDNEY

THE CAIRNGORMS,
HIGHLANDS
AND ISLANDS

CENTRAL &
NORTHEAST
SCOTLAND

SOUTHERN
SCOTLAND

NORTHERN
IRELAND

NORTHWEST
ENGLAND & THE
ISLE OF MAN

NORTHEAST
ENGLAND

NORTH
IRELAND

NORTH
WALES

THE MIDLANDS

SOUTHERN
IRELAND

MID
WALES

EAST ANGLIA
CAMBRIDGESH

SOUTH WALES

LONDON &
SOUTHEAST
ENGLAND

SOUTHWEST ENGLAND
& CHANNEL ISLANDS

CONTENTS

INTRODUCTION

We were trudging back from an incredibly soggy walk along the River Dart, having just found our way through the fog and mist atop Bellever Tor, when we spotted it. I say we, but really it was the dog; I was ready to get back in the car to dry off and head back to the hotel for a well-earned pint. He, on the other hand, had other ideas: as I walked on, I felt the lead tug behind me and turned to see him stuck still, frozen like he'd just locked eyes with Medusa, holding one paw off the ground and staring intently at the foliage beside the footpath. He was trembling and utterly immovable – no amount of pulling or cajoling with 'wozzis?' was going to move him, so I leaned in to see what it was that had caught his attention so completely: a tiny dormouse sat hunched over beneath a broad dock leaf along the river path as if sheltering from the drizzle, like a scene from a Beatrix Potter book.

Getting a firm grip on the lead to ensure he couldn't get any closer to it, I stood to watch the little hazel-coloured creature for a minute or so before it scuttled off into the undergrowth, totally unfazed by its interaction with what should be a maniacal rodent-killing machine. Had I not had my scared-of-his-own-shadow Manchester Terrier, whose ratting ancestors would be abhorred by his pitiful behaviour here, I likely would never have seen my first dormouse on that October morning – I was in too much of a hurry to get into the dry. Similarly, had the dog not demanded a 6.30am toilet walk on our first morning in an astonishingly sunny Shetland, I'd have never watched those two otters on the boat slipway pottering about on the shoreline and across the rocks. And in the Lake District, while I was aiming for big fell views and wide watery landscapes, it was his curious nose that held me back for a minute or so, forcing me to examine the moss- and lichen-carpeted rock he was so studiously sniffing, its colours so bright and details so intricate – a little wondrous world of its own that was just as mesmerising as that seen from the lofty viewpoint ahead.

Without our dogs, we'd miss an awful lot – not least their company, of course. And so travelling with your dog, in my opinion, is a must. And while you might not be able to take them everywhere, there are still hundreds (well over the 365 in this book) of places, from museums to castles to caves, where they'll be welcome by your side. Whether it's just a day out you're after, or you want to plan a road trip that the dog can come along on too, the UK and Ireland have plenty to offer, and the dog will help you see it all a little bit differently. I hope reading and using this book brings you as many adventures as we, Arty and I, have had while researching it.

←↑ Arty, the author's Manchester Terrier, enjoys his days out

How to use this book

This book is split geographically by region and within each chapter each entry is ordered from south to north so you can easily find brilliant things to do nearby one another. Most of the places are easy enough to look up on your chosen maps app, but sometimes where I need to reference a specific parking spot for a walk or a beach, I've used what3words to denote the location. The what3words locations look like this: ///travel.with.dogs. When you see one of these, you can find it on the map by visiting what3words.com and putting the three words with the dots in between into the search bar.

Each entry has all the information you need to plan a trip, but to save space I've used symbols to communicate the essential things you need to know. Here's what they mean...

 The **number of dogs** allowed in a property; where there's a + symbol, it means you can negotiate over the phone to take more dogs. (also appears in this format: 🐾2).

 The **number of people** in a self-catering property; where there's a +2 next to it, this indicates extra space for children in bunk beds or sofa beds (also appears in this format: 👤2).

 The activity is **free**.

 This is a **budget** activity and it likely costs less than £10 per person or there is a combined family ticket at a significant discount (also appears in this format: 🪙).

 This denotes a **luxurious hotel** or accommodation (also appears in this format: 🏛).

 Dogs are free to roam **off-lead**.

 There will be **livestock** nearby (also appears in this format: 🐑).

 This is an **indoor** activity.

 There's disabled parking and access for wheelchairs (also appears in this format: ♿).

 This is a great place for families (also appears in this format: 👪).

 You can get here without using a car.

 This place is a brilliant winter break option (also appears in this format: ❄).

 There's an enclosed garden or paddock (also appears in this format: ⛓).

 There are beaches nearby (also appears in this format: ☀).

 There's a charge to bring dogs (also appears in this format: 🐕).

 The average cost per night (also appears in this format: ▬).

What to pack

- **Food** – including their daily meals and a few treats for fun (or bribery).
- **Bedding** – while many hotels and accommodation might offer to provide a bed for your dog, bringing some of their own bedding, such as favourite blankets, ensures they can settle faster and feel more comfortable.
- **Poo bags** – and plenty of them. Nobody likes carrying dog poo around for hours on a walk, so get yourself a Dicky Bag (dickybag.com) or similar so you can keep hiking hands free.
- **Towels** – for those post-walk wipe-downs before you get in the car or inside your accommodation.
- **Spares** – accidents happen, so bring a spare lead, collar or harness, ID tag and bowl in case you leave something behind.
- **Toys** – for entertainment in your accommodation or at mealtimes. Food-dispensing toys, such as Kongs, will keep your dog's brain engaged and give them something to focus on while you're eating in a pub or restaurant.
- **A longline** – for those camping or glamping, a longline is handy for letting your dog roam further without them disturbing other guests or snaffling a sausage off the neighbour's barbecue.
- **A pet first aid kit** – including bandages, Hibiscrub or wound cleaner, tweezers for removing grass seeds or thorns, a tick hook, and antihistamines for insect bites or allergic reactions.

↑ Arty knows he doesn't have to carry all of this...

↓ Travelling with a dog needn't be stressful for either of you

Travel tips

In the car

If you're travelling by car, there are a few rules of the road you need to know – and some hacks to keep your dog happy and safe...

- **Keep them secure** – it's the law. Dogs need to be restrained in vehicles away from the driver, either with a harness and seatbelt/headrest leash, or inside a crate. Crash-tested crates, such as MIMsafe cages (mimsafeuk.com), are the best option for optimum safety.
- **Make it cosy** with blankets or bedding so your dog can easily relax.
- **Take regular breaks** at least every couple of hours to stretch legs and allow your dog to toilet.
- **Avoid stopping** at noisy service stations on motorways and look for rural farm shops or tearooms just off the main roads where you can have a more peaceful break from your drive.
- **Never leave your dog** in the car in temperatures above 22°C (71.6°F); in temperatures below this, if you do leave your dog, always crack a window for ventilation.

Planes, trains and automobiles

Whether you're going by train, taking a ferry or travelling on the bus, taking the dog on public transport can be a logistical challenge, but here's how to stay safe and sane as you go...

- **Avoid rush hour** – peak times can be stressful for dogs as space on trains and buses is limited. Stick to off-peak hours for a much more comfortable ride.
- **Always ask permission** – not all bus drivers are comfortable with dogs on board, so check with them first. The same rule goes for taxis.
- **Pack a blanket** or small, soft mat for them to lie down on so they can feel comfortable on the floor of the train or bus.
- **Bring enrichment toys** or long-lasting chews to keep them occupied and away from other passengers.
- **A portable water bowl** or bottle with a drinking vessel attached is an essential for any public transport journey.

Good dog etiquette

While the UK is a nation of dog lovers – evidenced by the sheer variety of places they're welcomed in this book – not all humans love dogs and while you're travelling, you're likely to come across at least a few people who have no interest in, or perhaps even a mild fear of, your pet. This means you need to be responsible, and you need to teach your dog how to be good in public spaces and social situations. Here's a little etiquette guide for exploring the UK and Ireland with your dog...

- **Be conscious of wildlife** – from seals on beaches to ground-nesting birds in summer, respect the ecology and wildlife in the area you're visiting and keep your dog under control either on the lead or with reliable recall.
- **Don't let them make the first move** – it's all very well if your dog loves attention from strangers, but you must teach them when is an appropriate time to interact. Ensure they don't jump up at strangers or lean in for unsolicited kisses with nearby faces.

- **Respect other dogs** – not all dogs love dogs either, so if you see a dog walking on the lead it's better to be safe than sorry and leash yours, too. Your dog doesn't need to 'say hello' to every single dog you pass.
- **Be cautious around water** – watching your dog splash and swim might be cute, but currents, riptides and swells can be dangerous, and too much time in water can be bad for their joints. Only let them swim when you're sure it's safe, and never let them do so for longer than 15 minutes.
- **Help them settle** – when you're dining out, bring a mat and some long-lasting chews or a toy such as a Kong to keep them busy while you eat. This will stop them from bothering other diners, too.
- **Let them explore** – when you arrive in a new place, such as a hotel or or cottage, take them for a brief sniff about the new environment before checking in. This will help calm them after a long drive and allow them to relieve themselves before heading inside. Make sure they don't cock their leg on walls once they are inside...

Travelling with nervous or reactive dogs

Not all dogs are made equal and some, for whatever reason, are made a little more nervous than others. For many dogs, this can manifest as reactivity, which means they might growl or bark at people, dogs, children or other animals they encounter. Travelling with a reactive dog isn't impossible – it just requires a little more thought and planning. I should know – I've been travelling with my reactive dog since 2020 and we've driven the length and breadth of the UK to bring you this book. Here's what we've learned...

- **Self-catering is king** – for reactive dogs, whether it's humans or animals that are the trigger, picking self-contained accommodation is often best. This means they're less likely to come across other dogs and won't be bothered by the sounds of elevators or other bedroom doors shutting along the corridor.

- **Avoid the school holidays** if possible – when school's out there's bound to be more dogs about, as thousands of families take their holidays during the summer and half-term breaks. If you can, travel in the low or shoulder seasons (winter, autumn and early spring) for a quieter, stress-free break.

- **Go slowly** – the more triggers your reactive dog experiences, the more stressed and uncontrollable their reactions will be, so take it slow. When going into a new situation or location, don't go headfirst into the experience – for example, if you're going to a museum, don't follow the crowds but start at the edges, gradually heading into the exhibition as your dog gets more used to it. Plan time for relaxing and sleeping, too, so they can decompress after a busy day.

- **De-stress them** – activities such as sniffing, chewing and licking can be soothing for dogs, so bring along long-

lasting chews or bones, a LickiMat or a snuffle mat and use them when you're enjoying some downtime in your accommodation.

- **Sit in the corner** – when you're dining out with the dog, ask for a table away from other dogs or in a quiet corner where you're unlikely to be bothered by people or waiting staff walking past too often.
- **Find a field** – don't be afraid to make use of the hundreds of secure dog fields around the UK and Ireland for a stress-free walk or game of fetch. Find one on websites such as dogwalkingfields.com and dogparksnearme.co.uk.

How to find great dog walks in new places

The daily dog walk is one of the greatest pleasures of being a dog owner, but in new places where you don't know the terrain and local byways, it can be something of a minefield. There are plenty of excellent walks recommended in the pages of this book, but here's how to find great dog walks wherever you go...

- **Download the essential apps**, such as the OS Explorer app (explore. osmaps.com), which shows national trails, footpaths and bridleways; AllTrails (alltrails.com); or for Scotland, use the Walk Highlands website (walkhighlands.co.uk).
- **Seek out waymarked trails** so you needn't worry about navigation. Most National Trust properties, official Forestry England/Scotland sites and Irish national parks have waymarked walks you can follow without the need for a map.
- **Just ask** – whether it's in the local pub or your hotel, there's bound to be someone who can give you a great local walking route.

↓ Arty in front of the mountains of Torridon, Scotland

SOUTHWEST ENGLAND & THE CHANNEL ISLANDS

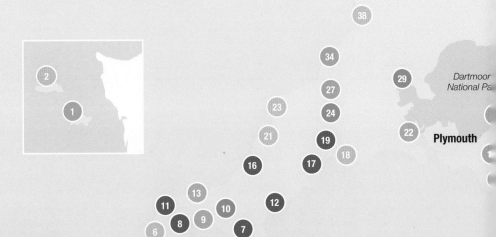

Dartmoor
National Pa

Plymouth

WALK

ST OUEN'S BAY TO GROSNEZ CASTLE ①

Jersey

START POINT: Les Laveurs Car Park, JE3 2FN
DISTANCE/TIME: 4km/1 hr each way

If you can drag yourself away from the sweeping sands and grassy dunes of St Ouen's Bay, a nearly 6.5km-long beach on the west coast of Jersey, there's a wonderful walk to be had along the coast path northwards to Grosnez Castle. Stroll along the dog-friendly sands of the beach before heading up on to the cliffs. North of Route des Havres, a number of paths criss-cross the headland's nature reserve, where relics of military action and even Neolithic remains lie abandoned within the landscape.

You'll pass the ruins of incomplete World War II artillery batteries and a German naval tower as you walk along

Swindon

Bristol

Bath

xmoor
onal Park

New Forest
National Park

Exeter

↑ St Ouen's Bay

the coastline, but the most intriguing is Le Pinacle, just west of the model aircraft field. Wander down off the main path to this important prehistoric site, which includes evidence of Neolithic, Chalcolithic, Iron Age and Bronze Age

settlements, as well as a Roman temple.

Heading north, you'll eventually reach the former medieval fortress of Grosnez. Dating back to 1330, all that remains of this once-French stronghold is a perfectly poised pointed arch and a few walls and staircases that look out over the rocky cliffs and endless ocean views.

Need to know: Dogs prone to chasing should be kept on the lead around cliff edges.

WHAT'S FOR LUNCH?
Stop for seafood on the cliffs at Faulkner Fisheries (faulknerfisheries. com) at the northern end of St Ouen's Bay.

GRANDES ROCQUES BEACH

Guernsey

One of the few beaches on Guernsey that's dog-friendly year-round, Grandes Rocques is a beautiful crescent of white sand on the north-eastern coast of the island. Rocky outcrops provide a vantage point from which to survey the entire stretch and perhaps spot marine life in small rockpools, while on a small promontory to the north lies a relic of this island's military history: Grandes Rocques Fort. Built in the late 1700s and once fitted with 24 powerful guns, it's now a ruin ripe for exploring with the dog.

Make a night of it: The Duke of Richmond Hotel is a regal spot in St Peter Port, just 15 minutes' drive from the beach, welcoming dogs with treats, toys and water bowls. dukeofrichmond.com

🐕1 <£300

Parking: GY5 7XF

TAKE A WILDLIFE SAFARI IN THE ISLES OF SCILLY

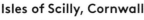

Isles of Scilly, Cornwall
stagnesboating.co.uk

Life on the Isles of Scilly very much revolves around its boatmen and women, as they offer the only way to get between these wild, low-lying islands that sit 45km off the coast of Cornwall. But around once a week, the sailors behind St Agnes Boating turn their ferry into a wildlife safari vehicle and take visitors, and their dogs, out on to the seas in search of wildlife. And wildlife aplenty there is.

These remote islands are a true haven for all manner of creatures, and they're home to myriad seabirds throughout the year. During breeding season (April through July), you'll spot puffins bobbing about on the water and the cute penguin-like guillemots nesting on the rocks. There are Manx shearwaters, razorbills and fulmars, too, and beneath the surface of the sea you're guaranteed to spot a seal or two on your travels – they're often curious about boats and sometimes even swim alongside. And if you're lucky, porpoises and dolphins might also make an appearance.

Getting there: Dogs can travel with you on the foot-passenger-only *Scillonian III* ferry, which departs Penzance daily (weather permitting). There is limited space for pets on the Skybus from Newquay, Land's End or Exeter too, where they ride in the cabin with you secured in a crate by your feet. islesofscilly-travel.co.uk

Make a night of it: Book into Karma St Martin's (see below), which sits right on the beach.

KARMA ST MARTIN'S

Isles of Scilly, Cornwall
karmagroup.com

Few hotels have better locations than Karma's handsome beachfront house on the island of St Martin's. Sitting directly on the beach, with lawns that lead down to a bright-white crescent of sand lapped by paradisiacal turquoise waters, it overlooks

↓ A labrador stands atop cliffs on the Lizard Peninsula

one of the many uninhabited islands
within this low-lying archipelago, where
seabirds and seals can be seen offshore.
The pace of life here is unhurried,
dictated by the tides and weather
systems that pass over the islands, and
it's best embraced by a slow amble along
its largely untouched coastline.
Where to walk: Walk north along the
hotel's beach and follow the coast path
clockwise around the island of St Martin's
for a wonderfully wild hike. It'll take
around three hours to complete a circuit
of the island and you'll pass artist studios,
honesty boxes with local flowers and

produce, and plenty of secluded coves
and sweeping beaches ideal for the dog
to explore.
Need to know: To reach St Martin's
you'll need to take the Skybus from
Newquay, Land's End or Exeter to St
Mary's Airport, or board the *Scillonian III*
ferry from Penzance to St Mary's. There
are multiple boat departures daily from
St Mary's to St Martin's. Dogs are allowed
everywhere in the hotel, including the
bar and restaurant.

WALK

LIZARD COASTAL WALK

5

Cornwall

START POINT: National Trust Car Park,
TR12 7PJ
DISTANCE/TIME: circular 11.2km/3 hrs

This remote peninsula at the bottom
of Cornwall is a supremely enchanting

spot, especially during winter when it's far quieter and the beaches are all open for dogs. This circular walk follows the South West Coast Path, tracking the craggy cliffs eastwards from the car park and dipping down on to pristine sands. In summer, the cliffs are painted purple with heather, while autumn brings sepia tones to the landscape. Look out for basking sharks lurking in the ocean and seabirds such as guillemots and gannets in the sky.

The footpath skirts past interesting historical infrastructure, from an old Victorian lifeboat station to a pair of wireless huts once used by Italian engineer Guglielmo Marconi during his radio experiments, and then turns inland along Green Lane towards Lizard village before returning to the car park.

WHAT'S FOR LUNCH?
There's a National Trust cafe open throughout summer at Kynance Cove. Check winter opening hours.

Need to know: Dogs are banned from Kynance Cove from 1 July to 31 August but other beaches are fine. Keep them on a lead near cliff edges. Download route directions from nationaltrust.org.uk.

NANJIZAL BEACH

Cornwall

A hidden cove only accessible on foot along the South West Coast Path from either Land's End (2km) or Porthgwarra (3km), Nanjizal is well worth the walk. It's all about drama and geology here, with towering cliffs, vast sea caves and enchanting rockpools.

Make a night of it: Artist Residence in nearby Penzance is both creatively quirky and homely all at once, with unusual artworks and design pieces throughout its rooms. **artistresidence.co.uk**

🐾2 🛏 <£200

Parking: Land's End (TR19 7AA) or Porthgwarra (TR19 6JR)

↓ Nanjizal Beach

CORNISH SEAL SANCTUARY

Gweek, Cornwall
sealsanctuary.sealifetrust.org

There are few places where you can responsibly get up close to seals when you've got a dog by your side, and it's rarely advised in the wild, but the Cornish Seal Sanctuary offers a chance to do exactly that. The rescue centre takes in injured or sick seals from the surrounding seas and nurses them back to health in their hospital. Those that can't be re-released retire here, enjoying a life of swimming and snacking. You can watch their antics from three different underwater viewing areas and meet a small colony of Humboldt penguins on their own private beach.

NEWLYN ART GALLERY

Newlyn, Cornwall
newlynartgallery.co.uk

There's no reason you should miss out on contemporary art just because you've got the dog with you – at least, that's Newlyn Art Gallery's policy. Just a stone's throw from the South West Coast Path, you can bring the dog in to see whatever contemporary exhibitions are showing at the time (provided that it's safe for four-legged visitors). Expect arresting photography, sculpture, painting and drawings that challenge preconceptions and promise to ignite your curiosity and imagination.

SWIM WITH YOUR DOG IN A 1930S LIDO

Penzance, Cornwall
jubileepool.co.uk

Built in the year of King George V's silver jubilee, this popular lido in Penzance – which underwent a multi-million-pound renovation and reopened in 2016 – sits right by the swirling seas and is usually only open to two-legged swimmers. But for one day each October, at the end of the season just before it closes for winter, dogs are invited to dive in alongside their owners for a dip in an historic pool. Don't expect it to be warm, though, as this pool – unlike the adjacent geothermal pool – isn't heated and instead enjoys temperatures just one or two degrees higher than the ocean itself. It's a great day out if you can bear a bracing swim – or if you come packing a wetsuit!

Make a night of it: Artist Residence in nearby Penzance is both creatively quirky and homely all at once, with unusual artworks and design pieces throughout its rooms. artistresidence.co.uk

WOODLAND COLLECTION HOLIDAYS

Cornwall woodland-collection.co.uk

Tucked away down a rural country lane, almost equidistant between two Cornish coastlines where dog-friendly beaches abound, is one of the most relaxing holiday destinations in the

↓ A daschund enjoys the surf on the beach opposite St Michael's Mount

county. Woodland Collection isn't blissful because there's an extensive spa or massage therapist on demand – there isn't. Nor is it because it's in the most peaceful spot in the country – though you're unlikely to meet the hordes that beeline for Cornwall in summer here. Woodland Collection Holidays, which comprises four modern three-bedroom homes each with their own garden, is idyllic for dog owners because the owners have thought of everything.

Got a dog who likes to wander without a care for your whereabouts? Just a few steps from each cottage is a fully enclosed field for wayward dogs to run free in so you don't have to worry about losing them. Each house has a fully enclosed garden, there are crates available to borrow so you needn't lug your own, and there's even a dog shower out the back of each property for muddy or sandy returns. There's a dog-friendly bistro next door, and they'll even organise a dog-sitting service if you want to head out without your pet.

Of course, the attraction goes well beyond the dog-friendliness of these cottages. Set within a former flower farm, where daffodils are still grown in spring and barley in summer, the houses are surrounded by natural beauty – and they're just a short drive from some spectacular dog-friendly beaches, too.

Where to walk: When you're not walking within the private meadows on the Woodland Collection Holidays site, the next best place is the National Trust's Godolphin Estate. More than 500 acres of forest, river and medieval gardens are at your disposal (dogs on leads), and there's even a dog-friendly tearoom.

Need to know: Each cottage has an enclosed garden with 1.5-metre-high fencing and there's a large secure paddock for exercising pets with unreliable recall; a 36-acre wildflower meadow with mown pathways in summer is a gorgeous place to let them explore if their recall is good. Dogs are allowed in bedrooms if you bring your own bedding and treats, balls, poo bags, dog shampoo and towels are provided.

PLACE

GEEVOR TIN MINE

Land's End, Cornwall geevor.com

Once part of a vast mining network across Cornwall and Devon, the Geevor Tin Mine is now a relic of what was Cornwall's most important industry. Perched right on the cliff edges of the Land's End Peninsula, hundreds of men descended into its depths between 1911 and 1990, when it closed down. You can follow in their footsteps in the 'Dry', the room where they would surface each day and change to go home. Rather eerily, it has been left almost exactly as it was – coats hung on lockers, boots lined up on top – that final day the mine was in use over 30 years ago.

While dogs can't join you down in the mine itself for safety reasons, there's plenty to do on the surface. The Hard Rock Museum isn't dedicated to the eponymous cafe brand aligned with rock 'n' roll music, but instead chronicles the subterranean landscape of Cornwall since mining first began as early as 4,000 years ago. There's mineral panning and equipment demonstrations to take part in, and plenty of opportunity to admire those endless sea views.

PLACE

ST MAWES CASTLE

12

Cornwall english-heritage.org.uk

Henry VIII built more than 30 fortresses between 1539 and 1547, many of which still stand today – though none is quite as well preserved as St Mawes. Teetering on the tip of the Cornish Roseland Peninsula, overlooking Carrick Roads and the harbour town of Falmouth, it has seen tensions aplenty, first with the Spanish and later, in the 1700s, the French. You can wander in and around its ramparts, see its centuries-old guns and visit the eerie oubliette where prisoners were held captive. There are informative exhibitions throughout its towers and plenty of mesmerising ocean views. For the ultimate adventure, take the ferry across Carrick Roads from Falmouth's Prince of Wales Pier – dogs travel free. While you wait for your return, nip into the St Mawes Hotel for a cup of tea and slice of cake.

→ A whippet surveys Godrevy Lighthouse

EXPERIENCE

TAKE A TRIP ON AN HISTORIC LIFEBOAT

13

Cornwall stivesboats.co.uk

After its 33-year stint as a St Ives lifeboat in the early 20th century, during which it completed hundreds of important rescues including more than 200 people and two dogs, the *James Stevens No.10* was eventually left to rot in a boatyard in Walton. It was returned to St Ives in 2002, and after several restorations it has landed in the capable hands of St Ives Boats, who now sail the vessel around the coastline surrounding this artsy Cornish seaside town.

Leaving St Ives Harbour, the boat – which would have been rowed by several sailors when it was a rescue vessel in the 1920s – cruises out past Carbis Bay, Lelant and Hayle, and on to the 26-metre-high Godrevy Lighthouse. Built in the 1850s, the lighthouse warned passing ships about the perilous Seven Stones Reef until 2012, when a modern steel structure was added on a neighbouring rock. On board, you'll hear tales of the lifeboat's adventures and the wrecks that litter the sea floor in the area, all while enjoying the spectacularly wild Cornish coastal views.

Alternatively, hop on their other boat – the more modern *Dolly P* – and head out to Seal Island, where a colony of grey seals loll about on the rocks.

Make a night of it: Woodland Collection Holidays (see page 22) have some of the best dog-friendly cottages in all of Cornwall.

BEACH

NORTH SANDS

14

Devon

At only 100 metres long, North Sands isn't Salcombe's largest beach, but this scenic, sheltered little bay is a gorgeous spot for an afternoon of sunbathing and swimming. Set amid leafy cliffs and looking out over the entrance to Salcombe Harbour, you can enjoy views of the boats going to and fro, either from the sand or the dog-friendly The Winking Prawn cafe over the road.

Make a night of it: The Hope & Anchor at Hope Cove is a cosy, dog-friendly pub with rooms just 15 minutes' drive from North Sands. hopeandanchor.co.uk

2 <£100

Parking: TQ8 8LD

EXPERIENCE

PADDLE YOUR WAY AROUND THE AVON

15

Devon singingpaddles.co.uk

Take to the water with the dog on board one of Singing Paddles' canoes. On a four-hour group tour of the Avon Estuary you'll learn about the area's ecology from passionate guide Dave, see wildlife such as green woodpeckers, sparrowhawks and egrets, and stop off on a secluded bank to make a campfire and indulge in a Devonshire cream tea.

Make a night of it: try Dittisham Hideaway's treehouses and shepherd's huts (see page 27).

PLACE

HEALEY'S CORNISH CYDER FARM

Penhallow, Cornwall
healeyscyder.co.uk

You can't visit Cornwall without trying some homegrown cider, and Healey's is one of the most ubiquitous with its Rattler drink fizzing in pint glasses across the county. Under the guise of education, you can sample more than 60 different products made with their apples, which grow in orchards spread out beyond the visitor building. Sample jams, gins and juices – and, of course, the refreshing Rattler – before taking a vintage tractor ride through the 20 acres of orchards. There's a gin distillery, a cafe serving cream teas, and for kids there's a small petting zoo with shire horses, pygmy goats and a family of snuffling Cornish black pigs.

PLACE

SHIPWRECK TREASURE MUSEUM

Charlestown, Cornwall
shipwreckcharlestown.co.uk

'X marks the spot,' the saying goes. But what about when that treasure is underwater? How do you find lost gold when it's buried beneath the ocean? This tiny but engaging museum explores exactly that, looking at the earliest scuba divers and their hefty suits, and documenting the treasures that have

been found, and some of the lives lost, beneath Cornish seas and beyond.

BEACH

PAR SANDS

Cornwall

A glorious south-facing, dune-backed beach with watersports equipment for hire (ABCwatersports.co.uk), Par Sands is a sparkling spot on a summer's day or a wonderfully quiet place for a game of fetch out of season. It's also one of the few Cornish beaches that's accessible for those with disabilities; hire a beach wheelchair at the nearby holiday park (01726 812868) and you'll be able to get right down to the shoreline.

Make a night of it: Nearby Fowey Hall is a superb family-friendly hotel with a spa. foweyhallhotel.co.uk

Parking: PL24 2AG

PLACE

EDEN PROJECT

Bodelva, Cornwall edenproject.com

From former clay pit to glorious garden, Eden Project is one of the most compelling rewilding stories in Britain. With more than 1,000 plant varieties now gracing its terraced gardens, there's a riot of colour all year round. Dogs are welcome everywhere except in the enormous temperate biomes, so instead take it in turns with your travel companion to head inside each of them to see exotic plants and curious little Sulawesi white-eye birds.

DITTISHAM HIDEAWAY

Dittisham, Devon

www.pawsandstay.co.uk/oak-at-dittisham

Shepherd's huts were once a modest form of accommodation – a home on wheels lugged across the countryside and set down at dusk for a night or two while the flock grazed and rested. Now, rather surplus to requirements for modern shepherds, they've become a permanent fixture on many a glamping site across the UK, and here at Dittisham Hideaway, any shepherd would have been lucky to lay their head within these positively palatial huts.

In fact, these dog-friendly boltholes are called shepherd's lodges rather than huts, owing to their fully plumbed-in bathrooms, kitchenettes and supremely comfortable double beds. There are five of them set into a hillside overlooking a plunging valley where a brook babbles below, each with their own patio where long nights spent toasting marshmallows by the fire are almost obligatory.

Inside, there's a log burner for chilly winter nights and sublime underfloor heating that the dog will love, and outside you'll find a wood-fired bathtub for soothing aching muscles after long walks. Your welcome hamper includes wine, orange juice, cereal and fresh bread, and a communal games barn has table tennis, chess and table football for your entertainment.

Where to walk: A walking booklet in your shepherd's lodge will detail some of the excellent local walks, such as the Dart Valley Trail, but don't miss the truly lovely Woodland Walk that's signposted around the site, too. You can walk into Dittisham village across the fields and down country lanes directly from the site (around 45 minutes).

WHAT'S NEARBY?

Agatha Christie's former home of Greenway (nationaltrust.org.uk), right on the River Dart, is just across the water from Dittisham village. Head across on the ferry – which you can call in a delightfully antiquated way by ringing the huge bell outside the Ferry Boat Inn – and explore its gorgeous landscaped grounds. Dartmouth is a 10-minute drive away (or a 30-minute ferry ride) and from here you can take a boat to Kingsway and then hop on the historic steam train (dartmouthrailriver.co.uk) where even the dog gets their own ticket. If you're really keen on trains, drive up to Totnes (25 minutes from Dittisham) and hop on the South Devon Railway (see page 30).

Need to know: Bowls and beds are provided for the dogs at Dittisham, as well as a welcome pack with treats and a tennis ball. There's a dog waste bin in the car park.

↓ A young puppy enjoys the rugs in a shepherd's hut at Dittisham Hideaways

FISTRAL BEACH

 21

Cornwall

On the edge of Newquay town and backed by one of Cornwall's best links courses (which also allows dogs on leads while you putt), Fistral Beach is a near 1km stretch of soft sand, grassy dunes and cliffs peppered with pretty red clover in spring and summer – plus, fantastic surf. In fact, its waves are so good, this is considered the epicentre of surfing in the UK and a number of high-profile competitions – including Boardmasters – take place here every year. This is an accessible beach, with beach wheelchair hire available from Fistral Beach Surf Hire (01637 850584).

↓ Fistral Beach at sunset

Make a night of it: The five-star The Headland hotel sits right on the beach and loves welcoming dogs. headlandhotel.co.uk
Parking: TR7 1HY

HAVE SOME HIGH-OCTANE FUN IN A FORMER QUARRY **22**

Menheniot, Cornwall
adrenalinquarry.co.uk

There aren't many places in the UK where you can do ziplining and axe-throwing with the dog by your side, but at Adrenalin Quarry they can join you for most activities, so long as they're kept

↑ Wildflowers on the cliffs above Watergate Bay

on the lead. This means you can take it in turns to zoom along the 50-metre-high zipwire over their turquoise lake, with the first member of your party returning to get the dog and walk back down as the rest enjoy the 490-metre-long ride. On the shores of the lake, there's a dedicated lawn area for dog owners with picnic benches for lunch in the sun, and if someone is willing to wait with the dog, the rest of your group can also enjoy go-karting or a stomach-churning ride on a giant swing that lunges out over a 50-metre drop above the lake.

Make a night of it: The Bodmin Jail Hotel (see page 30) is a 30-minute drive away.

(see page 30)

WATERGATE BAY

23

Cornwall

Just 5km north of Newquay, Watergate Bay is a seemingly endless sprawl of sand when the tide is out. Another surfer's paradise and home to a popular surf school, you'll see wetsuits in their hundreds during summer. In winter, though, it's deliciously quiet and there's ample space for ball chasing and exploring the rocky cliffs and caves behind it. This is an accessible beach, with beach wheelchair hire available from Watergate Bay Hotel (01637 860543).

Make a night of it: Watergate Bay Hotel has the best vantage point atop the cliffs overlooking the beach and two dog-friendly restaurants. watergatebay.co.uk

🐕2 🏨 🦮 ♿ ◄£200

Parking: TR8 4AY

THE BODMIN JAIL HOTEL

Bodmin, Cornwall
bodminjailhotel.com

On the edge of Bodmin town, between bucolic farmland and a busy working high street, a formidable prison building lords it over the Cornish landscape. Built in 1779 as a debtors' jail, the 220-cell stone prison housed men and women who had committed crimes of all kinds, from arson to murder. During its nearly 150 years as a detention centre, it saw more than 50 executions performed within its grounds – many of which were overseen by large crowds of jeering onlookers.

Today, though, the only crowds you'll find are in the dining rooms of what is now a surprisingly plush hotel, and there's not a jeer to be heard. With cells knocked through to create spacious bedrooms – all with original exposed brick walls and those tiny barred windows – a restaurant in the old chapel and a bistro in the courtyard, Bodmin Jail has been given a new lease of life, and serving life here now would be no bad thing at all.
Where to walk: The Camel Trail heads west from the hotel and into a small woodland along the River Camel before looping back into Bodmin. Alternatively, drive east to Cardinham Woods (forestryengland.co.uk), where there are waymarked walks ranging from 1.3km to 6.4km.
Need to know: The hotel provides hypoallergenic treats and dog beds in the rooms, and dogs can dine with you in the Courtyard Restaurant and will even get a sausage at breakfast. For late-night loo breaks, there's a patch of grass over the road from the hotel entrance.

BYGONES

Torquay, Devon bygones.co.uk

Take the kids – and the dog – on a Victorian adventure at this eccentric museum. Explore 15 different shops, packed with 19th-century memorabilia including wooden toys and old-fashioned sweets, and clamber on the 27-ton steam train before watching the 8.5-metre-long model railway chug around its tiny tracks.

RIDE THE RAILS IN SOUTH DEVON

Devon southdevonrailway.co.uk

Take a trundle along the tracks of the South Devon Railway, where dogs ride for just £1 and you'll get to watch the bucolic landscapes between Buckfastleigh and Totnes zoom past on this 22km return journey by steam.
Make a night of it: Two Bridges Hotel within Dartmoor National Park has cosy bedrooms and a brilliant dog-friendly restaurant. twobridges.co.uk 🐕2 £200

THE CAMEL TRAIL

27

Cornwall

START POINT: Scarletts Well Car Park, PL31 2RS (or Wadebridge, PL27 7AL)
DISTANCE / TIME: point-to-point 19.5km or 9.5km/5 hrs or 2.5 hrs

Trains used to chug along the tracks of the North Cornwall railway until the 1960s, when the line was closed and the tracks were left to get swallowed up by nature. Since then, the line between Bodmin and Padstow has been cleared and it's now a pleasant, flat trail following the winding Camel River all the way out to the coast.

Along the nearly 20km route from Bodmin you'll pass the sloping vines of the Camel Valley vineyard, whose sparkling wines make an excellent post-walk toast, and the wooded hills of the Cornwall Area of Outstanding Natural Beauty (AONB). Beyond Wadebridge, where the shorter route begins, you'll follow along the Camel Estuary and will eventually smell the salty sea air as you wend your way into Padstow. If you arrive in town on time, pair the walk with a visit to the dog-friendly National Lobster Hatchery (nationallobsterhatchery.co.uk), where you can meet a host of impossibly cute baby lobsters.

WHAT'S FOR LUNCH?
You can hardly eat out in Padstow without dining on a Rick Stein menu, so head to St Petroc's Bistro (rickstein.com), where dogs can join you in the bar for fresh Cornish fish and serious French cooking.

Need to know: This is a popular cycling trail, so beware of whizzing wheels as you walk. The number 11 bus will take you back to where you began in either Wadebridge or Bodmin.

↓ Flowers along the Camel Estuary

OLD WALLS VINEYARD

Bishopsteignton, Devon
oldwallsvineyard.co.uk

English wine is developing in leaps and bounds, and with each new harvest comes better flavours from the Old Walls Vineyard crop. Spend some time among the vines here and sample a bottle or two from the comfort of their cosy one-bed lodges or in the dog-friendly on-site bistro. Come during autumn and you can even get involved with the harvest, picking the best grapes to go into the next vintages.
Where to walk: Dogs will love exploring the nearby coast path or running on the beach at Ness Cove.

↓ Inside The Duke at Spring Park

THE DUKE, SPRING PARK

Spring Park, Devon
www.pawsandstay.co.uk/duke

For something a little bit different, meet The Duke. Set within its own little private wildflower meadow, this 1940s showman's caravan has serious character. On the outside it's all bright red paintwork with intricate decoration, while inside it has the feel of a cosy, eccentric artist's cottage, with printed wallpaper, an antique wood burner and patterned quilts on the double bed.
Where to walk: Venture beyond your wildflower meadow into the Tamar Valley AONB, where three rivers dissect a rather romantic English country landscape and several trails offer great walking, including the Tamar Trail and Drake's Trail.

SEE THE ANCIENT CLIFFS FROM THE SEA

(30)

Devon stuartlinecruises.co.uk

Get up close to the dramatic red cliffs of the Jurassic Coast on one of Stuart Line Cruises' cheerful red, yellow and blue boats. Departing from the traditional seaside town of Exmouth, this three-hour sailing takes you eastwards to admire the 185-million-year-old coastline. This is the oldest section of the UNESCO World Heritage Site, encompassing geology that goes back to the Triassic era. You'll spot seabirds nesting in the cliff faces, peer into sea caves, and you can even order a cream tea on board.

Make a night of it: Hotel du Vin in nearby Exeter has stylish dog-friendly rooms and an outdoor pool.

hotelduvin.com 🐾1 🏳 <£100

MAN O'WAR BEACH

(31)

Dorset

The view from the clifftops of the near-perfect crescent of pebble beach here is one you can never tire of. Grassy banks steeply slope down on to this slim but spectacular stretch of beach on the Jurassic Coast, where the ocean takes on a Caribbean quality in summer, all turquoise and shimmering in the sunshine, tempting bathers in from the pebbles. Don't be put off by its name – you won't find the eponymous jellyfish here. The beach got its moniker thanks to the rocky outcrops that jut into the ocean, as it's said they resemble warships of centuries past, so swimming in the calm, sheltered waters is safe and very much encouraged.

Most exciting of all, though, is that

this beach is one of the many where you can find prehistoric fossils lurking on the ground and within the cliffs. Keep a keen eye out for curious patterns on the stones beneath your feet; perhaps spirals from shell-dwelling ammonites or the long, thin spearhead shapes of the belemnite, both of which existed here between 200 and 66 million years ago. Also don't miss a walk along the coast path here, which overlooks one of Dorset's most famous views: the perfect natural arch of Durdle Door.

Make a night of it: Dog-loving staff at The Smuggler's Inn, 20 minutes' drive away in Osmington Mills, will welcome you all. smugglersinnosmingtonmills .co.uk

Parking: BH20 5PU

↘ Corfe Castle at sunrise

STAY

MOONFLEET MANOR
32

Weymouth, Dorset
moonfleetmanorhotel.co.uk

Overlooking the Fleet Lagoon and seemingly endless Chesil Beach, which is famous for its fossils, Moonfleet Manor is a special little place on the Dorset coast – and not just because of those views. This hotel is made for families, with up to two dogs welcome in each room and some seriously impressive kids' facilities, plus free childcare for up to 90 minutes a day. Expect indoor pools, indoor soft play and games rooms, organised fossil walks and even mini golf.

Where to walk: The South West Coast Path lies right on your doorstep here, so you can walk the length of the lagoon and beyond.

PLACE

CORFE CASTLE
33

Dorset nationaltrust.org.uk

It's on crisp winter mornings, when a low mist hangs in the air and the sun can be seen poking its head above the surrounding hills, that Corfe Castle is at its most mystical. Its crumbling, thousand-year-old ruins are set atop a grassy mound, with just hints of the keeps, towers and defences that once protected this royal residence. It has seen its fair share of battles, but now lies peacefully surrounded by bucolic Dorset countryside and is an ideal place to walk with the dog.

ST NECTAN'S GLEN

 34

Cornwall st-nectansglen.co.uk

START POINT: PL34 0BE
DISTANCE/TIME: 3km/allow 2 hrs there and back

While the Cornish coast draws walkers to tackle the beautiful South West Coast Path, inland Cornwall doesn't get the attention it deserves – and that includes St Nectan's Glen. This walk along an easy-to-follow trail, which starts just east of the car park from St Piran's Church, will take you through a lush, rainforest-like woodland with the trickling Trevillet River by your side. Expect bristling ferns and moss-covered rocks – this is a Site of Special Scientific Interest (SSSI) – as well as British garden birds, kestrels and even woodpeckers. You'll stroll over wooden bridges and walkways, passing the 'money tree' – a fallen tree trunk with pennies stuck in its bark like armadillo scales – before ending up at the entrance to St Nectan's Waterfall.

There's an entry fee to see the falls and you'll have to get your feet wet in order to get a good view, but it's well worth it to watch the fairy-tale spouts of water tumbling between the rocks into a crystal-clear, tranquil pool. Within the attraction itself, there's more walking to be done, with various waterfalls and viewing platforms, and a nature trail around a forest with old oaks, apple trees, towering Corsican pines and shimmering silver birch.

WHAT'S FOR LUNCH?
There's a cafe serving lunches, Cornish coffee and cakes with outdoor seating for dog owners.

Need to know: Dogs should be kept on the lead to protect the ecology of this SSSI.

BEACH

BEER BEACH 35

Devon

Walk down the plunging hill that leads on to the shingles of Beer Beach and you'll find yourself surrounded by white limestone cliffs within a delightfully sheltered bay. Dogs can roam the eastern end of this beach year-round, where boats lean to on the pebbles, having spent the morning out on the ocean seeking fish to sell ashore, and a few ramshackle cafes set amid the beach huts serve up English breakfasts and cream teas. With its calm waters, this bay is a fine spot for swimming and rentable deck chairs make a comfy spot to relax after a dip with the dog. Don't forget to pick up a fresh catch from Beer Fisheries on your way back to the village – fresh crab, mussels, cockles and scallops abound in this modest little fishmonger overlooking the beach. For a meal with a view, eat dinner in the clifftop garden of the Anchor Inn, where you can watch the sun set over the sea as you dine on the catch of the day.

Make a night of it: Westleigh B&B is all about dogs. They provide a dog bath, plenty of towels, dog food, bowls, homemade treats and even toys for your pet all included in the price, plus they have walking and sitting services should you want to spend an afternoon without the dog. westleighbeer.co.uk
Parking: EX12 3AQ

PLACE

THE DONKEY SANCTUARY 36

Sidmouth, Devon
thedonkeysanctuary.org.uk

Set across 134 acres of farm and woodland, this huge donkey sanctuary is home to around 50 donkeys all year round. Meet them in the enclosure and barns, learn about why they need to be rescued, and finish off with lunch in the dog-friendly Kitchen restaurant, which serves seasonal local produce and freshly baked cakes.

WATCH A SURFING COMPETITION WITH A DIFFERENCE

37

Bournemouth, Dorset
shakasurf.co.uk

While Cornwall's famous Boardmasters festival doesn't allow dogs, Bournemouth's own version – Dog Masters – is all about four-legged surfers. The UK dog surfing championships is held every July on Branksome Dene Beach, a soft, yellow-sand stretch just a 30-minute walk from Bournemouth Pier, and features live music, street food and, of course, surfing dogs.

Make a night of it: Soak up Miami surf vibes at The Nici, which has dog-friendly rooms with direct access to the lawns and your pets are welcome in the bar for dinner. thenici.com

SUMMERLEAZE BEACH

38

Cornwall

Right on the edge of Bude town centre, this wide, sandy beach sits on the mouth of the River Strat where you can see the Bude Canal connect to the sea. It's a surfing hotspot and is immensely popular in summer, with dogs required to be on leads between 10am and 6pm from May through September. Come in winter, though, and your dog can zoom on the sand as much as they like, and you'll only find a handful of hardcore surfers donning their wetsuits at weekends. Hire beach wheelchairs from the Summerleaze Beach Office (01288 352226).

Make a night of it: A 30-minute drive north of Bude, Philham Water Cottage is a pleasingly rustic little bolthole with a thatched roof and small stream running adjacent to its garden. It's wonderfully cool in summer and cosy with the log fire in winter. sawdays.co.uk

Parking: EX23 8HJ

CLOVELLY VILLAGE

39

Devon clovelly.co.uk

Life is lived at a slower pace in Clovelly, a tiny village set along a steep main street that tumbles down to an old fishing quay below. There are museums exploring its fishing history and local writers, glorious seafood suppers, and a herd of donkeys that once pulled sledges up and down its steep streets.

SALISBURY CATHEDRAL

40

Salisbury, Wiltshire
salisburycathedral.org.uk

Dating back to the 1200s and a masterpiece in religious Gothic architecture, Salisbury Cathedral dominates the city's skyline from almost any angle. Its intricately decorated tower and spire – all 123 metres of it – reaches high above any building in the area and is the tallest church spire in the UK, while inside you'll find the largest secular cloister of any religious building in Britain, too. A pleasingly green lawn surrounds the cathedral, great for a game of fetch before you head inside with the dog to admire its spectacular vaulted ceilings and artistic font.

BEACH

SAUNTON SANDS

41

Devon

While the focal point of most beaches is ahead of you as you walk on to the sand, here it's what lies behind this straight stretch of soft golden grains that will intrigue the most. Known as Braunton Burrows, behind Saunton Sands is a warren of grassy dunes that was designated a UNESCO Biosphere Reserve in 1976 thanks to its collection of rare plant and animal life. Keep the dog on the lead in the Burrows to protect the ecology and look out for 11 different species of orchid, 33 different types of butterflies and even a few reptiles – including adders.

Devon's own breed of Ruby Red cows graze the shrubbery as part of a land management system, and deer can sometimes be seen snacking on the plants, too. It's a fascinating and peaceful place for a stroll before heading on to the sand for swimming, surfing or simple games of fetch on the beach. Beach wheelchairs are available for hire from Saunton Sands Beach Shop (01271 890771).

Make a night of it: Located a five-minute walk from the beach, Saunton Beach Villas' self-catering lodges are some of Devon's most dog-friendly places to stay, with no limit on the number of dogs you can bring, enclosed gardens and plenty of blankets to protect the furniture. sauntonbeachvillas.co.uk
🐾10+ 👤4-8 ⛲ £200
Parking: EX33 1LQ or EX33 2NX

↓ Two dogs play chase on Saunton Sands

Arty posing outside Salisbury Cathedral →

ROBIN HOOD'S HUT

42

Goathurst, Somerset
landmarktrust.org.uk

This curious little building has two faces: from the back, it's a quaint and unassuming yellow limewashed cottage with a thatched roof and creaking wooden door. It looks like the sort of place that might have once belonged to a modest farmer or a servant working for the wider estate. But from the other side, where you can gather the full, mesmerising effect of its hillside vantage point overlooking the undulating Somerset countryside, it's a peculiar, folly-like structure with a circular Gothic umbrello and handsomely pointed arches, sitting unashamedly out of place within this bucolic setting.

Built in the 1760s by a member of the Halswell family, who owned the entire estate, including the grand Halswell House at the bottom of the hill, the 'hut' was left to crumble after the estate was split and sold off in the 1950s. The roof caved in and threats of demolition were made, until a trust took it up and restored its former glory. Today, it's managed by The Landmark Trust and while much of the estate is out of bounds to the public, this little slice of history remains accessible for those who choose to stay. There's a double bedroom, simple kitchen and cosy living room with a wood burner, but best of all are those near-endless views over the Somerset Levels.

Where to walk: A short drive south takes you to Kings Cliff Wood, a native forest where you can join the Macmillan Way.

Need to know: The garden is largely enclosed by a 1-metre-high estate fence.

DEVON BANKS CARAVAN AND CAMPING PARK

43

Bratton Fleming, Devon
facebook.com/devonbanksholidays

If it's a night under canvas you crave, there are few campsites better set up for dogs than Devon Banks. This adults-only site sits on the edge of Exmoor National Park and has just five pitches within its quiet borders, and beyond those there's access to some fine walking country in north Devon. But you needn't leave the grounds to enjoy exercising the dog, as there's a 3-acre field, secured with 1.8-metre-high stock fencing, with agility equipment and a straw bale scurry to test your pet's hurdling skills.

Where to walk: Exmoor National Park has fabulous walking trails all over, but one of its most dramatic with epic sea views is the Valley of the Rocks (see page 42).

PUTSBOROUGH SANDS

Devon

Dogs can enjoy 3.2km of beach just north of the cafe at Putsborough Sands (the southern end is restricted for dogs in summer), and with rolling surf and soft golden grains, it's a natural playground for all. Surfers and body boarders flock here in summer, and in winter it's particularly lauded for its glorious early evening sunsets.
Make a night of it: Hunker down in the glorious Coulscott House Holiday Cottages (see right).
Parking: EX33 1LB

↓ Putsborough Sands

PEACOCK COTTAGE AT COULSCOTT HOUSE HOLIDAY COTTAGES

Combe Martin, Devon
www.pawsandstay.co.uk/peacock-cottage

Set within a bucolic private estate in north Devon, Coulscott is the sort of place that's hard to leave. There are seven dog-friendly holiday cottages here – a favourite being the homely Peacock Cottage – sleeping between two and 17 people, most with their own

private enclosed gardens and hot tubs, and all oozing with character. But the real excitement comes when exploring the estate itself. Kids have endless entertainment on their doorstep: a heated indoor pool, paddocks of alpacas and pygmy goats, outdoor playgrounds and indoor games rooms. Adults seeking a bit of quiet can sign up to yoga classes, use the communal hot tubs, or sit at The Lookout – a hillside deck with calming views of the Coulscott valley, best paired with a cocktail or glass of wine.

Where to walk: For dogs, this area is heavenly. There's a 5-acre enclosed dog walking field on the estate itself, offering an opportunity to let them run free not far from the cottage, or you can stroll the 3km to the coast to dog-friendly beaches such as Wild Pear Beach or the rugged, cliff-backed Broad Sands.

Need to know: Dogs must be on leads unless in the exercise field or in an enclosed garden. There's no limit on the number of dogs allowed in each property, but smaller cottages may not be suitable for more than three dogs – call ahead to check.

↓ Footpaths through the Valley of the Rocks

VALLEY OF THE ROCKS

46

Devon

START POINT: The Esplanade, EX35 6HW
DISTANCE/TIME: circular 5km/2 hrs

This is an easy and wheelchair-accessible walk around the craggy, dramatic Valley of the Rocks that was formed during the Ice Age. Take the water-powered cliff railway up into Lynton town before following the tarmac coastal path along the precipitous cliff edges to enter this undulating, rugged beauty spot with its curious rock formations and glorious sea views. Look out for wild goats teetering on the rocks, and if you're lucky, you might even meet an Exmoor pony.

WHAT'S FOR LUNCH?
Charlie Friday's Coffee Shop (charliefridayscoffeeshop.co.uk) does cracking fry-ups, pancake and waffle brunches and fantastic falafel.

Need to know: Dogs should be kept on leads due to steep cliff edges. Directions can be found at explore.osmaps.com.

↓ View over Cheddar Gorge

CHEDDAR GORGE TRAIL

Cheddar, Somerset

START POINT: Cheddar Visitor Information Centre, BS27 3QE
DISTANCE/TIME: circular 6.4km/3 hrs

Get your climbing legs on for this spectacular walk around England's largest gorge, which is almost 5km long and an astonishing 122 metres deep. The trail begins from the visitor centre before joining a public footpath from the top of Cufic Lane. Here, you'll begin ascending the hills through woodland before coming out at the cliff viewpoint, which looks down on the road that passes through this dramatic, rocky gorge with its countless pinnacles and craggy outcrops. Formed over a million years ago as glaciers melted to form a river, today it's pockmarked with caves and unusual rock formations.

The footpath follows along the northern edge of the gorge heading eastwards, with dizzying views down on to the winding road below, before crossing over on to the other side for an alternative perspective as you loop back. While it's tempting to keep your eyes fixed on the valley beneath you, don't forget to look up; peregrine falcons can be seen soaring the skies here. Also look backwards – there are impressive views of Glastonbury, the Somerset Levels and Bridgwater Bay.

If you have time, don't miss a visit to the caves, too, where dogs are welcome on a lead. Gough's Cave was where the oldest complete skeleton in Britain was found. Monikered Cheddar Man, it's around 9,000 years old and we're still learning about the prehistoric population thanks to research on his remains.

> **WHAT'S FOR LUNCH?**
> Cheddar cheese, of course, at Café Gorge (cafegorge.co.uk) which does toasties, ploughman's platters and cheese quiches.

Need to know: There are stiles and kissing gates to navigate here so it may not be suitable for larger breed dogs; leads are advised due to sheer drops above the gorge. This route is waymarked but detailed directions can be found at nationaltrust.org.uk.

HILL HOUSE B&B

Ford, Wiltshire hillhousebandb.co.uk

It's easy to settle into a different rhythm at Hill House. Perhaps it's the patience required for warming the deep wood-fired hot tub, which invites you to languish on the patio chairs for a couple of hours before it's ready to engulf you. Or maybe it's the view that slows you down: watching the clouds or stars pass overhead, or gazing at the valley beneath you, where sheep graze on the sloping hillside and ancient woodland swaddles Ford village below. Sitting on the edge of the southern Cotswolds, this place can be the gateway to bucolic walks amid handsome villages such as Castle Combe, pub dinners at the nearby White Hart Inn, or it can simply be a bolthole to escape within. For once you're in the shepherd's huts here – each boldly designed with rich colours, printed fabrics and Shaker-style kitchens and en suites – the outside world will feel of little consequence.

Each of the two huts here are gloriously secluded from the main house, with enclosed gardens, wood-fired hot tubs and fire pits for cosy evenings outside. Treats from the local farm shop are provided in the fridge, and there's even a s'mores kit for toasting marshmallows by the fire.

Where to walk: There's a lovely trail from Ford village through undulating pasture and ancient woodland into Castle Combe, one of the Cotswolds' most attractive – and most photographed – villages. Maps can be found in the shepherd's hut.

Need to know: There is often livestock in the surrounding farmland and fences won't always keep dogs prone to jumping within your garden.

↓ Arty enjoying the Hill House B&B shepherd's hut

↑ Westonbirt Arboretum is a dog-walking heaven year round

PLACE

WESTONBIRT ARBORETUM

49

Westonbirt, Gloucestershire
forestryengland.uk

Cherry blossom and daffodils in spring, a lush green canopy in summer, and iridescent yellow and red leaves in autumn; one day is surely not enough to see Westonbirt's many outfits. With 27km of marked footpaths, it's a dog walking and picnicking heaven, with a few intriguing attractions up its sleeve, too.

In spring, see nature come to life again and head to the rhododendron collection to see award-winning purple flowers in bloom and seek out the spectacular magnolia trees with their white and pink flowers. Stroll down pleasingly named tracks like Oak Avenue and Maple Loop, all part of Silk Wood, where the dog can roam free off-lead.

Summer days are best spent picnicking on the grassy Downs or finding shade amid the woodland, perhaps on the Treetop Walkway that offers an aerial view of the forest, and the Acer Glade is most impressive in autumn, when these elegant Japanese trees turn from green to fiery red and shocking yellow. Wintertime here is equally pleasant, too, with fewer visitors and the satisfying crunch of frosty leaves and grass under foot.

LONDON & SOUTHEAST ENGLAND

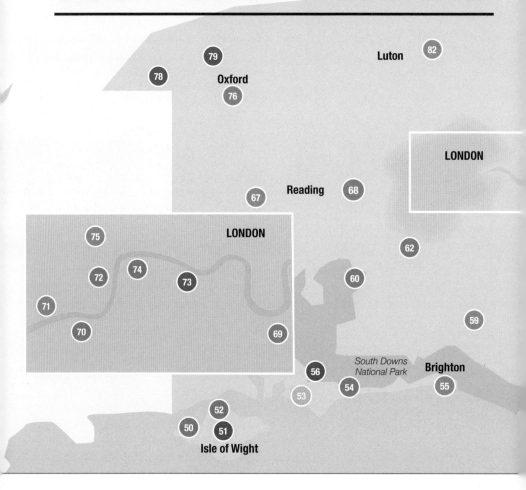

79

78

Oxford
76

Luton
82

LONDON

Reading 68

67

75

LONDON

72 74

73

71

70

69

62

60

59

56

South Downs
National Park

Brighton

53

54

55

52

50

51

Isle of Wight

TAPNELL FARM 50

Yarmouth, Isle of Wight
tapnellfarm.com

Once you're settled in at Tapnell Farm, there's very little reason to leave – especially if you're holed up in one of their self-catering geodesic domes overlooking the Solent, or the chocolate-log-shaped cabins, each of which has its own hot tub for long evening soaks best enjoyed as the sun sets over the arable landscape. This working farm is a joy for families with young children – and the dog, of course.

There's a farm park for meet-and-

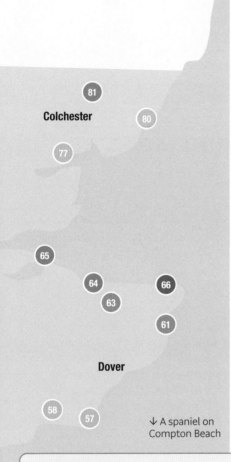

Colchester

81
80
77
65
64
66
63
61

Dover

58
57

↓ A spaniel on
Compton Beach

greets with all manner of creatures, from goats and sheep to alpacas and even wallabies. Next door to the animal enclosures is a farm shop stocked with local treats, including an excellent range of Isle of Wight beers and produce from the farm itself. And a buzzy restaurant serves up homegrown comfort food, with beastly burgers and moreish loaded fries to fill rumbling bellies. In summer, there's a sunflower meadow and an aqua park, while soggy days can be spent in the Clubhouse playing table football or pool.

You could fill several days here with activities and walks and trips to the nearby beaches, but there's plenty of pleasure to be had in simply whiling away the days from the decking of your cabin or safari tent, or long evenings spent cooking and eating in the woods while making use of the communal outdoor pizza oven.

Where to walk: The 9.7km Tapnell Trail (maps available from the shop) is a pleasant, largely flat waymarked walk that goes directly from the farm itself and crosses crop fields, a fruit farm and a small woodland area before skirting the edge of Compton Down. When you're away from the livestock, the dog can run

WHAT'S NEARBY?

A 10-minute drive from Tapnell Farm is the soft, reddish sand of Compton Beach, which sits just over the brow of Compton Down on the south coast of the island. Undeveloped aside from a National Trust car park and backed by crumbling ochre cliffs, the western end of this beach is dog-friendly year-round. Low tide reveals rockpools teeming with sea life, and at Hanover Point, keen eyes will spot evidence of creatures from the past: a 60cm-long *Iguanodon* footprint that's now over 125 million years old is immortalised in the reddish rocks.

free, and if you're feeling energetic you can climb over the downs and on to the coast path to look out over the ocean. **Need to know:** Needless to say, there's a lot of livestock here and you can't take your dog into the farm park itself. The rest of the site isn't really suitable for dogs afraid of or reactive to sheep or cows. Dogs must be kept on a lead within Tapnell Farm's main areas, but you can walk them off-lead around the crop fields and along the Tapnell Trail provided that they can be kept under control. Bring a longline so you can tether your pet while relaxing outside your accommodation.

PLACE

CARISBROOKE CASTLE

Carisbrooke, Isle of Wight
english-heritage.org.uk

It has Roman history, but with walls dating back to 1100, Carisbrooke Castle is truly a testament to Norman engineering. For almost 1,000 years, these turrets, keeps and crenelations have stood tall on its mound in the centre of the Isle of Wight, keeping out the French and Spanish in the 16th century and locking in its prisoners during the Civil War of 1642 – including Charles I. In its later life, the castle became a summer residence for Princess Beatrice, Queen Victoria's youngest daughter, and in the late 1800s, architect Percy Stone made restorations on its gatehouse and chapel, the latter of which is now an ornate little church.

Today, kids, adults and dogs will delight in exploring its ramparts. You can all climb the walls and walk along its battlements for excellent views over the Isle of Wight, or play bowls on the green. There's a pretty planted garden that was

designed for Princess Beatrice, and in the stables you'll find a herd of donkeys. These gentle giants have been integral to the castle since the 16th century, when they were used to draw up water from the well, and today there are regular demonstrations of how it worked.

STAY

PINKMEAD ESTATE

Isle of Wight pinkmeadestate.co.uk

While Pinkmead might not sit right on the coastline of the Isle of Wight, the clink of sail masts at the adjacent marina on the river is there to remind you that you're not too far away from the sea. Though why you'd feel the need to venture out beyond the vineyard estate's boundaries is a mystery: you still have shimmering waterside views as the lawns extend right down to the banks of the Medina River, and the beautiful little six-person bungalow is so well equipped with ample adventures and activities, as well as plenty of space – 24 acres to be exact – that you can do not very much at all if that's the way you're inclined. Pinkmead is a veritable holiday destination in itself.

The house sits slap bang in the middle of a huge lawn, where a small boathouse has kayaks and paddleboards you can take out on the water from the estate's private jetty, and a handful of seating areas invite al fresco lunches overlooking the river or the next-door wetland nature reserve. On the deck surrounding the bungalow is a small wooden sauna and hidden around the back of the house is a golf cart you can take for trips around the wider estate and vineyard. There are

Pendleton bikes to borrow, and while the estate isn't yet producing wines, there'll be a bottle of their own gin in your welcome hamper to help get the party started.

Speaking of parties, this house has three bedrooms, but it can sleep up to 10 if you make use of the sofa bed in the separate yoga studio and standalone 'Kitchen Garden' house, which can be turned into a bedroom to go alongside its state-of-the-art cooking area and dreamy bathroom with a large, garden-facing tub. After all, with all that space and such divine views, it would be a shame not to bring a few friends – and their dogs – along, too.

Where to walk: The house sits right on a disused railway line that now connects Newport and Cowes for walkers and cyclists, but more rural walks can be enjoyed in Parkhurst Forest (forestryengland.uk), where dogs can roam off-lead on its various trails.

WHAT'S NEARBY?
The seaside town of Cowes is a lovely day out, best reached via water taxi on the Medina, with a handful of waterfront restaurants – The Globe (globecowes.co.uk) is dog-friendly and has a great seafront beer garden. Osborne House (english-heritage. co.uk), the former summer residence of Queen Victoria, is a 20-minute drive north and dogs are welcome around the grounds, and Carisbrooke Castle (english-heritage.co.uk), just 20 minutes south of the estate, is also dog-friendly.

Need to know: No beds or bowls are provided here so you'll need to bring your own. The huge garden is enclosed by foliage and fencing at the back and by water at the front, so if you've got a swimmer in your midst it might not be entirely secure.

EAST HEAD BEACH

53

West Sussex

A 15-minute walk west along the beach from the car park at West Wittering lies one of the last natural coastal areas of Sussex: East Head. This little triangle-shaped spit of land is, unlike the rest of the Sussex coast, uninterrupted by groynes and coastal defences. Instead, it's a daily-changing mass of sand topped with dunes and marram grass, shaped by the movement of the tides and wind. Thanks to its natural composition, it has become a favourite habitat for certain birds in winter – look out for godwits, sanderlings and oystercatchers – and

↓ Sand dunes on East Head Beach

summer sees skylarks nesting in its grasses.

This rare environment is also home to sand lizards and rare moth species, including the pink-and-green elephant hawk moth, and come high tide, you might spot common seals splashing about in the water hunting for fish. Due to its fragile nature, dogs must remain under control and on a lead within the dune system (which is best avoided during nesting season), but they're free to race about on the sandy beach.

Make a night of it: Plush Tents Glamping has fully furnished yurts just a 25-minute drive away, complete with wood burners for colder nights and proper double beds. There are vintage Airstream caravans, too. plushtentsglamping.co.uk

2 2-5 £200

Parking: Beach Car Park, PO20 8AJ

BAILIFFSCOURT HOTEL & SPA

Atherington, West Sussex
hshotels.co.uk

You wouldn't think this hotel was built in the early 20th century – its stone archways, golden sandstone masonry and tiny single-pane Tudor-style windows look far older than 1927. But that's because they are. Bailiffscourt is a peculiar but brilliant amalgamation of salvaged materials and antiques – doorways from medieval chapels welcome you into lounges and bedrooms filled with furniture from the centuries before. Its thatched cottage and Norman

↓ Climping Beach

↑ A boxer roaming on Brighton Beach

chapel only add to the illusion that this collection of handsome buildings has been here for several hundred years. But antiquated, the rest of it is not.

Dinner – which for dog owners can be served by the fireplace in the snug lounges – is a menu of rich, expertly curated dishes with ingredients largely sourced within an 8km radius, and the modern spa (not dog-friendly, unfortunately) has a heated outdoor pool from which you can hear the ocean crashing on the pebbles at Climping Beach.

Where to walk: The shingle beach is dog-friendly all year round. There are also footpaths from the beach that take you inland and up to Hobbs Farm, then back down the lane to the hotel – this is a lovely 45-minute circuit.

Need to know: Bailiffscourt has special dog-friendly packages from around £510, which includes dinner, bed and breakfast, plus bowls, blankets, balls and treats for the dog, and a Ruff & Tumble drying coat to take home, too.

EXPERIENCE

EXPLORE THE LANES IN BRIGHTON

Brighton, East Sussex

Brighton is a supremely dog-friendly seaside city, with a vast pebble beach where dogs can run around year-round west of the pier. But if a whole day spent on the beach isn't your thing, wander up into the city to the famous Lanes, where a tangle of pedestrianised streets are lined by independent shops and cafes. Whether you want to buy crystals, handmade clothing, ceramics or antique maps, The Lanes – particularly North Laine – has it all, and many of the shops allow dogs; just ask at the door.

Make a night of it: A short walk from The Lanes and the beach is Oriental, a supremely dog-friendly B&B where animals stay for free. orientalbrighton .co.uk 🐕1 <£100 ☀

FISHBOURNE ROMAN PALACE

56

Chichester, West Sussex

sussexpast.co.uk

The site of Fishbourne Roman Palace was once a military barracks, used during the early stages of the invasion of Britain by Roman forces. But once they had conquered the land here, the barracks became surplus to requirements and so, as any wealthy civilisation would, they built a palace in its place. Today, what remains is protected inside a series of warehouse-like buildings, where you'll find some of the most impressive mosaics from the time. There's also a reconstructed Roman garden, and the dog can join you throughout the site on a short lead.

BEACH

DUNGENESS BEACH

57

Kent

Dungeness is a love it or hate it kind of place. Some might say it's depressing and ugly, while others fall head over heels in love with the bleak beauty of its enormous, flat expanse of shingle, littered with rusting winches from former fishing fleets and abandoned boats. A clear-sky day helps, bathing the beach in golden light, but if you're into melancholy, the landscape takes on an eerie air in winter when the skies are grey and few visitors bother with its shores.

Fresh fish lunches are available from the Snack Shack (**dungenesssnackshack.net**). **Make a night of it:** Bring family and friends to stay in Living Architecture's striking Shingle House, a stunning four-bed house right on Dungeness Beach. living-architecture.co.uk

Parking: Dungeness Road, TN29 9ND

BEACH

CAMBER SANDS

58

East Sussex

You'll have to walk over sand dunes and through tufty grasses to reach Camber Sands, a brilliant 3km-long sandy beach

on the East Sussex coast. Within the dunes lies a special ecosystem where rare moth species thrive, and in winter it becomes home to hen harriers, sanderlings and short-eared owls. The beach is flat and wide and, when the winds are right, popular with kite-surfers, who bounce around on the horizon. There is a dog exclusion zone between 1 May and 30 September so bear right out of the car park to avoid it in summer.

Make a night of it: Beside the Sea Holiday Cottages has a clutch of beautiful dog-friendly cottages sleeping up to nine people. besidetheseaholidays.com

🐕2 👤2-9 🅿️ £200

Parking: New Lydd Road, TN31 7RB

↓ A pair of dobermans run on Camber Sands

RIDE THE BLUEBELL RAILWAY

59

Uckfield, East Sussex
bluebell-railway.com

Starting at Sheffield Park Station in Uckfield or from East Grinstead Station and traversing 17.7km through the dreamy Sussex countryside, the Bluebell Railway was one of the UK's first preserved heritage lines. The Lewes and East Grinstead Railway opened in the late 1800s, but less than a hundred years later, it closed down in 1958. Reinvigorated by a team of passionate volunteers who have restored it, it's now a beautiful journey – made even more spectacular when a carpet of bluebells is laid out on the floor of the woodland it passes through.

Make a night of it: Keep on with the railway theme and book The Hoover Hut – a former railway cargo carriage turned glamping cabin. canopyandstars.co.uk

🐕1 👤2 🏠 🅿️ £100

THE MERRY HARRIERS

60

Hambledon, Surrey sawdays.com

Sometimes getting away with the dog simply means a superb meal, some solid walking territory and a cosy bed for the night, and The Merry Harriers offers exactly this. The pub, sitting half an hour outside the M25 south of Guildford amid the rolling Surrey Hills,

↑ The dog-friendly shepherd's huts at The Merry Harriers

has plenty of character and a pleasingly large beer garden that fills up with locals and walkers in summer. There's always water available for the dogs, and plenty of treats behind the bar, and food is proper pub fare, with ham, egg and chips or shepherd's pie on the menu.

Bedrooms are either in the Garden building out the back of the pub, which each have direct access to the outside for ease, or in their handsome shepherd's huts next to the car park. The latter are particularly tempting, with log burners and lovely colourful furnishings inside and teak loungers and a fire pit out the front. There's also a wood-fired hot tub for private use in the paddock, and if you fancy meeting the local llama herd, just ask at the bar.

Where to walk: There's an excellent 45-minute circuit from the pub (turn left out of the front door and keep bearing left) that makes a brilliant morning walk along a bridle path, but for longer rambles head across the road and through the car park towards Winkworth Arboretum (nationaltrust.org.uk).

Need to know: There are llamas living on site and the pub is situated on an occasionally busy lane, so dogs must be kept on leads at all times. Dog beds and towels are provided in the rooms.

EXPERIENCE

TAKE A HISTORY LESSON IN DEAL

61

Deal, Kent thehistoryproject.co.uk

Dogs join for free on Deal's history tours. This town might be small, but its history is plentiful, with links to Henry VIII, Julius Caesar, Nelson and Churchill. You'll follow your energetic guide around the town's main sights and look out to sea to a sandbank known as the mysterious 'ship swallower'.

Make a night of it: Stay right in the town at the handsome Royal Hotel, which has its own nod to the town's maritime history in the bar. theroyalhotel.com
🐕2 🏠 ◀£200

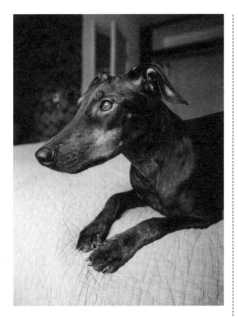

dog, and plenty of opportunities for sampling the estate's best wines. Take a walking tour with one of the on-site guides to see secret corners of the vineyard not open to the public or hop on the land train (dogs welcome) that travels up to the best viewpoints, where you'll enjoy a glass of sparkling at the top.

For a more sedate affair, retire to the hotel's wine library, where you can sit with the dog and watch the vines flutter in the breeze through its floor-to-ceiling windows as you partake in their brunch and bubbles offering or a food and wine pairing experience. Expect superbly smoked chicken and moreish

↖ Arty watching the vines from his bedroom at Denbies Vineyard Hotel
↓ The sloping vines at Denbies Vineyard

STAY

DENBIES VINEYARD HOTEL

Dorking, Surrey denbies.co.uk

You needn't step foot on the Continent to enjoy a wine-themed weekend away, as there's a special little spot in the Surrey Hills that rivals the likes of Champagne and the Loire for its fine wines and fabulous food. Spread across 265 acres on an estate that's had royal connections since the 1850s – when it was owned by master builder Thomas Cubitt, who brought Prince Albert here – Denbies sits on the edge of Dorking, watched over by the 224-metre-high Box Hill to the east and sloping woodlands to the west.

From the front doors of its small and pleasingly low-key hotel, which is hunkered down between rows of vines behind the visitor centre, there are myriad adventures to be had with the

cured venison, and a handful of carefully selected wines that pair perfectly with each item. It's here where dinner is served, too, which often includes local game and Surrey Hills fruit and vegetables.

Of course, all cobwebs can be blown away on the endless footpaths around the estate. You might just need to adjust your expectations on returning home – if only all dog walks could be bookended by food and wine pairings.

Where to walk: The North Downs Way passes right through the middle of the estate, offering excellent walking terrain through the vines and up into the western hillsides, where forests of silver birch skirt the edges of the National Trust's Polesden Lacey estate. If you've boundless energy and strong legs, you can also cross the main road outside the vineyard and tackle the steep slopes of Box Hill for exceptional views over the Surrey Hills.

WHAT'S NEARBY?
Dorking town centre has some curious independent shops and antiques emporiums well worth exploring (ask before you head inside with the dog), and Dorking Museum does dog-friendly walking tours. The Stepping Stones in Westhumble is an excellent dog-friendly pub just a 30-minute walk away.

Need to know: Dogs can be off-lead but must remain under control around the estate. Beds and bowls are provided for dogs in the rooms. Be aware that weekends get incredibly busy here with local dog walkers and families, so this isn't the best stay for nervous pets.

MESS ABOUT IN BOATS WITH CANOE WILD

Kent canoewild.co.uk

Small and medium-sized dogs are welcome in the canoes on Canoe Wild's trips up and down the Great Stour, just outside Canterbury. You can hire your own by the hour and go for a roaming paddle or join a sunrise or sunset tour that will take you all the way to Grove Ferry. If you're lucky, you might spot beavers along the way!

Make a night of it: The Cook's Cottage (see below) is a gorgeous little bolthole just 25 minutes' drive from Fordwich.

THE COOK'S COTTAGE

Whitstable, Kent pawsandstay.co.uk

Whitstable is a supremely dog-friendly town, with a high street that's packed with intriguing independent shops – including the excellent Millie and the Tiger (millieandthetiger.co.uk) pet shop – and a pebbly beach that's dog-friendly year-round. And just a few steps away from all this is The Cook's Cottage on Sydenham Street, where you'll find a charming little fisherman's cottage with a dog-proof garden to boot.

Thoughtful is the word of the stay

WHAT'S NEARBY?

Whitstable's lovely little high street is an excellent diversion and dogs can join you in many of its shops (just ask before you enter), and the pebble beach is perfect for games of fetch (they must be on leads in peak season, though). Look out for the oyster beds laid by the Whitstable Oyster Company, whose nearby The Lobster Shack ([thelobstershack .co.uk](thelobstershack.co.uk)) is a very good dog-friendly option for lunch on the water.

here – everything in this three-bed home is thoughtfully placed and beautifully presented. Its decor has a delightful French farmhouse meets rustic sailor vibe, with white-painted floorboards and solid wood ship wheels hanging on the walls, and a kitchen that's made for passionate cooks, with plenty of spices and oils to work with, too. There's a fireplace complete with kindling and logs in the dining room for cosy dinners in, but it's outside where the real magic lies – an outdoor kitchen with a ceramic egg barbecue, a summerhouse with a projector and a big dining table and plenty of lush pot plants make this a beautiful space. And it's completely enclosed by 1.8m fencing.

Where to walk: For a peaceful walk, head inland to Blean Woods (rspb.org.uk), where woodpeckers and nightingales can be heard in spring and sparrowhawks hunt in winter. Dogs should be kept on leads so as not to disturb the wildlife here. Another excellent lead walk is on the 12km Crab and Winkle Way between Whitstable and Canterbury. As part of the National Cycle Network, it's largely traffic-free, and the number 4 bus will return you to the coast once you've explored historic Canterbury. For an off-lead adventure, head to Reculver, where you can see the crumbling towers of a medieval church as well as remains of a Roman fort before letting the dog loose on the beach nearby.

Need to know: Dog bowls and plenty of treats, tennis balls and poo bags are provided at The Cook's Cottage. They're not allowed on the furniture in the summerhouse or in the bedrooms, but they can snuggle on the sofa with you downstairs in the evening. There's on-road parking only here and it can get busy, so be prepared to unload the car at the end of the road by the house before looking for a space to park elsewhere.

↓ A dog on the beach at Whitstable

↑ The view from Sandy Toes Beach House, Isle of Sheppey

SANDY TOES BEACH HOUSE 65

Isle of Sheppey, Kent
pawsandstay.co.uk

If it weren't for the twinkling lights in Whitstable across the water, you might feel like you're living at the end of the world at Sandy Toes. It's a 20-minute drive across the island from the Kingsferry Bridge, and once you've passed the somewhat scruffy town of Leysdown-on-Sea with its numerous holiday parks, the fact that there are any more houses along the single-track road is quite the shock. But houses there are – 14 in fact, all off-grid and looking directly out to sea.

'Beach House' might seem like an exaggeration at first sight – this little seaside home looks like no more than a ramshackle wooden hut with windows, improbably still standing despite the occasionally blustery gales that batter this end of the Isle of Sheppey. But it's certainly more robust than it looks, and despite being off-grid – powered by solar panels or a generator when there's not enough light – it still has a few mod cons: central heating, hot showers and a fully equipped kitchen to name but a few.

But what's inside Sandy Toes Beach House matters very little – though its shabby chic interiors and enormous log burner are indeed idyllic on rainy

↑ The ramshackle hut that is Sandy Toes Beach House, Isle of Sheppey

afternoons – for it's the beach and nature reserve outside that'll get you, and the dog, most excited. You're almost at the easternmost tip of the island here, where wetlands meet the sea and a sandy beach peppered with oyster shells is on your doorstep. The light is quite mesmerising, and it's especially spectacular in the peace of winter, when the sun rises late directly over the ocean and remains low in the sky for much of the day, and there are no souls to be seen except oystercatchers sticking their beaks in the sand for snacks.

Where to walk: There's a lovely, flat 12km walk right from the beach here to The Ferry House and back. Head south towards the hamlet of Shellness and then bear right into the Swale National Nature Reserve (dogs on leads) when you hit the houses. You might spot marsh harriers hunting in the skies and little waders in the wetland waters – bring binoculars for birding in the hides – before reaching grazing pasture near the village of Harty. Stop in at the medieval church before carrying on through the village and down to the coast for lunch at the pub, which serves inventive small plates (locally shot pheasant goujons and game sausage rolls) and Kentish cider. The walk back goes across Harty Marshes and ends back on the beach.

WHAT'S NEARBY?
Queenborough is the island's biggest town and from here you can take the Jetstream boat tours around the island, out to the WWII Maunsell Forts, or to the wreckage of the SS *Richard Montgomery* – an American warship that sank here in 1944.

Need to know: There's enclosed decking with fencing up to a metre or so and dogs are allowed on the beach off-lead year-round. No beds are provided for dogs, so it's a bring-your-own situation.

CRAB MUSEUM 66

Margate, Kent crabmuseum.org

You've probably never thought about how crabs might have cured human ailments, but these undersea creatures have been used to make vaccines safe since the 1970s. It's random knowledge like this – ideal for pub quizzing – that you'll come away with from the Crab Museum, a small but fascinating exhibit in Margate that allows dogs on leads to join their owners on a crustacean exploration.

CRUISE THE KENNET & AVON CANAL 67

Berkshire abcboathire.com

You'll find a deep sense of peace sets in once you're cruising on the Kennet & Avon. This relatively quiet canal stretches all the way from Bristol to Reading, and heading west from Aldermaston Wharf you'll pass through the swells of the North Wessex Downs and through the southern Cotswolds. Pick a sturdy vessel from ABC Boat Hire and spend a week cruising here, and you'll wake up with the kingfishers and otters before spending long, languid days on the water, using the centuries-old locks and bridges just as they were intended.

THE SAVILL GARDEN TO THE LONG WALK

68

Windsor, Berkshire

windsorgreatpark.co.uk

START POINT: The Savill Garden, TW20 0UU
DISTANCE/TIME: 6km/1 hr

The centre of so many royal moments throughout history, Windsor Great Park is a wonderful 5,000-acre estate with trails and cycle paths crossing its manicured green lawns and woodland areas. The most famous footpath, of course, is The Long Walk, where countless royals have paraded by carriage to cooing crowds.

WHAT'S FOR LUNCH?
Sit outside at The Savill Garden Kitchen, or if you want to sit inside, The Fox & Hounds pub (http://www.thefoxandhoundsrestaurant.com) is a short diversion out of the park on Bishopsgate Road

Need to know: Directions can be downloaded from the park's own website. Note that there may be deer so dogs must remain under close control or on a lead.

GREENWICH PARK CIRCULAR

69

Greenwich, London

START POINT: St Mary's Gate, SE10 9JL
DISTANCE/TIME: 2km/30 mins

You could aimlessly wander for hours in Greenwich Park, but this is a lovely 30-minute walk with gorgeous views of the Naval College and Canary Wharf looming across the river. Starting at St Mary's Gate, you'll head towards the Royal Observatory where the Meridian Line cuts across the park, and then climb up the hill and on to Lovers' Walk, where you can divert on to One Tree Hill to gaze out at the city.

WHAT'S FOR LUNCH?
Fish and chips or a hearty roast dinner at the Greenwich Tavern (greenwichtavern.co.uk) opposite St Mary's Gate.

Need to know: Directions on alltrails.com under 'Greenwich Park Circular'. Dogs are allowed off-lead but must be under control.

↓ Views over Greenwich Park

ART'OTEL LONDON BATTERSEA POWER STATION

70

Battersea, London
artotellondonbattersea.com

London's plethora of museums and galleries are, sadly, not dog-friendly, but that doesn't mean that cultured dogs should be left out of the art scene here – and this hotel is an excellent alternative to the V&A or Royal Academy. While you might not see a Goya hanging on the walls or get to gaze into the eyes of a Michelangelo, there's ample art to see here, from the ceramic pieces lining the shelves in the lobby to the hanging modern art by Jaime Hayon in the breakfast restaurant on the ground floor. Even the furniture – a mix of mid-century modern and Bauhaus design – is artistic, and the lobby has some striking architecture around the elevators.

Unless you've got a young dog who will want easy access to the outdoors, it's all about the upper floors here – the higher the bedroom, the better the view. On one side you'll be able to look out at the renovated Battersea Power Station while on the other you might overlook Battersea Dogs & Cats Home, where your pet can watch the rescues roaming in their sensory gardens below each morning. Don't forget to make the most of the rooftop pool and hot tub, where sunset makes the power station towers glow orange.

Where to walk: In this part of south London you're a mere few minutes away from Battersea Park, where there's plenty of space for off-lead adventures and a few intriguing installations, including the London Peace Pagoda.

WHAT'S NEARBY?
The Battersea Power Station mall is just across the road and welcomes dogs in the majority of its shops, which range from indie bookshops and high street retailers to designer stores like Jo Malone and Lululemon.

Need to know: Beds and bowls are provided. The ground-floor restaurant is dog-friendly; if you want to enjoy the fabulous Portuguese and Spanish dishes in JOIA on the 15th floor, leave the dog in the bedroom and put the privacy button on.

TREAT YOUR DOG TO LUNCH AT LOVE MY HUMAN TOWNHOUSE

71

Chelsea, London
lmhtownhouse.co.uk

There are dog-friendly cafes, and then there's Love My Human Townhouse. Less dog-friendly and more dog-first, with human-friendly elements too, this pet-obsessed cafe is really built for dogs. Anything goes here, with dogs encouraged to sit at the tables and on sofas, and they're catered for with a vast array of dog treats, from natural chews to homemade dog-safe donuts. There's a full dog menu, because why doesn't your pet deserve its own brunch of scrambled eggs or a hearty lunch of beef Wellington with pumpkin purée? And if it's a special occasion, they'll even do a three-course meal for your dog, with a main course, celebration cupcake and a puppuccino, along with a birthday serenade.

There are treats for owners, too, including cream teas, Asian salads, open sandwiches and an excellent breakfast menu – and your cappuccino comes with chocolate sprinkles in the shape of a dog bone. But it's upstairs where things get serious: they have a crèche and roof terrace, which, if you're so inclined, you can hire for a fee to put on your own dog birthday party for up to six dogs and ten people, and there's a wellness room for pampering puppies and elderly dogs alike. They offer massages, reiki and even acupuncture for dogs that need a little pick-me-up.

Make a night of it: Native Hyde Park is a lovely 45-minute walk from the cafe through the handsome streets of Kensington & Chelsea and out the other side of the vast Hyde Park. nativeplaces .com

ST ERMIN'S HOTEL

72

Victoria, London
sterminshotel.co.uk

In the heart of Victoria, just a few minutes' walk from St James's Park, this hotel is one for the well-heeled dog owner. Its spectacular lobby with intricate plasterwork and a pair of symmetrical curved staircases is a prime spot for a photo shoot before heading up to your room, where bowls, beds and toys await for the dog.

Where to walk: St James's Park is just a few minutes' walk from the hotel's front door and there you'll find trails that circle around the lake, past Buckingham Palace and into neighbouring Green Park.

TOWER BRIDGE

73

London towerbridge.org.uk

Since 1886, the steeples of Tower Bridge have been dominating the skyline along the River Thames. Back when it was first built to the plans of Sir Horace Jones they were some of the tallest constructions in the City of London. It was a feat of engineering, with 11,000 tonnes of steel used and a sophisticated bascule system that lifted the bridge to allow tall ships to pass through. It used 20 tonnes of coal per week and it was lifted up to 30 times a day.

Today, it stretches across the river with a backdrop of glassy skyscrapers

and still occasionally lifts its platforms for visiting vessels. And this is where it gets fun: a walkway connects the top of its twin towers and its floor is made of glass, meaning you can stand right above the bridge as it lifts and watch the boats sail through. Looking eastwards through the windows within the walkway you'll see Wapping on the north bank and Bermondsey on the south bank of the Thames, with the towers of Canary Wharf in the distance. Westward views include the 'Gherkin' and 'Walkie Talkie' buildings, as well as The Shard and City Hall below.

Dogs are welcome throughout the bridge's towers and walkways, where exhibitions chart the creation and adaptation of the bridge's build and lift system. There's an extra exhibition that's not to be missed in the Engine Rooms on the South Bank, where there's even more detail about the bridge's inner workings.

↓ A corgi posing in front of Tower Bridge

BANKSIDE HOTEL

Southwark, London
banksidehotel.com

If it's those sexy city views you're after for your adventures in London, Bankside Hotel has rooms to impress: St Paul's and the shimmering towers of the City beyond are visible from some of their best bedrooms. Inside, the views are pretty good, too. Monochrome decor and stand-out designer pieces – think geometric lamps, unusual artworks, mid-century modern-style furniture – make the hotel's interiors a calming and cool space to spend your downtime. Creativity is at the heart of this property, as it employs an Artist in Residence each season for their Art Yard Maker's Studio – a room dedicated to exhibiting and enabling independent artists' work – and you can head there to see who's making on any given day (the dog is welcome, too).

There's a brilliant bar for your afternoon aperitif and a terrace for when the sun's out, and you can even bring the dog to dinner while you snaffle a spread of burrata, beetroot hummus, Cornish plaice and aubergine and pesto flat breads.
Where to walk: Head out of the door and on to the South Bank, where if you walk east along the river you'll spot

WHAT'S NEARBY?
Tower Bridge (see opposite page) is well worth heading over to for its dog-friendly glass walkway views, and great dinners and al fresco drinks can be had in nearby Gabriel's Wharf, which buzzes with office workers on sunny weekday evenings.

Shakespeare's Globe and Tate Modern, and to the west you will pass the Oxo Tower, National Theatre and London Eye. What's nearby?

Need to know: There is a weight restriction – maximum 25kg – on dogs here, so unfortunately cultured Labradors should book elsewhere. Dog beds and bowls are provided, as well as a host of treats. The hotel has a 'canine concierge' service that'll offer tips on the best places for off-lead walks and shopping for the dog.

EXPERIENCE

WAKE UP IN SCOTLAND ON THE CALEDONIAN SLEEPER

75

London/Scotland sleeper.scot

There's a special romance to train travel – watching the country whiz by as you gaze out of the window, speeding towards pastures new. Overnight train travel, though, is even more alluring, and it's especially exciting on the Caledonian Sleeper with the dog snoozing by your side. This long-distance sleeper train is one of just two in Britain, and it's the only one that allows you to share a cabin with your dog. It connects London with Scottish cities such as Edinburgh, Aberdeen, Inverness and Glasgow, or to the likes of Fort William – the gateway to the Highlands, where dog walks are more than just an amble through the fields and instead mean conquering mountains such as Ben Nevis or exploring loch-side forests in nearby Glencoe.

Cabins are small but sophisticated, with en-suite toilets and showers and a small basin with a stowaway table

beneath. Some come with a double bed, while others have surprisingly comfortable bunks, made even more cosy by complimentary eye masks and ear plugs. But it's not what's inside the train that's most enticing – take the journey in summer and you can stay up late to watch your departure point fade away into fields or foothills. If you don't mind leaving the dog to settle in the cabin, you can head into the Club Car to meet fellow travellers and talk about your impending adventures over hearty dinners of beef bourguignon or Scottish fish. Every cabin has a window, though, so you could simply order a glass of something to your room through the intercom and relax on the bed as the world goes by.

The next morning, you'll wake to witness a new land spreading out beside you. The route to Fort William is particularly spectacular, travelling past Loch Lomond & The Trossachs National Park as it wends its way north, where gnarly mountains that look like a giant's knuckles bulge beyond the windows. In winter, the landscape is almost entirely sepia thanks to the mix of bracken, brambles and browning heather covering the hillsides, while summer brings brighter greens and brilliant purples. Breakfast is served in the Club Car – complete with tattie scones and Lorne sausage – or delivered to the room for those who don't want to leave the dog alone. On arrival yet more adventures await, be it pounding the city streets in Edinburgh or London, a boat trip on the loch in Inverness, or a hike in the Nevis Range from Fort William.

Need to know: Dogs must be on a lead in train stations, lounges and on board unless in your cabin, where they aren't allowed on the bed. The floor space is relatively small, so any animal larger than a Labrador might find it uncomfortable for sleeping. The sleeper lounges are all dog-friendly so you've got somewhere to relax before boarding.

OXFORD ARCHITECTURE AND PUBS

Oxford, Oxfordshire

START POINT: Oxford train station or Seacourt Park & Ride, OX2 0HP
DISTANCE/TIME: circular 5km/1.5–2.5 hrs

Dogs aren't allowed inside Oxford University buildings, but you can still see plenty of them on a self-guided stroll – and this sandstone city really lends itself to walking. Starting from the train station, head east into the centre along the A4144. You'll cross Castle Mill Stream, then hit George Street, which is lined by several bars and restaurants. Keep heading east on to Broad Street and you'll find your first college on your left: the handsome golden-stone Balliol College – also look out for the Martyrs'

Cross brickwork on the road, which commemorates the stake burning of three Protestant martyrs in the city in the 16th century.

Around 200 metres further along Broad Street things get really exciting: Blackwell's Bookshop (dog-friendly inside) is home to the office where Tolkien once held meetings with its owner, and on the south side of the street is Sir Christopher Wren's Sheldonian Theatre and the glorious 18th-century neoclassical Clarendon Building, behind which lies the world-famous Bodleian Library, housing more than 13 million books. Head into the quad behind the theatre and Clarendon and you'll also spot Oxford's answer to the Bridge of Sighs, Hertford Bridge, on New College Lane. Head out and under the bridge, then take a left into St Helen's Passage – a narrow alleyway leading to The Turf Tavern, an ideal pit stop, and then on to Holywell Street.

At the eastern end of Holywell, turn right on to Longwall Street, then left on to the High Street and immediately right on to Rose Lane. At the end of here you'll

↓ The sandstone city of Oxford

find yourself in Christchurch Meadow Walk, which connects to a vast green pasture where the dog can roam under close control. A total of 13 British prime ministers studied here at Christ Church college, and if you come in term time, you might spot some future politicians in Oxford gowns rushing about between exams.

Head out of the meadows past the college and on to St Aldate's, where you can head north past Carfax Tower to finish with a drink in Morse Bar, named for the detective at the centre of the Inspector Morse books, whose writer often drank here at The Randolph Hotel on Beaumont Street, or the university-owned Lamb & Flag on St Giles'. Almost directly opposite the Lamb & Flag and closed at the time of writing is The Eagle and Child, one of the many locations where C.S. Lewis and J.R.R. Tolkien were known to knock back a few. From here, it's just a 15-minute stumble back to the train station past

the Ashmolean Museum and Worcester College.

Need to know: Oxford's streets can be incredibly busy with tourists in spring and summer, so come in winter or late autumn for a better experience – the city has a beautiful sepia glow when the leaves have turned. If you're driving, use the Seacourt Park & Ride (OX2 0HP) in Botley and take the bus up to George Street to begin your walk.

BEACH

WEST MERSEA BEACH

Essex

If it's a typical day out at the beach you're after, West Mersea is one of Essex's top stretches of sand. Multicoloured beach huts line the back of the beach, and there's plenty of room here for bucket-and-spade activities. Huts can be hired through The Little Beach Hut Company (thelittlebeachhutcompany.co.uk), and dogs can roam free for most of the year, but it's best to keep them on a lead when

it's busy during summer.
Make a night of it: The White Hart Inn in West Mersea town is a fantastic little pub with colourful bedrooms and excellent local seafood. sawdays.co.uk

Parking: Victoria Esplanade, CO5 8BH

PLACE

BLENHEIM PALACE

78

Woodstock, Oxfordshire
blenheimpalace.com

It doesn't matter which angle you see it from, Blenheim Palace is a breathtaking building. Its baroque design is the genius of Sir John Vanbrugh, although genius wasn't the term the Crown would have used at the time, as it was dismayed at the sheer extravagance and cost of his creation. Today, though, cost needn't be an issue as you can enjoy its opulent sandstone exterior from the expansive grounds it sits within, which are free to access via a few slightly hidden public footpaths. Park in Woodstock town

centre and wander north along the A44 where, just after a zebra crossing beyond the bridge, you'll find a pair of gates leading to a driveway, where a public footpath enters the estate. Stroll around lakes, through woodland and up to the towering Column of Victory – an excellent vantage point for views of the palace.

PLACE

COTSWOLD WILDLIFE PARK & GARDENS

79

Burford, Oxfordshire
cotswoldwildlifepark.co.uk

Taking the dog to the zoo may have never crossed your mind, but Cotswold Wildlife Park and Gardens makes it safe to show your dog a whole world of wildlife beyond its own kind, as you can stroll the 160 acres of landscaped gardens and enclosures here with your pet on a short lead. A fantastic family day out for those with young kids, this wildlife park has some absolutely enthralling animals. See lions skulking or sunbathing, watch

↓ The Blenheim Palace Estate

rhinos grazing on pasture, and look up to see the towering giraffes gazing down at you.

There are some unusual characters, too, including the snout-nosed Brazilian tapir, giant anteaters and reindeer, as well as a huge array of monkeys. Look out for the emperor tamarin, a squirrel-sized monkey with an impressive tufty white moustache. There are, of course, some areas where it's not safe for dogs, including the bat and reptile houses, the farmyard and the Madagascar exhibit, where you can walk through the lemur's enclosure. They must also be kept away from the Flamingo Lake and Wolf Walkway, but provided that an adult stays with the dog, the rest of your party can explore.

Tired feet will be grateful for the miniature train that travels around the park, and there's a cafe with outdoor seating, though the best way to enjoy a day here is with a picnic – there are benches overlooking the rhinos, zebras, camels and giraffes.

THE NAZE (80)

Essex

The most easterly peninsula in Essex is a haven for wildlife both on land and in the sea. Barn owls hunt in the grasslands atop the orange, fossil-rich cliffs that tower over the sandy beach, while harbour porpoises are sometimes seen in the waters beyond the shoreline. In rockpools on the beach, you might find crabs, whelks or even scallops.

Make a night of it: The Pretty Thing campsite has dog-friendly bell tents for hire just a 20-minute drive away. theprettything.co.uk 🏕1 👥2-4 🐾 <£100
Parking: 9 Sunny Point, CO14 8LD

DEDHAM AND CONSTABLE COUNTRY (81)

Dedham, Essex

START POINT: The Sun Inn, Dedham, CO7 6DF
DISTANCE/TIME: circular 7km/2 hrs

Any walk that begins and ends at a pub is brilliant, but this is a superb ramble to work up an appetite in the countryside where John Constable was so inspired to create his famous paintings. From The Sun Inn, head out of the village towards Dedham Hall and follow the footpath north-east to the river. Here, stroll eastwards with the River Stour to your left and enjoy its twists and turns through the occasional copse and vast fields of green pasture. After just more than a kilometre, you'll come to a bridge where you can cross the river and enter the tiny hamlet of Flatford. You might recognise its bucolic beauty from Constable's famous pieces, such as *The Hay Wain* or *Boat-Building near Flatford Mill*.

This painting-perfect hamlet is now National Trust-managed, and you can walk its lanes with the dog on a lead, admiring historic buildings from the outside, such as Willy Lott's House and Flatford Mill. Stop for a cuppa in the dog-

> **WHAT'S FOR LUNCH?**
> The Sun Inn in Dedham (thesuninn dedham.com) serves fabulous roast dinners on a Sunday, or a thoughtful menu of local produce mid-week – the Merrifield Farm duck is a winner. They also have dog-friendly rooms if you feel like staying over.

friendly tearoom before heading back the way you came or take an alternative route: cross back over the river and follow the footpath south, then turn westwards back to Dedham across the fields.

Need to know: Dogs can be off-lead on the south side of the river, but once in Flatford, they need to be on a lead.

↑ Crowds enjoying The Big Dog Walk at Dogfest, Knebworth House

EXPERIENCE

TAKE YOUR DOG TO A FESTIVAL AT DOGFEST KNEBWORTH HOUSE 82

Knebworth, Hertfordshire
www.dogfest.co.uk

If you can imagine Glastonbury, but instead of bands it's dog experts, and instead of people it's dogs, then you're picturing DogFest, the UK's biggest and most chaotic dog-friendly festival. This two-day dog extravaganza, with fun dog shows, an obedience ring, a stage with expert speakers and fun dog displays, plus interactive activities such as hay bale racing and agility, is a riot for both humans and dogs. They'll get to play in ball pits and leap into the canine swimming pool while you eat street food, learn training tips from the likes of TV behaviourist Adem Fehmi, and browse stalls selling everything you could possibly want for your dog.

Make a night of it: Roydon Marina Village has lovely dog-friendly lodges with their own hot tubs and plenty of great walks on the doorstep. roydonmarinavillage.co.uk 🐾2 👤6 £200

THE MIDLANDS

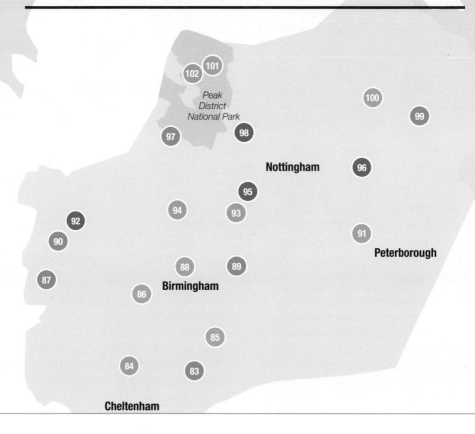

Peak District National Park

97
101
102
100
99
98
Nottingham
96
95
94
93
91
92
90
Peterborough
88
89
87
86
Birmingham
85
84
83
Cheltenham

THE FISH HOTEL

83

 £300

Broadway, Worcestershire
www.sawdays.co.uk/the-fish-hotel

You'd be forgiven for thinking The Fish Hotel was built for dogs rather than humans. The entire estate is an adventure playground for our pets, with endless public footpaths and waymarked trails to explore. Accommodation, which comes with a dog bed, bowl and treats, is either in plush bedrooms with direct access to the outside or in one of their Scandi-style treehouses, complete with outdoor decking. There's an outdoor warm-water bathtub complete with pet-friendly shampoo for post-walk paw washing, and – the pièce de résistance – just beyond the hotel's main building lies an enclosed paddock with a handmade wooden agility course just for dogs.

Fear not, though, for dog owners are well cared for, too. Expect fluffy white gowns, enormous impossible-to-leave beds and, on the treehouse decking, twin outdoor tubs complete with a button for ordering boozy bubbles direct to your bath. What's more, a dog-friendly seafood restaurant serves up refined fish dishes with international twists.

Where to walk: With a public footpath running right through its grounds offering access to the 164km Cotswold Way, it is perfectly placed for short ambles around its own waymarked nature trail, or longer hikes over the undulating landscapes. Grab a map (and a pair of wellies) from the hotel's boot room and you're all set for adventures large and small.

Need to know: Dogs must be kept on a lead around the estate and there may be livestock on site.

in the Malvern Hills. This walk takes in the spectacularly preserved Iron Age hillfort atop Herefordshire Beacon, where 4,000 people once lived prior to Roman invasion in small, round thatched huts. You'll climb to the top of Herefordshire Beacon, an excellent vantage point for surveying the landscape at 338 metres high, then on to Swinyard Hill for more 360-degree views. The walk loops back via a man-made cave before returning to the car park.

Need to know: Directions can be downloaded from visitthemalverns.org.

WALK

BRITISH CAMP TO SWINYARD HILL ⑧⁴

Malvern

START POINT: British Camp Car Park, WR13 6DW

DISTANCE / TIME: circular 5.5km/2 hrs

The Midlands is often thought of for its industrial history, but there are remnants of civilisations gone by that were here well before the car and chocolate factories moved in, much of which can be seen

EXPERIENCE

BOARD A BOAT TO TASTE THE BARD'S GIN ⑧⁵

Stratford-upon-Avon, Warwickshire shakespearedistillery.com

It's unclear whether Shakespeare drank gin, but we know he liked drinking – perhaps a little too much, actually, as one of the many rumours surrounding his

↓ The river running through Stratford-upon-Avon

death was one particularly heavy session with a fellow playwright. But still, there are few better ways to appreciate his home town than raising a glass to his life's work on the idyllic River Avon with a G&T in hand.

It's a pretty little thing, the Avon. Its banks are thick with reeds that teem with ducks and moorhens, and weeping willows drape themselves over its silvery waters, as if bowing to passers-by. After a gin or two, guided by Shakespeare Distillery's own gin nerds, you might just find yourself inspired to write a sonnet, too...

Make a night of it: Get more of those river views from The Arden Hotel. theardenhotelstratford.com

SEE THE SEVERN VALLEY BY RAIL 86

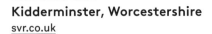

Kidderminster, Worcestershire
svr.co.uk

Whether you're a rail enthusiast or not, the sight of a chuntering steam train is always exciting – and riding one is even better. The Severn Valley Railway has 25.7km of track connecting Kidderminster to the Shropshire town of Bridgnorth, passing through beautiful Midlands countryside with stops at four small historic stations. Dogs ride free, and they can join you in the Engine House, where the stock of heritage locomotives lie in wait for their turn on the rails.

Make a night of it: Just 25 minutes from Kidderminster is the idyllic two-bedroom Lakeside Retreat, where you can enjoy wild swimming and endless walks around the beautiful estate. sawdays.co.uk

WALCOT HALL

Lydbury North, Shropshire
walcothall.com

Something special is afoot in the woods surrounding Walcot Hall, a Georgian country pile set amid the Shropshire Hills that is home to the rather creative Parish family. Creaking ancient oaks and handsome old Douglas firs – some of the oldest in the country, no less – create a rich green canopy throughout the arboretum in spring and summer, while hiding away in little clearings or on patches of green pasture lies an array of enticing structures in which to lay your head for the night. Be it a regal red showman's caravan, a retro fire truck or a Central Asian-style yurt with its own decking overlooking a plunging valley, there's a plethora of unique places to stay here, all entirely dog-friendly.

Perhaps most dog-friendly of all is

Norbury Hall, a small but magnificent wooden building sleeping up to six people that once housed Walcot village's meeting place. Set behind the estate's farmhouses within its own paddock, today it has been made homely with antique rugs and walls lined with fragrant cedar – the creamy, perfumy smell hits you the moment you open the door. Stained-glass windows in the living area and kitchen create beautiful light patterns as the sun breaks through in the morning, and a log burner promises cosy evenings in – though if you're here in summer, you'll want to make the most of the changing colours in the sky from the bench on the front veranda, a perfect sundowner spot.

Where to walk: Walks around the Walcot estate offer plenty of intrigue for both human and dog. In the arboretum itself, you'll find a wizened oak draped with pairs of old, decaying boots for reasons entirely unclear, and a pair of small ponds with rowing boats to borrow for floating picnics on a summer's day. You could easily spend an hour exploring the arboretum and formal gardens down by Walcot Hall itself, but plenty of public trails lead away from the estate and into those undulating Shropshire Hills.

The nearest hill for wonderful views is Bury Ditches, which you can reach via Lower Down (head out of the gate at the southern end of the yurt field and follow the farm track to the village). From this 2,500-year-old hillfort, you can see south to the Clun valley and forested hills beyond, but even more impressive is the structure of its ancient fortifications, still visible as mounds and ditches today.

> **WHAT'S NEARBY?**
> Rather conveniently located at the end of Walcot's near kilometre-long driveway is the reliably welcoming Powis Arms, where local ales and seasonal produce satiate tiring ramblers. There's even ice cream for the dog, too.

Need to know: Some accommodation here has enclosed outdoor space, including Norbury Hall. Dogs are welcome to roam off-lead in the arboretum if they're under control; beyond this, keep them on a lead and beware of livestock throughout the estate.

↓ The view from the veranda at Norbury Hall

DELVE INTO BIRMINGHAM'S BIZARRE HISTORIES

88

Birmingham, West Midlands

birminghamwalkingtours.co.uk

If you think you know Birmingham, you might want to think again. Kevin Thomas, a passionate Brummie photographer with a penchant for quirky local history, will undoubtedly be able to tell you a few things you never knew about this spirited city. His walking tours take in some well-known neighbourhoods – such as the Jewellery Quarter or city centre – but always put an eccentric twist on their history. There'll be no long lectures on architecture or industry here; expect a run-down of the city's lost pubs, with stories of revelling and rioting, or explore some of Brum's more gruesome history with his 'Five Ways to Die in Birmingham' walk, which travels between plague pits and cemeteries.

If cemeteries are your thing, he even does two-hour tours of the little-known Birmingham Catacombs. It might sound a touch dry, but there's little chance you'll be bored to death when you can pay your bittersweet respects to the likes of Alfred Bird of Bird's Custard or John Wellington Starr, inventor of the lightbulb whose own light extinguished in 1846 on a trip to England from his home in Cincinnati. **Make a night of it:** Sitting right on the Birmingham Canal, Malmaison is a handy city-centre escape with a dog-friendly bar. malmaison.com

ASTLEY CASTLE

89

Astley, Warwickshire

landmarktrust.org.uk

There aren't many places you can stay in the UK that have been hosting visitors – royals, nobles and plain folk like us – since the Saxon period. And from inside Astley Castle, you wouldn't know just how old its walls are and just how many stories they could tell, if only they could talk. Its interiors are a triumph of minimalist modern design and architecture, with a mix of mid-century modern and farmhouse-style furniture and a few splashes of regal colour in green velvet curtains and red-painted dining chairs, all fitted neatly within a once-decaying ancient structure.

While Astley enjoyed an illustrious history – proudly owned by two Yorkist queens in the 16th century and later

WHAT'S NEARBY?

If you can drag yourself away from your regal surroundings, a trip into Birmingham city centre offers intrigue by way of unusual dog-friendly walking tours around its historic Jewellery Quarter and beyond (see left), as well as plenty of green space for the dog to explore – the city has more than 8,000 acres of green space. Coventry is just a 20-minute drive south of Astley Castle and has a stunning ruined cathedral that can be explored with the dog; it sits right next to its modern counterpart, a gob-smacking Brutalist construction that's divided opinion since its opening in the 1960s.

↑ An aerial view of The Owl House

inspiring Mary Ann Evans, better known as George Eliot, in her short story *Scenes of Clerical Life* – if it weren't for The Landmark Trust, Astley might have been lost to the ground forever in the 1990s. After centuries of private and royal ownership, and then a brief stint as a hotel, Astley began to crumble in the 1980s after a disastrous fire ripped through its bedrooms, and when The Landmark Trust got its hands on the property, it was a ruinous mess almost beyond repair.

Rather than rebuild and restore, they froze in time the decay that was occurring, building in and around its tumbling walls, preserving their ruin while reviving their purpose. Today, its cracks are most obvious from the outside, where new modern brickwork sits comfortably within the original manor house walls, propping up centuries of history. So lauded was this innovative way of restoring an ancient construction, the castle won the RIBA Stirling Prize for architecture in 2013 and continues to be praised today by the hundreds of lucky visitors who book a stay in its four bedrooms, which look out on an open

estate ripe for roaming with the dog.
Where to walk: There's lots of land to explore around the castle itself, but a footpath leads north from the estate to Ansley village, where you can stop in at The Lord Nelson Inn for a pint, or drive into Nuneaton to explore the 43-hectare Whittleford Park.
Need to know: The gardens around Astley Castle aren't enclosed, so dogs need to be kept under control or on a lead.

STAY

THE OWL HOUSE 90

Pulverbatch, Shropshire
www.pawsandstay.co.uk/owl-house

Adventure at The Owl House begins as soon as you arrive: a wheelbarrow awaits by your parking space in the woods to cart all your belongings to the cabin, and it's a pleasant five-minute amble through the forest, across a field and along a stream to your own enclosed patch of wilderness. Set within the branches of an alder tree is your own little wooden oasis – an open-plan studio built from oak frames and clad with cedar shingles with vast decking overlooking a small valley. Here, the only sounds are the local flock and the babbling stream at the bottom of the hill, and perhaps the owners' dogs racing about their garden a few fields away.

Your dogs can roam freely around the grounds of the treehouse while you sip coffee on the deck or soak in the large outdoor tub – push the button on the wall to start the bubbles – and inside, an exceptionally efficient log burner keeps the entire place toasty warm whatever the weather. You can tell owners Kerry and Dave have been in this business a while as they've thought of everything, from the torch in the little box in the car park to help you find your way home through the trees after a night in the pub to the honesty wine rack full of bubbles and Bordeaux. There's a complimentary welcome stash of beer, wine, biscuits, eggs and butter, and in the freezer you'll

find homecooked meals made by a local chef to purchase if you can't bring yourselves to leave. And frankly, why would you? The south-facing dining area is blessed with warming evening sun and on a clear night, sitting beneath the stars by the fire pit is utterly blissful.

Where to walk: With quiet country lanes and ample footpaths leading to villages with charming pubs, there's plenty of opportunity for stretching your legs. Romp across the fields to Picklescott for Ludlow Brewing Co beers in The Bottle & Glass Inn (**bottleandglasspicklescott.co.uk**), a traditional old free house with comfort food aplenty on the menu, or walk slightly further to Pulverbatch, where The White Horse Inn (**thewhitehorseinnpulverbatch .co.uk**) does mighty roasts. For a longer walk, head to the National Trust's Carding Mill Valley and Long Mynd (**nationaltrust.org.uk**).

WHAT'S NEARBY?
The lovely market town of Shrewsbury is just a 30-minute drive from here and you can take the dog into the old prison for a somewhat disturbingly immersive experience (see page 78). Further immersion is available to the east at Ironbridge, where Blists Hill Victorian Town (**ironbridge.org .uk**) is a recreation of a 19th-century community with costumed actors and real, old-timey shops.

Need to know: Dogs get a pack of treats, poo bags and balls on arrival and there are plenty of bowls and towels. There's good stock fencing here but it's only around a metre high so won't keep in bouncy dogs. There's livestock on site (though not within your enclosed paddock) and wild deer often roam the forests nearby, so dogs with a prey drive are best kept on leads when arriving or departing the treehouse.

↑ A border collie enjoys the welcome mat at The Owl House

↓ Rutland Water

WALK

HAMBLETON PENINSULA

91

Rutland

START POINT: Oakham Road, LE15 8HJ
DISTANCE/TIME: 8km/2 hrs

When Anglian Water wanted to create a reservoir in the fields surrounding the village of Hambleton, villagers were predictably up in arms. Since its creation, though, Rutland Water has become this little community's greatest asset – the views from many of its waterfront houses are simply serene, and the footpath that tracks the shoreline is a wonderful and easy 8km walk. Park up on Oakham Road before you reach the hill that leads into the village, or in the small car park on the left-hand side (///throats.negotiators. princes), and walk eastwards to take the footpath at ///cyclones.makes.pickle. From here, you'll start to get glimpses of the water – sparkling on sunny days and a deep, melancholy grey when the clouds dull the light – as you navigate the undulating northern side of the peninsula. You might wander among grazing sheep, or if you come before a cold winter sets in, you could spot ospreys soaring in the skies anytime from spring to autumn – the Rutland Osprey Project reintroduced the birds here in 1996 and there have been hundreds of chicks born since.

As you round the end of the peninsula, detour to its far eastern tip to see the county's iconic Normanton Church on the opposite bank before making the westward stride back along the southern edge. With the right conditions, you can watch windsurfers catching the breeze on the water as you stroll back to the car.

> **WHAT'S FOR LUNCH?**
> Head into Hambleton village proper for some sustenance, either in the bar of The Finch's Arms (finchsarms. co.uk) or drive into Oakham for burgers at The Grainstore Brewery (grainstorebrewery.com).

Need to know: Dogs must be on leads throughout due to grazing sheep.

SHREWSBURY PRISON

Shrewsbury, Shropshire
shrewsburyprison.com

Shrewsbury is a handsome little market town in north Shropshire, but one of its buildings has a particularly dark history: the 18th-century prison. Not only did this vast fortress of a building host dangerous criminals, but it was also a place of public executions until the mid-1800s, and private executions continued until 1961. Now it's a highly interactive museum where you can take guided tours with the dog on a lead – just be sure to behave, or you might find yourself in the stocks.

HEART OF THE FOREST TRAIL (SOUTHERN CIRCUIT)

Leicestershire

START POINT: Moira Furnace, DE12 6AT
DISTANCE/TIME: circular 8km/2 hrs

Don't come to the National Forest expecting sweeping views and dramatic landscapes. This region of the Midlands, sandwiched between Birmingham, Derby and Leicester, is almost as flat as a pancake. It is neither the oldest forest in Britain nor the largest, but its story is truly captivating and its trails

↓ The greenery of Ashby Canal

– of which there are many, including a 121km long-distance route – are the best way to understand it. This is a story of regeneration.

Moira Furnace is the beginning of the Heart of the Forest trail and it's here you'll begin to get an idea of this region's history: an old blast furnace and a disused canal set the scene for an industrial adventure. This was mining country back in the 1930s, with coal, limestone, granite and brick clay extracted from beneath the earth. But today you wouldn't know it, because the National Forest was established in the 1990s and since then, its management company has planted thousands of trees across 518 sq km in one of the most impressive rewilding projects in the country.

From Moira, the trail tracks a little along the disused Ashby Canal, once the method of transporting coal from here

to the railways. It opened in 1804 but was abandoned in the 1940s, and now it's just mallard ducks and swans that cruise down its still waters and nest in the thick reeds. After heading north-east, you'll then change tack and turn southwards to enter Hicks Lodge. This former coal mine, where trucks with 2-metre-tall tyres and huge diggers once rattled along its grey, dusty tracks, is a testament to the wider transformation of the whole National Forest. What was once a blackened landscape with few natural features aside from one small cluster of trees – still seen on the eastern side of the lake – is now a beautiful nature reserve with bird hides for watching sand martins and a large shimmering lake.

Also unrecognisable is Donisthorpe Colliery, now a young native woodland area, and an information board with pictures of its mining days shows the stark difference in scenery today. But most charming is Thortit Pit site, not for its looks – though it is a handsome forest these days – but for the story behind its moniker. The discovery of coal here was a surprise to many, which led to many locals exclaiming 'Who'd have thought it!' The name stuck, and you'll still hear residents refer to it as Thortit Pit today. Looking at the contrast – the past versus the present – you too might just find yourself muttering 'Who'd have thought it' under your breath as you explore this once barren, now beautiful area.

> **WHAT'S FOR LUNCH?**
> There's a cafe at Moira Furnace as well as Hicks Lodge, where you can dine inside or out with views over the lake.

Need to know: You'll have to cross a few roads on this trail and navigate a couple of dog-friendly stiles. There may be livestock along the route. Download the map from nationalforest.org.

↑ Autumnal woodland in later afternoon sun

LADYHILL TRAIL, CANNOCK CHASE

94

Staffordshire

START POINT: WS15 2UQ
DISTANCE/TIME: 1.6km/20 mins

Cannock Chase is a near 70 sq km landscape made up of fragile heathland, working farmland and planted forestry, which produces over 19,000 tonnes of timber each year. Among all this lie thousands of unique habitats harbouring protected wildlife, including lizards and bright little yellowhammers, and insect life such as emperor moths and dragonflies – some of which you might just see on the Ladyhill Trail.

This short, flat route – which is suitable for wheelchairs and pushchairs – might only take 20 minutes to complete if you don't dawdle, but dawdle you should. The trail takes you from the car park and into the woodland, where sculptures of characters from favourite children's story *The Gruffalo* can be found hiding in the trees. There are 'Fairy Trees', where clever carvers have etched doors and staircases into the most robust trunks, and at the end of the trail you'll find yourself in Pingle Slade, a clearing perfect for picnics that also has an agility trail for dogs. Teach your pet to weave and jump on the apparatus, which has been created using locally felled wood.

> **WHAT'S FOR LUNCH?**
> If you're not bringing your own picnic, head south in the car to The Swan With Two Necks (theswanwithtwoneckslongdon .co.uk). This unusually named pub has real ales, an open fire and serves proper, traditional pub comfort food.

Need to know: This is a hugely popular trail for families so is best for dogs used to children and with excellent recall.

CALKE ABBEY

95

Ticknall, Derbyshire
nationaltrust.org.uk

This regal, baroque-style mansion plonked in the middle of the Derbyshire countryside has had many owners, but none were quite so eccentric as Sir Vauncey Harpur-Crewe, who filled the home with all manner of curiosities – from taxidermy birds to hundreds of shells from beaches all over the world. He was a natural history buff, and so Calke Abbey became home to a number of unusual collections towards the end of the 18th century.

Today, it's these collections and the general state of decay that earns this house its alternative moniker: 'the unstately home'. Calke is a time capsule of a period in which British country estates were struggling, and it shows in the mansion's messy staterooms, where peeling wallpaper and piles of children's toys have been left as they were on the day it became the property of the National Trust.

Not only is the house decaying on the inside, but its grounds have also been left to go wild in places, making it an intriguing and sometimes haunting 600-acre estate to explore with the dog. Look out for the 'Old Man of Calke', a 1,200-year-old oak tree that looks as if it's been ripped from the pages of a Brothers Grimm tale.

Once you've seen the formal gardens and admired the mansion's handsome sandstone exterior, take the dog on a romp across the fields and beyond the estate's reaches: a footpath bears south-west from the main driveway and across cattle pasture, before reaching a tight bend on a single-track road. Just 150 metres south along the road you'll find The Milking Parlour (tollgatebrewery.co.uk), home to one of Derbyshire's favourite breweries, Tollgate, and their pizza kitchen. It makes an excellent lunch stop before heading back up to Calke Abbey to see inside the house (assistance dogs only; leave yours in the car or with a member of your party in the dog-friendly stable yard).

BELTON HOUSE

96

Grantham, Lincolnshire
nationaltrust.org.uk

Visit the attractive grounds of a fantastic Restoration-style country house, where sheep roam its manicured lawns and more than 20,000 snowdrops pop up with each new year. Walk the dog through its formal pleasure gardens and let the kids loose on its excellent outdoor adventure playground or on the miniature train. The on-site cafe is dog-friendly.

THE TAWNY

97

Stoke-on-Trent, Staffordshire
thetawny.co.uk

Even on the soggiest, most drab of days, The Tawny hotel and its highly manicured grounds feel like a special little English paradise. This 'deconstructed hotel', where bedrooms are independent

can even get a breakfast hamper for lazy mornings in bed.

For dogs, there are treats left in the room and a toy to keep them entertained, but the best part is the 8km of footpaths that wend their way around the ponds, leading down into a rainforest-like woodland where they can sniff out black deer tracks or peer into rabbit holes. Listen out for the call of tawny owls, too, which reside here year-round and can sometimes be seen hunting at dusk.

Where to walk: Beyond the spectacular grounds of the hotel lies the beautiful Consall Woods RSPB reserve, which has lakes and woodland to drift among as you spot flycatchers, bright redstarts and nuthatches. Of course, you're right on the edge of the dramatic Peak District here, where gritstone outcrops and majestic mounds like Mam Tor make for rather epic walking. Head to The Roaches, where you can park on the side of Roach Road and then head up on to one of the most dramatic escarpments in the area.

dwellings of varying different designs – think shepherd's huts or treehouses or log cabins – is set amid a classical English country garden with follies and flowers and fabulous trees.

The estate, which was previously known as the Consall Hall Gardens Estate, began life in the hands of the English gentry in the 13th century. Later, a Georgian manor house was built on the land and, in the 1900s, William Podmore took over its gardens, redesigning its entire landscape to look much like what you see today: ponds, lush plants and spectacular views from all corners, be it on its bridges or from its handful of unique follies.

The Georgian manor house is long gone, but in its place stands the towering modern restaurant where creative seasonal menus make it a veritable dining (dog-friendly) destination, and across the 70 acres of grounds are a smattering of bedrooms housed in unusual buildings. Each one promises romantic views across the estate and an outdoor hot tub on a private deck, and if you can't bear to leave the room, there's excellent pizza and flatbread delivered to your door. You

> **WHAT'S NEARBY?**
> It's highly likely you'll hear the Churnet Valley Railway before you see it, as the tracks run not far from The Tawny and its whistle often rings around the grounds of the hotel as it passes by. This heritage steam railway is dog-friendly (though it's £10 a ticket for your pet) and it offers a scenic 35.4km round trip through the Staffordshire countryside, with stops at Froghall, Consall or Cheddleton.

Need to know: Dogs must be kept on leads throughout the site when around fellow guests, but it's safe to let them off in the lower gardens provided that they have adequate recall and remain under close control.

CRICH TRAMWAY VILLAGE

98

Matlock, Derbyshire tramway.co.uk

Crich Tramway Village is an open-air museum with a difference. Not only can you see vintage transport, from open-top trams with fancy wrought-iron barriers to luxury tramcars that look more like boats, but you can ride them, too – and so can the dog. They trundle along tracks between various stops, including a mock period high street with buildings that have been rescued from demolition in towns across Britain. It has its own working pub and sweet shop, and elsewhere you can walk through their woodland sculpture trail or visit the 'Electrifying the Future' exhibition to learn how trams changed the world.

BAINLAND LODGE RETREATS

99

Bainland Country Park, Lincolnshire bainland.co.uk

Whether you've got a special occasion to celebrate or you're just having a big family get-together, Bainland Lodge Retreats is a brilliant place for multi-dog, multi-generational escapes. This high-end lodge park – think Center Parcs but with a bit more swank – has accommodation in all shapes and sizes, from two-bed cabins with hot tubs and enclosed decks to sprawling 24-person lodges with private pools and large lawned gardens.

There's plenty to keep you entertained indoors, with pool tables and arcade machines in some of the lodges,

↓ Atmospheric evening in Steep Hill

enormous kitchens and dining tables for big group dinners, and hot tubs to bubble away in out the back (the larger lodges even have two tubs so the entire party can dive in). But beyond the swish interiors of your lodge, there's even more entertainment outside. Try your hand at becoming the next Robin Hood at the archery range, where the dog can relax at the back while you compete to see who can shoot the most accurate arrows in an array of games led by an instructor. Or scale the outdoor climbing wall while the dog watches from below. Kids will love the pedal street karting, mini Land Rover track and the on-site alpaca herd, and the indoor pool is available for private hire so the whole family can enjoy a dip.

Where to walk: Bainland's side gate opens out on to a public footpath, which, if you head south, will take you to Ostlers Plantation (note that you'll need to cross a relatively quiet but fast road; forestryengland.uk), where the dog can wander off-lead among the conifers and monkey puzzles. Many of

its footpaths are concrete – a hangover from the former airfield that once lay here – and there are fascinating remnants from WWII operations, including bomb stores from the 'Dambusters' squadron. In autumn, the heather that fringes the footpaths comes into purple bloom, and in summer you must watch out for the piri piri burrs, which will make any long dog coat matted within minutes.

Need to know: The lodge gardens are all enclosed with 1.8m fences though some have shorter fences around the side gate entrance. Dog bowls are provided but you need to bring beds. The excellent on-site restaurant, The Nest, is dog-friendly and offers delivery to your accommodation.

EXPERIENCE

BUS ABOUT LINCOLN

Lincoln, Lincolnshire lincolnbig.co.uk

Lincoln is one of the most dog-friendly cities in the UK but there's one major drawback: some of its best attractions sit on top of a punishingly steep hill called, well, Steep Hill. Fortunately for older dogs and less energetic owners, the excellent open-top, hop-on-hop-off bus tours can ferry you between sights while offering insightful commentary along the way. You can catch it at any of its nine stops, including the Brayford Waterfront and the historic Cathedral Quarter, between March and October. Don't miss a tour of the cathedral with one of the expert guides (dogs welcome) and try to time your visit with a dog-friendly day at the adjacent Norman castle.

Make a night of it: Stay just 30 minutes away at the ultra-dog-friendly Bainland Lodge Retreats (see page 83).

WHAT'S NEARBY?

The handsome little town of Woodhall Spa is a 30-minute walk from Bainland Lodges and has a few intriguing little shops and a couple of good dog-friendly pubs. A 10-minute drive south takes you to Tattershall Castle, an imposing 15th-century castle with one impressive intact tower (no dogs inside) and lovely grounds to explore. A little further afield is Lincoln city centre, where dog-friendly attractions abound. A breathtaking cathedral, a Norman castle, a Victorian prison and a hop-on-hop-off bus tour (see right) could keep you busy for days, but a mooch around its many dog-friendly shops on Steep Hill and the pubs of the Cathedral Quarter is equally entertaining.

↑ Winnats Pass

GO UNDER-GROUND IN THE PEAK DISTRICT

101

Castleton, Derbyshire
speedwellcavern.co.uk

The southern Peak District is known for its skyward hills, such as Mam Tor (see page 87) and Kinder Scout, but below these rocky summits lies a fascinating underworld, packed with stories of danger and fortune, for this is mining country. Beneath the dramatic landscape around Castleton lies a network of caverns, some natural, but many man-made, created when precious minerals and metals were discovered here in the 18th century.

At the base of the spectacular Winnats Pass, Speedwell Cavern offers a unique opportunity to see a former mine by boat. Descend the 105 steps, which were built in 1778, down into the belly of the mine and you'll board a small boat on an underground river that now flows between two caves. Your guide will take you into a tunnel and regale you with tales of the miners who once worked here looking for lead to send to the surface, before docking at the 'Bottomless Pit', a large underground lake. Dogs can join you in the boat and explore the cave at the end of the underground river but note that it can be noisy and incredibly dark, so it's best for confident dogs only.
Make a night of it: The Devonshire Arms at Beeley is a supremely dog-friendly pub with rooms serving excellent meals by a cosy log fire. devonshirehotels .co.uk 🐕 2 🐾 <£200

MAM TOR CIRCULAR WALK

102

Derbyshire

START POINT: S33 8WA
DISTANCE / TIME: circular 5km/2 hrs

The lofty peak of Mam Tor is an almost irresistible vantage point in the Derbyshire Peak District. At 517 metres high, on a clear day you can see right across to the even loftier Kinder Scout. The terrain is tough, not because of scree or uneven footpaths – it's a stone-surfaced path that's easy to navigate – but because there are steep, breathtaking inclines to tackle. The reward, though, is well worth the racing heartbeat: gentle drama of the green Derbyshire Dales to the south and the Edale Valley to the north.

Need to know: Directions via the National Trust website (**nationaltrust.org.uk**). Dogs must be on leads due to grazing sheep and steep terrain. Speedwell Cavern is a dog-friendly attraction nearby (see page 85).

WHAT'S FOR LUNCH?
An excellent ploughman's at Ye Olde Cheshire Cheese Inn (**cheshirecheeseinn.co.uk/en-GB**) in Castleton, at the bottom of one of Britain's most arresting roads: Winnats Pass.

← The footpath to Mam Tor

EAST ANGLIA & CAMBRIDGESHIRE

117 116 115

114 113

109 112

110
Norwich

111

108

107

106

105
Cambridge

104

103

HARE FIELD CABIN 103

Sudbury, Suffolk
canopyandstars.co.uk

If it's peace and quiet you're after, this modest little countryside cabin is the way forward. On the edge of the village of Foxearth you'll find Hare Field Cabin stranded between a pair of fields. Huge floor-to-ceiling windows and doors look out on to the crops that grow here in summer – often a sea of bright yellow rapeseed – and a pretty little patio with loungers and a fire pit offers an opportunity to get close to nature.
Where to walk: There are countless ways to walk here, with footpaths leading in all directions from the cabin to pretty medieval villages such as Long Melford. For dogs with poor recall, Brookfield Place Kennels has a secure field for hire (brookfieldplacekennels.co.uk).

→ A black labrador sitting on the deck outside Hare Field Cabin

THE FOOD MUSEUM

104

Stowmarket, Suffolk

foodmuseum.org.uk

In a region that's been called the 'breadbasket of Britain', it's fitting to find the country's only museum dedicated to food. Owners of hungry Labradors need not turn the page here as there's no risk of actual food being pilfered or snaffled by dogs – except in the on-site cafe. This museum focuses very much on the process behind food and learning about where our breakfast, lunch and dinner comes from.

It's an outdoor museum with historic buildings set across 75 acres of leafy grounds, where you can follow a sculpture trail or bob in and out of its structures to see various exhibitions. You might explore a medieval barn – the oldest building there – or see the Boby Building's various tools used throughout the ages to gather food from fields and orchards. You can nip inside farmers' homes, where exhibitions tell the stories of residents and their agricultural lives, and there's wartime history here, too. A pair of huts thought to have been taken from Mendlesham Airfield were most likely used by the US 8th Air Force during WWII.

There are various demonstrations, tastings in the Bone Building (no dogs inside, they'll need to wait outside) and talks throughout the year, so keep coming back to learn more. Dogs are welcome all over the museum except in the Bone Building and Abbot's Hall; they must be on leads throughout.

↓ A terrier posing outside one of Cambridge University's colleges

WALK

CAMBRIDGE TO GRANTCHESTER RIVER WALK 105

Cambridge

START POINT: Cambridge Market Square, CB1 0SS
DISTANCE/TIME: 5.7km/1.5 hrs each way

This point-to-point route starting in Cambridge city centre is a superb meander for taking in those famous university colleges and exploring a little of the Cambridgeshire countryside. It wends its way west from the city centre and over Clare Bridge, then southwards along The Backs, where you'll get arresting views of King's College across the River Cam. If a game of fetch is in your dog's agenda, this is the place for it before you walk on along the riverbank towards Grantchester. The footpath passes through various nature reserves and livestock paddocks, and then turns west into the village where thatched cottages and timber-framed pubs abound.

> **WHAT'S FOR LUNCH?**
> The Red Lion in Grantchester (**redliongrantchester.co.uk**) welcomes dogs in the bar area, where you can feast on cheese platters, fish and chips or cracking Sunday roasts before walking back into the city.

Need to know: Dogs are allowed off-lead if they are under control but note there may be livestock along the river. This is an easy-to-follow walk even with Google Maps, but OS directions can be downloaded from **gps-routes.co.uk**. If you don't fancy the walk back, the 118 bus leaves from Burnt Close and takes just 15 minutes to return to Cambridge.

COVEHITHE BEACH

106

Suffolk

This little-visited beach in Suffolk is a beautiful expanse of soft sand and pebbles. Its remoteness makes it ideal for busy summer months when the county's more popular beaches bring in dog bans or become overcrowded with visitors. The evidence of coastal erosion is stark here, as remnants of woodland that once sat atop the cliffs can often be seen scattered on the beach and the original road to the sands now stops abruptly at a cliff edge. Don't walk this way, but instead follow a footpath clearly marked from the village that takes you across fields to a safer beach access point. Down on the sand, you can walk for miles in either direction, or simply set up with a picnic on your towel to enjoy the sound of the encroaching seas.

While here, also don't miss exploring the part-ruined St Andrew's Church before or after heading to the beach – during its medieval heyday it was a sizeable building, but now just a smaller 17th-century thatched church remains ensconced within its original ruin. At just 375 metres away from the cliffs, experts predict this little village will no longer exist in a hundred years.

Make a night of it: A 45-minute drive south from Covehithe is Letheringham Mill, a collection of luxurious holiday homes set within 7 acres entirely surrounded by water to keep them safe. letheringhammill.co.uk

🛏5 👤2-8 🏠 ❄ ♨ £200
Parking: NR34 7JW

↓ Driftwood on Covehithe Beach

ELY CATHEDRAL

Ely, Cambridgeshire elycathedral.org

Come to admire the sheer splendour of Ely Cathedral, a 1,300-year-old building that was marooned on an island until the surrounding Fens were drained 400 years ago. Today, it welcomes thousands of visitors to its truly spectacular monastic buildings, chapels and the fascinating octagonal tower, and dogs are welcome too (as well as inside the Stained Glass Museum nearby; **stainedglassmuseum.com**).

↓ Ely Cathedral on a summer's day

BECCLES MARSH TRAIL WALK

Suffolk

START POINT: Beccles, NR34 0AJ
DISTANCE/TIME: 6.4km/2.5 hrs

Summertime on this Norfolk Broads trail is a spectacular sight: wildflowers of yellow and purple bloom in the grasses, while butterflies and dragonflies flit between the foliage. If you come early in the morning, you might even spot a kingfisher diving for its breakfast, or a harrier hunting from the sky. The trail also takes in an ancient Iron Age causeway, and dykes that were created during the medieval period.
Need to know: Dogs must be kept on the lead. Download the route from **visitthebroads.co.uk**.

WHAT'S FOR LUNCH?
The most dog-friendly place in Eccles is Paws for Tea tearoom (07974 110376) which serves homemade quiches, sandwiches and cakes – plus an array of treats for the dog.

↓ A dog on a boat in the Norfolk Broads

NORWICH CATHEDRAL

Norwich, Norfolk cathedral.org.uk

With the largest monastic cloister of any cathedral in England and the second-tallest spire after Salisbury Cathedral (see page 37). While it's the size of this nearly thousand-year-old church that will capture you initially, it's the details that deserve the most attention – not least the 1,200 medieval roof bosses, carved protrusions in the ceiling that here illustrate stories from the Bible. The shiny copper font has unusual origins, having been repurposed from the nearby Rowntree's confectionery, and in the centre of the cloister there's a labyrinth to conquer.

EXPLORE THE NORFOLK BROADS BY BOAT

Norfolk broadstours.co.uk

Windmills, birdlife and winding rivers flanked by reeds and grasses make up the enchanting landscape of the Broads National Park. Within this thriving ecosystem lives some of the UK's rarest wildlife, including bitterns, water voles, European eels and swallowtail butterflies, which can grow up to 9cm in size. The best way to see it all, of course, is on the water and Norfolk Broads Direct run river trips on their double-decker *Belle of the Broads* vessel, which was built right here in Wroxham. You can also hire day boats for your own exploration if you're confident playing skipper.
Make a night of it: There's no need to book a hotel here, as Norfolk Broads Direct has cruisers sleeping up to six people so you can spend an entire week on the water with the dog if you so wish. They'll even provide lifejackets.
broads.co.uk 🐾2 <£200

WREN'S NEST

Wendling, Norfolk
thefirepitcamp.co.uk

Neither hut nor cabin nor tent, Wren's Nest is a truly unique construction. This domed building – deceivingly small on the outside and surprisingly spacious inside, like some sort of natural, fairy-tale Tardis – is made from locally felled hazel branches, dug 1.8m into the ground and bent over to create a frame for its custom canopy. It has hard wooden flooring, raised like garden decking to keep it from getting too cold, and is insulated with natural sheep's wool for extra warmth, so this is an idyllic winter escape. Not least because, in the real depths of the season,

↑ Arty in the dog bed at Wren's Nest

when Fire Pit is in semi-hibernation as its seasonal bell tents have been put to bed, you'll be the only guests on site here.

You won't be alone, though, as myriad animals call this rural little spot just outside Norwich home, including the owls that you'll hear hooting through the night and the squirrels whose feet tip-tap on the top of the Wren's Nest canvas come sunrise. This is a supremely magical place when all is quiet, aside from the roar of the log fire in the belly of the Nest, and when it comes to leaving, you'll no doubt find yourself disappointed to return to a life within bricks and mortar.

Where to walk: There aren't many walks on your doorstep here as footpaths are few and far between, but hop in the car and you're just 25 minutes from the 500-year-old Oxburgh Estate (nationaltrust.org.uk), where you can amble around formal gardens or take in the trails through park and woodland.

Need to know: Wren's Nest sleeps six people and allows two dogs. The family-run Fire Pit Camp has a brilliant pizzeria on site, which is open most days for takeaway even throughout winter.

There's a large field for the dog to run around in, but it's not fully enclosed so only dogs with excellent recall should be trusted off-lead. Bring a longline and camping tether for wayward dogs.

WHAT'S NEARBY? The handsome Georgian town of Swaffham is just 12km west of Fire Pit Camp and is well worth a diversion for its excellent Saturday market and dog-friendly pubs and cafes – try the Market Cross Cafe Bar (facebook .com/marketcrosscafebar). Of course, Norwich city centre is equally enticing for its collection of excellent independent shops and green spaces. Head to Eaton Park or Mousehold Heath for a walk, then make your way to the city's towering cathedral (see page 93) to explore its vast and intricate interiors. Stop in at the quirky Norwich Playhouse Bar for a drink, and for a spot of dog-friendly culture, the Sainsbury Centre Sculpture Park has works by Antony Gormley and Henry Moore.

WINTERTON-ON-SEA BEACH 112

Norfolk

Beyond the small town of Winterton and a vast grassy dune system, this beach spreads out along the coastline and has a wide expanse of soft sand, which is still sizeable even when the tide is in. Dogs can run around off-lead as there's plenty of space even during the busy summer months. Come winter, dogs will need to be kept on a lead as this stretch is a breeding ground for seals, which have their white fluffy pups between November and January. Never approach seals; they can be dangerous.

Make a night of it: Book East Ruston Cottages' Hidden Gem to sleep right next to the dunes. eastrustoncottages.co.uk

🐕4 👤4 <£200
Parking: NR29 4AJ

THE WALNUT 113

Happisburgh, Norfolk
eastrustoncottages.co.uk

When a holiday cottage owner goes out of their way to welcome your pet to their home, it puts you at ease immediately, and this is exactly what Stella and Paul do at The Walnut in Happisburgh. There are few places quite as dog-friendly as this flintstone cottage: dog beds of various sizes are scattered throughout the house, there are crates available to use if you wish, and you'll find a little pack of goodies on the kitchen table when you arrive, including treats for the dog. All the little things are taken care of too, with spare leads and poo bags aplenty, and even a selection of toys. In the enclosed garden you'll find a patio and fenced-in paddock, and a hot tub for the humans to enjoy.

↓ Dog walking on Winterton-on-Sea Beach

Where to walk: An excellent 8km romp across the fields and along the coastline is from the cottage to Walcott's Kingfisher Fish Bar (<u>01692 652999</u>) for a chippy lunch. Head towards Happisburgh village, with its attractive red and white lighthouse, then follow the coast path (or its diversions – there's lots of coastal erosion here) on to Walcott. The beach here is wide and sandy, and the dog-friendly chippy overlooks the sea.

Need to know: There are few rules here – dogs can snooze with you on the sofa (throws provided) – but the main one is that you mustn't leave your pets alone in the property. A dog-sitting service is available for dog-free nights out, though. The two-bed cottage sits on a quiet road surrounded by fields and advertises itself as reactive dog friendly, meaning those with nervous dogs who bark at passers-by or other dogs needn't worry.

↓ Arty on Cart Gap Beach in winter

BLICKLING ESTATE WALK

114

Blickling Park, Norfolk
nationaltrust.org.uk

START POINT: Blickling Hall Car Park, NR11 6NF
DISTANCE/TIME: circular 7km/1.5 hrs

There are any number of routes around the Blickling Estate's 4,600 acres, but this one takes in some of its highlights – and has showstopping views across its handsome grounds to the elegant Jacobean mansion at its centre. You'll pass the 13th-century church of St Andrews in the village and a hidden little ice house tucked away in a plantation on Silvergate Lane, before heading west through woodland and meadows where you can gaze across at Blickling Hall.

You'll come across a tower that was the grandstand for an 18th-century racecourse here (it's now a National Trust holiday cottage) before heading into Great Wood, where ancient oaks, beech and chestnut trees have been creaking for over 300 years. The final intriguing point of interest is a huge pyramid mausoleum, where the 2nd Earl of Buckinghamshire and his two wives are interred within 190,000 Portland stone blocks. The walk ends with lovely views of the River Bure

WHAT'S FOR LUNCH?
A menu of pub classics with a few more unusual features (think Thai seafood curries, pheasant schnitzel, light and crispy tempura vegetables) can be enjoyed at the 18th-century Buckinghamshire Arms Aylsham (<u>bucksarms.co.uk</u>) next door to the start point.

before heading back to the visitor centre. **Need to know:** Look out for the blue arrow waymarkers on white-topped posts to follow this route without a map; otherwise, directions can be downloaded from nationaltrust.org.uk.

STAY

4 COASTGUARD COTTAGE

Weybourne, Norfolk
pawsandstay.co.uk

You can't stay much closer to the sea than at this cosy terraced cottage that sits right on the Norfolk Coast Path. Inside it's all antiques and log fires and seafaring equipment like the wall-mounted barometer, while outside there's a small enclosed garden and the wonderful restriction-free Weybourne beach on your doorstep. A short walk away is the dog-friendly Ship Inn, but even dog-friendlier is the Wiveton Bell, which has its own dog menu (15 mins by car).

Adventures abound nearby. Boat trips to Blakeney Point (see right) in winter are the highlight, as here thousands of seals loll about on the sand between November and January to give birth to their fluffy white pups. Try your hand at crabbing from the quay in Blakeney – just remember to put your catch back – and stop in at Cookie's Crab Shop (salthouse.org.uk) for a platter of local seafood before heading home.
Where to walk: The coastline here has spectacular walks – Holkham to Wells-next-the-Sea is particularly lovely, but you can head out of your front door and in either direction for excellent sea views from the clifftops.
Need to know: Dog bowls, treats and towels provided; the garden fence is

only around a metre high so not suitable for dogs that jump. Small, determined escapologists might well be able to get through the gaps in the fence, too.

EXPERIENCE

GO SEAL WATCHING SAFELY

Norfolk beansboattrips.co.uk

By far the safest way to see Norfolk's enormous seal colonies each winter is by boat. Bring your binoculars and jump on board Beans Boats, which cruise around to Blakeney Point in North Norfolk, where thousands of these blubbery creatures flop about on the sand.
Make a night of it: Book into the 4 Coastguard Cottage (see left) right on the Norfolk Coast Path.

BEACH

HOLKHAM BEACH

Norfolk holkham.co.uk

Holkham Beach is a gloriously wide expanse of sand on the north Norfolk coast reached via a boardwalk through a pine woodland. Winter sunrises are particularly magical here, and a dog-friendly cafe serves warming cups of tea and freshly made sandwiches.
Make a night of it: The Victoria in Holkham village is a lovely pub with rooms and a dog-friendly dining room. holkham.co.uk 🐕2 🅿 <£200
Parking: 33 Lady Anne's Drive, NR23 1RJ

NORTHEAST ENGLAND

141
140
139
138

Northumberland National Park

137 Newcastle upon Tyne 136
135
134

133
132
Middlesborough 129 130
128
131
127 126
125 *North York Moors National Park*
124
122 123
York
121 120
Hull
118 119

EXPERIENCE

TAKE A WALKING TOUR OF HULL'S BEST PUBS

118

Hull, East Riding of Yorkshire
tourhulll.com

There may be no other Hull resident with a passion for his home town like Paul Schofield, and it especially shines through on his pub walks. Whether or not it's anything to do with the local ale he imbibes is beside the point: this man is a font of Hull knowledge and he delivers it with the gusto of a Labrador in a steakhouse. Book a private pub tour and learn the quirks of Hull's old town streets – including the story behind the Land of Green Ginger and the smallest window in Britain –

while stopping in some of its oldest drinking houses.

Make a night of it: Stumble home to Hideout Apartment Hotel, whose sleek, modern apartments are an excellent place to sleep it off. www.hideouthotel.co.uk 1 2-4 £200

NORTH STAR SANCTUM

119

Fitling, East Riding of Yorkshire

northstarsanctum.co.uk

A 30-minute drive from Hull city centre takes you out into a flat rural landscape where arable farms abound, interrupted only by single-track lanes and the occasional village. North Star Sanctum – named for its spectacular starry skies on clear nights – is a remote collection of six swish lodges, each built by experienced owner Simon and decorated by his intrepid wife, Rupal, who has given each lodge (sleeping up to four people) a different theme based on their travels as a couple. Stay in the Kasbah to be transported to Marrakesh with intricate lanterns and bold prints, or book into the Lotus for an Indian-inspired stay. Each lodge has a private little patio out the back with its own hot tub, and dogs will love sniffing around the lawns throughout, where rabbits can be seen grazing in the mornings.

Where to walk: There's a lack of public footpaths in this area, but a short drive away is Burton Constable Hall & Grounds (burtonconstable.com), where lakeside strolls and woodland walks abound (there's livestock so dogs must be on leads). You can dine inside the Stables Kitchen cafe, too.

WHAT'S NEARBY?
The sandy Mappleton Beach is the local highlight, just 10 minutes' drive from North Star Sanctum, and if you get there at dawn, you'll be in for a mesmerising sunrise.

Need to know: There are no enclosed gardens here, so you'll want to pack a longline and a camping tie-out.

↓ The beach at Mappleton

HORNSEA SOUTH BEACH

East Riding of Yorkshire

Fine sand and shingle make up the shores of Blue Flag Hornsea Beach. Grab a portion of fish and chips from Port of Call (facebook.com/PortOfCallHornsea/) on the promenade, then head on to the sand for a game of fetch. Stay south of Sands Lane car park in summer as there are restrictions to the north between 1 May and 30 September.

Make a night of it: Stay at North Star Sanctum (see page 99), just 20 minutes south of Hornsea.

Parking: Sands Lane, HU18 1PZ

EXPLORE YORK BY BOAT

York, North Yorkshire
cityexperiences.com

The storied city of York is made for walking the dog, its picturesque streets offering pleasant ambling. But skip the crowds and join City Cruises for a sail on the River Ouse for another perspective on this historic city, with live commentary and refreshments on board.

Make a night of it: No1 Guesthouse oozes modern Scandi chic while being just a 10-minute walk from the historic centre of town. guesthousehotels.co.uk

🐕1 🏠 <£200

↓ The River Ouse in York

↓ The ornate exterior of Castle Howard

CASTLE HOWARD

122

York, North Yorkshire
castlehoward.co.uk

This is the North East's most spectacular stately home. Ground was first broken here in 1699 but it took 100 years to build this truly spectacular palace of opulence. It was the brainchild of John Vanbrugh and architect Nicholas Hawksmoor, who had visions of a perfectly symmetrical baroque masterpiece, but instead it turned out to be a vast house with unmatching wings and an almost 9,000-acre estate. Come to see the impressive exterior of the main house, walk (dogs on leads) among bluebell woodlands and formal gardens, and seek out some of its intriguing temples and monuments.

NORTH LANDING (FLAMBOROUGH)

123

East Riding of Yorkshire

Ensconced by grass-topped chalk cliffs, North Landing is a small but beautifully formed curve of sand and shingle, with rocks strewn out into the ocean, where pools teem with life at low tide and fishing boats are occasionally left on the sand. This used to be the hub of the region's fishing fleet, but the business has dwindled in recent years, leaving just one or two keen vessels – some of which will even take you out for a view of the nearby RSBP reserve, Bempton Cliffs, where half a million seabirds reside in summer. Speaking of summer, it can get a little crowded with both people and birds – noisy kittiwakes, cormorants, shags and sometimes puffins can be seen nesting in the cliffs by the beach – so come in winter

if you prefer a quieter day out.

An old lifeboat station atop the slope that backs the beach here is now a great little cafe serving fried breakfasts, burgers for lunch and ice creams for those sunny afternoons. There's great swimming thanks to the cove's sheltered nature, and blustery walks along the coast path on the clifftops must not be missed – the coastline here is soul-stirring.

Make a night of it: North Star Sanctum (see page 99) is just an hour's drive from Flamborough.

Parking: YO15 1BJ

WALK

BEMPTON CLIFFS TO FLAMBOROUGH HEAD

124

East Riding of Yorkshire

START POINT: YO15 1JF
DISTANCE/TIME: 9km/2 hrs 10 mins each way

As coastal walks go, this one is truly spectacular. Sure, the cliffs here are impressive – their chalky white faces looming above a greyish ocean – but it's the wildlife that's going to wow you most. This point-to-point walk is best done in the height of summer in June when half a million seabirds reside on the tiny crags of the cliffs, creating a cacophony for the ears and nose – the guano is pungent. There are pretty black guillemots, squawking gannets and a good number of orange-beaked puffins nesting in the tufty grasses. The route starts at the RSPB Bempton reserve, where wooden platforms overhang the cliff edges for the best views of the birds, before following the coast path southwards to Flamborough Head. There are spectacular views of the magnificent cliffs all the way along, with intriguing geological features such as natural arches and sea caves to explore.

The walk finishes at Hidden Beach, but a little inland from here is a tall, white stone 17th-century lighthouse that's well worth a visit. Stop for lunch before making the two-hour hike back the way you came.

> **WHAT'S FOR LUNCH?**
> The Headlands Family Restaurant (headlandsrestaurant.co.uk) sits at the end of the walk next to the new lighthouse, serving moreish cakes and hearty fish and chips.

Need to know: Dogs must be kept on a lead for the entire walk due to cliff edges; they can be off-lead on North Landing Beach (see page 101). Directions available on alltrails.com.

RIEVAULX ABBEY

Rievaulx, North Yorkshire
english-heritage.org.uk

Once a thriving 12th-century monastery where Cistercian monks lived a peaceful life in an isolated valley, Rievaulx Abbey is now one of the most remarkable ruins in Britain. You can walk the dog among its dramatic archways and along what would have been the nave of the former church before stopping in at its museum, which houses medieval carvings and gold coins found during site excavations.

↓ Arty standing on the ruins of Rievaulx Abbey

WALK

LEVISHAM STATION WALK, NEWTONDALE

126

North Yorkshire

START POINT: Levisham Station Car Park, YO18 7NN
DISTANCE/TIME: circular 10km/3 hrs

The sound of steam and the shrill blast of a whistle is never too far away on this lovely circular walk through Newtondale. Starting from the 1912 time capsule that is Levisham Station, where the North Yorkshire Moors Railway passes through on its way to and from Whitby, it follows the valley floor then climbs into the trees, where soft, thick mosses and plumed ferns coat the forest floor, before returning.

↓ The Scandi-style hut at A Place in the Pines

WHAT'S FOR LUNCH?
Head to The Fox and Rabbit Inn (foxandrabbit.co.uk) in Lockton for proper hearty, homecooked food, where dogs can snooze on the carpet while you dine.

Need to know: Directions are available from northyorkmoors.org.uk but this walk is also waymarked as 'Levisham Station Walk'.

STAY

LARK, A PLACE IN THE PINES

127

Osmotherley, North Yorkshire
www.canopyandstars.co.uk/lark

This cabin in the woods on the edge of the North York Moors is all about handmade Scandi chic. Lark has

↓ Overlooking Robin Hood's Bay from Ravenscar

been carefully crafted by its creative owner, Matt, and sits within a small pine woodland next to a glassy pond. Matt's eye for design means there are spectacular vaulted ceilings lined with wooden panels, large windows that let streams of natural light brighten its living room, and a pair of silver outdoor tubs right outside the main bathroom covered by the roof's canopy to keep you cosy in the bubbles even when it's raining.

Where to walk: The best walks end at a pub, and from here you can mooch along footpaths for 3km to Osmotherley, where The Golden Lion (goldenlionosmotherley

.co.uk) will quench any thirst with a local Northallerton ale. Alternatively, head south through Thimbleby village and take the footpath towards Silton Forest (forestryengland.uk), where the dog can enjoy an off-lead adventure through the woods.

Need to know: Dog towels, bowls, beds and a hose for washing them down after muddy walks are all provided. Dogs are allowed on the sofa but not the human beds. There are Herdwick sheep on site so keep dogs under control.

WHAT'S NEARBY?
A half-hour drive south and into the National Park will take you to the fantastic ruins of Rievaulx Abbey (see page 103), where you can clamber in and out of the remains of a 12th-century monastery. Drive another 25 minutes further south and you'll find yourselves at Castle Howard (see page 101), a magnificent baroque stately home with domes and fountains and fabulous gardens to roam.

 WALK

RAVENSCAR  128

North Yorkshire

START POINT: Visitor Centre, Ravenscar, YO13 0NE
DISTANCE/TIME: circular 2.2km/45 mins

Enjoy spectacular sea views, bluebell woods and a little industrial history on this National Trust trail on the North

Yorkshire coast. The trail begins by crossing a lush green golf course and passes through woodland towards an old alum works. The return has a brilliant viewpoint with lovely views out to Robin Hood's Bay and crosses the site of a former brickworks before following an old railway line back to the start. There's free Tramper mobility scooter hire for those with reduced mobility.

WHAT'S FOR LUNCH?
Grab a light lunch or scone with jam at the Ravenscar Tearooms (ravenscartearooms.co.uk).

Need to know: Dogs must be on leads near livestock and cliff edges. Directions available at nationaltrust.org.uk.

STAY

THE RIVER LODGE

129

Egton Estate, North Yorkshire
www.canopyandstars.co.uk/theriverlodge

If you've ever dreamed about running away from it all to a log cabin in the woods, this is the place to live out your fantasies. The River Lodge is blissfully remote, made from wood inside and out,

WHAT'S NEARBY?
About 10km away on the coast is Runswick Bay, where you can try fossil foraging with the dog (see page 109), while there are boat trips in Whitby (see opposite). Also don't miss Whitby Abbey, the eerie and dramatic inspiration for a location in Bram Stoker's *Dracula*.

↑ A border collie on the beach at Runswick Bay

and sits just beside a wild river where salmon and seatrout abound beneath the surface. It'll be just you, the dog and whatever wildlife graces you with its presence, be it squirrels, buzzards or the whistling red kites.

There's plenty to explore nearby but be sure to save some time for bathing in the outdoor tub on the deck, or simply staring up at the sky on a clear night – the sheer number of visible stars is utterly astonishing.

Where to walk: The Coast to Coast trail (coasttocoast.uk) is right on your doorstep here, so you could tackle the footpaths to Whitby and Robin Hood's Bay for a day-long hike. Alternatively, it's a good two-hour hike up to Egton High Moor (and another two hours back), or you could head west and do part of the Esk Valley Walk.

Need to know: Beds, bowls and treats are provided for your dogs. There may be livestock on site so dogs must be kept under control.

SEE WHITBY FROM THE WATER

130

North Yorkshire
endeavourwhitby.com

Dogs haven't always been a pirate's best friend but they can be on the appropriately named *Bark Endeavour*. This mighty vessel is a replica of HMS *Endeavour*, the ship Captain James Cook sailed on during his 18th-century expeditions, and today it welcomes visitors to cruise around Whitby harbour. Look out for the ruined abbey atop the cliffs above the town and keep an eye on the water – dolphins and porpoises can often be seen swimming beneath the surface.

Make a night of it: Book a stay nearby at Runswick Bay Cottages, where old fisherman's homes make delightful seaside escapes. runswickbaycottages.co.uk 🐾2+ 👤2-8 £200

↓ Arty waiting for the train at Pickering Station

GO ROAD TRIPPING WITH DEFENDER CAMPING

131

North Yorkshire
defendercamping.com

Even staunch non-campers will be swayed by the fantastic set-up that comes with the Defender Camping vehicles, as each one has state-of-the-art kit and – most importantly – a comfortable roof tent for sleeping at night. You'll pick up your Land Rover Defender from the HQ on the northern edge of the North York Moors National Park, then head off in any direction that suits. Within half an hour, you could be in the wilds of the park, where you can ramble in the Fryup Dales, hop on the North Yorkshire Moors Railway steam trains or roam the heather-clad hills of Square Corner, which is anything but square. Alternatively, the wilds of the Yorkshire Dales or the Lake District await further west, or northwards you could drive into Northumberland and set up camp in the national park, which has some of the darkest and therefore starriest skies in Britain.

Defender Camping's Land Rovers are top-of-the-range, with six gears, an onboard computer for music and directions, and heated seats. They're a pleasure to drive, but the real fun is in setting up camp. The cars come with 2.5-metre side awnings for extra space, camping chairs, all the cooking equipment you could need, an optional Ooni pizza oven, fire pit and even a portable toilet if you're going off-grid. Plus, dogs are kept safe in MIMsafe's crash-tested car crates. All you need to bring is your sleeping bag and a blanket for the dog.

GO FOSSIL HUNTING IN RUNSWICK BAY

North Yorkshire facebook.com/
RunswickFossilWalks

The coastline on the edge of the North York Moors National Park is old – millions of years old, in fact. Join one of the fossil walks on Runswick Bay beach and you'll come away with your own piece of history – ammonite fossils, left by creatures that died here 66 million years ago, abound. Your guide will bring the equipment, so you just need to bring the dog and a keen eye for spotting those historic finds.

Make a night of it: Runswick Bay Cottages has a series of lovely fisherman's cottages just above the beach.
runswickbaycottages.co.uk

2+ 2-8 <£200

SALTBURN-BY-THE-SEA

North Yorkshire

Not only is Saltburn Beach a gloriously wide sweep of soft sand with wonderful views of the surrounding cliffs and the grassy hilltops that back it, but it's also got some intriguing history and a few entertaining dog-friendly attractions.

The town that surrounds this vast beach was built up by the Victorians as it became a popular seaside resort, a status that made it proud home of the North East's only pleasure pier – once more than 450 metres long, it's now just 205 metres after storms battered its original construction. Another delightful legacy from the Victorians is the clifftop tramway, which ferries passengers from the town down to the pier or vice versa.

↓ A border collie on Saltburn Beach at sunset

First opened in 1884, it's now the oldest water-balanced funicular in Britain and welcomes dogs inside its carriages for an easy ride up or down the cliffs. Railway nerds will also want to hop aboard the miniature railway, which has been operating here since 1947.

On the beach itself, dogs can enjoy racing about at its southern end beyond the pier all year round – conveniently, this is where the dog-friendly Ship Inn (facebook.com/ShipSaltburn/) sits right by the sand, serving up excellent homemade pies and local ales.

Make a night of it: The River Lodge in Egton Bridge (see page 106) is a perfect escape just 30 minutes' drive from Saltburn.

Parking: Marine Parade, TS12 1DP

(see page 106)

PLACE

BEAMISH: THE LIVING MUSEUM OF THE NORTH

134

Beamish, County Durham
beamish.org.uk

Who said history needs to be dry? At Beamish: The Living Museum you'll meet real people in period costume who can tell you stories of bygone eras, be it life on a 1950s farm or the work of a miner in an old colliery. Dogs can wander the historic streets with you here, ride an old-timey tram and nip into the local pub, The Sun Inn, for a pint – the 1900s-built pub was moved from Bishop Auckland to the museum after it closed down. Kids will love visiting the old sweet shop and bakery for treats, while dogs can snaffle some handmade biscuits from the gift shop.

EXPERIENCE

RIDE AN HISTORIC RAILWAY IN TANFIELD

135

County Durham
tanfield-railway.co.uk

Billed as the oldest railway in the world, this delightful steam-powered heritage train line chunters through the countryside just south of Newcastle. The conductor's whistle will see you off from Tanfield Station on a 9.7km round trip along the Causey Burn river before returning for tea and cake in the traditional cafe.

Make a night of it: Burnhopeside Hall is a 15-minute drive from the railway station and has several resident dogs for yours to mix with. **sawdays.co.uk**

🐾2 <£200

LONGSANDS BEACH

136

Tyne and Wear

Just a 20-minute drive from Newcastle city centre on the northern side of the Tyne lies a 1km stretch of golden sand. Popular with surfers, volleyball players and local families, this beach has space for everyone and dogs are welcome to run around all year. There are grassy dunes skirting the back of the beach and a handful of lovely cafes for lunch or ice cream, and if you're craving green space, Tynemouth Park has plenty just behind the sand.

Make a night of it: The Clifton Hotel is just a hop over the estuary from Tynemouth and has charming, cosy bedrooms for solo travellers, couples and families. theclifton.co.uk 🐾**2** 🐾 **<£100**

Parking: NE30 4JF

↓ People and dogs milling on Longsands Beach in Tynemouth

EAST FARM LUXURY GLAMPING

137

Great Whittington, Northumberland
eastfarmglamping.co.uk

Sitting on a small patch of land amid farm fields and surrounded by natural shrubs and wild grasses, East Farm Luxury Glamping has two positively chic accommodation options: a pondside cabin with decking and pergola decorated with fairy lights, or a shepherd's hut with a small patio garden that's surrounded by a wonderfully colourful wildflower meadow. Expect wood-fired hot tubs in each and modern boho decor, and evenings spent by the outdoor fire pit watching the dark Northumberland skies overhead.

Where to walk: Hop in the car and make your way south to Hadrian's Wall, where you can join the 117km trail that follows this crumbling Roman ruin. Corbridge Roman Town (**english-heritage .org.uk**) is also worth a visit with the dog.

↓ The author and her dog on top of a hillfort in Breamish Valley

WALK

BREAMISH VALLEY HILLFORT TRAIL

138

 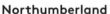

Northumberland

START POINT: Bulby's Wood Car Park
DISTANCE/TIME: circular 7.2km/3.5hrs

This thrilling circular walk starts with a steep climb, but don't let that put you off. Once you're up on the Cheviot Hills around the Breamish Valley, the views are well worth it and the visible history is truly compelling. The route connects a series of prehistoric settlements, from the rubble ramparts left behind at Brough Law hillfort to centuries-old cultivation terraces. There are five hillforts to find, each slightly different in the way they've been preserved, and in between them lie sheep grazing pasture and swathes of gorse that flowers a merry yellow between January and June.

It's within these hills that archaeologists have made myriad discoveries, including Bronze Age burial cairns that are 2,000 years older than the hillforts themselves. Middle Dean hillfort is the most distinct of them all, while inside Cochrane Pike hillfort you can spot the markings of four roundhouses that would have been home to people more than 2,000 years ago.

> **WHAT'S FOR LUNCH?**
> A picnic by the river in Bulby's Wood is a fabulous way to end the day, or nip into the Ingram Café (**facebook .com/cafeingram/**) just down the road to replace those calories with cake or cheese toasties.

Need to know: Directions can be found on **northumberlandnationalpark.org.uk**, but the route is waymarked as the Hillfort Trail, too. There are sheep and cows, so dogs must remain on the lead or under control.

BAMBURGH BEACH

139

Northumberland

Beaches rarely get better than Bamburgh. You've got a golden (sand) trifecta of treats here: towering dunes for sweeping coastal views, a wide and flat expanse of beach that seems to never end, and a formidable castle lording over it all like some sort of sleeping giant. It is, without doubt, one of Britain's finest – not least because the dog can run around here all year with no restriction. Beach wheelchairs are available for hire from Beach Access North East (beachaccessnortheast.org).
Make a night of it: In the heart of Bamburgh village, Windley Cottage is unassuming from the outside but delightfully bougie on the inside, with bold John Lewis decor and fancy kitchen appliances. crabtreeandcrabtree.com

Parking: Bamburgh, NE69 7DD

FORD AND ETAL ESTATE

140

Northumberland ford-and-etal.co.uk

Sitting north of Northumberland National Park and around 16km from the coastline, Ford and Etal is something of a hidden highlight in the North East. This pair of villages, now part of a single estate, has been settled on since 2000 BCE, though little remains of its prehistoric communities. But plenty of history can still be found in its pair of very different but equally intriguing castles,

↓ Arty on the battlements at Bamburgh Castle

a battlefield where a king fought in the 16th century, and a handful of industrial remains that are now working exhibits. There's so much to do here you could spend an entire day with the dog – and so you should.

A pleasant starting point for any visit is at the Heatherslaw Light Railway, the northernmost steam railway in England that follows the River Till. You'll find a traditional working corn mill and lovely dog-friendly cafe here, well worth exploring before you step aboard the tiny train's enclosed carriages to watch the bucolic estate and Cheviot Hills pass by in the distance. You'll trundle the 3km northwards to Etal village, where you can hop out after 25 minutes to explore a 14th-century castle that saw battle with the Scots in the 1500s and now lies in ruin alongside the river. A pit stop in The Black Bull pub nearby is a smart idea before a walk along the footpaths back to Heatherslaw and on to Ford (directions available from the Heatherslaw visitor centre).

The walk to Ford passes the village's impressive castle, first built in the 13th century and remodelled in the Victorian era. The village itself is a comely little place, with pretty cottages and the arresting Lady Waterford Hall. Nip inside the 19th-century schoolhouse to see its vaulted, timber-framed ceilings and walls decorated with Pre-Raphaelite murals, painted by Lady Waterford herself, who inherited the estate in the early 1800s.

Elsewhere on the estate, accessible by car, you'll find the Hay Farm Heavy Horse Centre, which is home to rare breeds of sturdy steeds, a dog-friendly cafe, and a vast collection of horse-drawn machinery. There are carriage rides during school holidays, too. History buffs should make for Flodden Battlefield, where a brutal, bloody battle between the Scots and the English saw 10,000 Scottish lives lost, including King James IV. Beer fanatics can stop in at Cheviot Brewery's taproom for pizza and proper English ale on draught (there's also dog-friendly accommodation here, see below). For a more remote dog walk, head up to the Ford Moss Nature Reserve and Colliery, where a 3km path offers safe passage across the boggy ground amid an ecosystem that feeds adders, common lizards and red grouse.

STAY

CHEVIOT GLAMPING

Slainsfield, Northumberland
cheviotbrewery.co.uk

Tucked away within a pine forest on the edge of the Cheviot Hills, this place is an intimate retreat among nature. Glamping pods fashioned from shipping containers and bell tents on insulated platforms sit amid lush green lawns, overlooking a paddock where the resident alpacas roam, while two self-catering cottages with suntrap patio gardens – fully enclosed and complete with fire pits and furniture – sit within the main building. Accommodation is simple, letting the great outdoors do the wooing here – and woo it does, especially at night when the stars are sublime in the sky.

But the best part of this peaceful glamping site is that it sits right next door to Cheviot Brewery and comes with its own tap room and pizzeria, where fresh ale is available on draught throughout the week (Fridays only in winter) and local chefs come to bake their best dough in the outdoor pizza oven. On a sunny afternoon, after a long dog walk in the Cheviot Hills, a few pints on the terrace beneath the pergola dripping with hops is a blissful way to end the day.

Where to walk: A 30-minute drive from here is the start of the Breamish Valley Hillfort Trail (see page 112), which takes in a series of prehistoric settlements on hilltops with glorious views over the undulating Cheviot landscape. But there are plenty of shorter walks on the public paths and bridleways that surround the glamping site, including routes over Etal Moor and Brownridge Moor. Ask at the taproom for ideas or use the OS app on your phone (explore.osmaps.com).

WHAT'S NEARBY?
The site sits within the exceptionally dog-friendly Ford and Etal Estate (see page 113) so there's lots to do nearby, with Hay Farm Heavy Horse Centre where you can ride carriages pulled by gigantic shire horses, or you can visit an old castle or Victorian schoolhouse. A 30-minute drive takes you out to the coast, where you can explore Holy Island, a popular pilgrimage site with more excellent walks, a craggy castle, a ruined monastery and a mead distillery.

Need to know: There's communal cooking facilities for those in tents and pods, and showers for the campers. Only the self-catering cottages have enclosed gardens, so a camping tie-out and longline might be necessary for those in pods and tents. Dogs must be kept on a lead throughout the site due to the presence of alpacas.

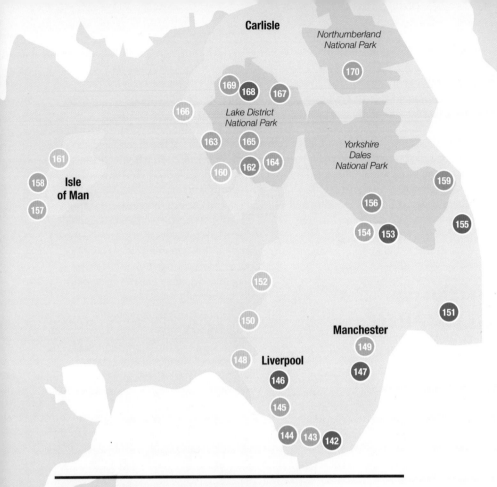

Carlisle

Northumberland
National Park

170

169 168 167

166

Lake District
National Park

163 165

Yorkshire
Dales
National Park

160 162 164

161

159

Isle
of Man

158

156

157

155

154 153

152

151

150

Manchester

149

148 Liverpool

147

146

145

144 143 142

NORTHWEST ENGLAND & THE ISLE OF MAN

HACK GREEN SECRET NUCLEAR BUNKER

142

Baddington, Cheshire
hackgreen.co.uk

What looks like a fairly unassuming, windowless concrete box from the outside has a very different feel on the inside. Hack Green Nuclear Bunker has played a pivotal role in protecting North West England throughout history. Its life began as a bombing decoy to protect

Crewe's railway station, but it then became part of RAF Hack Green in 1941, when it used radar systems to detect incoming attacks. In the late 1950s, following the end of WWII, it was then converted to an air traffic control centre helping civilian and military planes cross the skies safely, and it was left empty and in peace in the mid-1960s. But then the Cold War came along and the Home Office had new ideas for Hack Green – ideas that cost £32 million, the equivalent of almost £500 million today.

Its control rooms became nuclear fallout filter rooms, they built a generating plant for power, and an emergency water supply was established for a worst-case scenario. It was a secretive underground Tardis that could keep 135 personnel alive during a nuclear attack, and today it's open for all to see. You can drift through its vast complex of rooms with the dog, examining the original radar equipment and looking at the original (decommissioned and entirely safe) WE 177 400-kiloton nuclear weapons that would have been used to retaliate against an attack on home soil. It's an eerie but compelling place to spend a day.

UNLEASHED AT WRENBURY HALL

143

Nantwich, Cheshire
unleashedwrenbury.co.uk

Dogs that love to run but don't have great recall will thrive in Wrenbury Hall's enclosed woodland. Totally secure with fencing around 1.5 metres high, it's a perfectly safe place to let your dog off-lead to explore on its own. There's a lake for those who love to swim and woodland for sniffing about. It's available for private hire, but there are regular socialisation sessions for dogs of all ages, too.

Make a night of it: Stay at The Pheasant Inn, which has spectacular walks from its doorstep and excellent roast dinners on Sundays. thepheasantinn.co.uk 🐾2 🐾 <£200

↓ Arty posing for the camera at Unleashed, Wrenbury Hall

↓ The garden at Barton Bank cottage

STAY

BARTON BANK COTTAGE

Barton, Cheshire www.sawdays
.co.uk/barton-bank-cottage

The Cheshire countryside is a lovely place to escape to with the dog: endless fields for roaming across, undulating hills with excellent bucolic views, and several lovely towns and cities to explore if an urban adventure takes your fancy. And all of this is accessible from the tiny but terrific little cottage in Graham and Chris' back garden. The one-room, studio-style home is well equipped for such a small space: a four-poster bed adorned with twinkling fairy lights, a cosy leather sofa facing the exceptionally toasty wood burner, and a kitchen with all the essentials – plus a few non-essentials such as biscuits and Lindt chocolates.

Outside your front door is a small fenced-in paddock where the dog can run about or play fetch, and you've a small covered deck area for al fresco breakfasts if the weather allows.

Where to walk: There's a short (40-minute) walk from the front door across fields to the next village and back along the lanes, though beware of some curious cows and horses along the footpath. The best walking route nearby is on the Sandstone Trail: start from Bulkeley Hill Wood and head through the forest northwards to join the trail. You can walk all the way up to Beeston Castle (**english-heritage.org.uk**), but a stop at The Pheasant Inn in Burwardsley is a must – their roast dinners are divine.

If you've got a dog with unreliable recall, Unleashed at Wrenbury Hall (see page 117) is just a 25-minute drive from Barton Bank Cottage and makes for a lovely afternoon's entertainment for your pet. Bring a picnic to make the most of it.
Need to know: A dog bowl is provided,

WHAT'S NEARBY?

Chester city is a brilliant day out – there are boat trips (see below) and lovely walks around the city's ancient walls and Roman sites, as well as the handsome Grosvenor Park. The National Trust's Quarry Bank (see page 120) is an hour's drive away and is a captivating landscape of former industrial architecture and infrastructure with pretty gardens and a 400-acre estate. For something completely different, head east to Hack Green Secret Nuclear Bunker for Cold War history in a surreal setting (see page 116).

as are firewood, lighters and kindling for the burner. The paddock is fenced in but determined small dogs will be able to sneak underneath to escape, though the owners are usually happy to shut the driveway gates to ensure they can't get far. There are horses living on site in an adjacent field.

join the ChesterBoat team on one of their vessels for an alternative view of Chester. Their half-hour cruise is a perfect introduction to the city's waterway and the history that surrounds it, and for anyone who loves to be nosy, it's an excellent way to see some of the fanciest riverside homes belonging to Chester's well-heeled residents. The boat turns to travel back just as the city gives way to countryside, but if you'd like a longer meander on the Dee, book the two-hour tour that goes all the way out to the ornate, blue-painted Aldford Iron Bridge. Bring your binoculars for kingfisher spotting and a picnic, and get a round in from the on-board bar to make a proper afternoon of it.

Make a night of it: The Queen at Chester Hotel, right by the train station and less than a kilometre from Grosvenor Park, is supremely dog-friendly, with dining areas for those with pets and dog welcome packs in the rooms. thequeenatchesterhotel.co.uk

EXPERIENCE

SEE CHESTER CITY BY BOAT (145)

Chester, Cheshire chesterboat.co.uk

The city of Chester is synonymous with the Romans, and on any walk around the centre you can hardly avoid its millennia-old walls, amphitheatre and gardens. It's well worth a wander, and the dog will love Grosvenor Park, but beyond all this lies a slightly less obvious history along the River Dee – one of Viking invasions, Roman trade and a hidden harbour that's now become a racecourse.

Walk down to The Groves, the city's tree-lined waterfront promenade, and

PLACE

NATIONAL WATERWAYS MUSEUM (146)

Ellesmere Port, Cheshire
canalrivertrust.org.uk

There was always a hubbub of organised chaos at the confluence of the Shropshire Union Canal and the Manchester Ship Canal in Ellesmere Port, with its trading docks, Victorian warehouses and blacksmith's forges a hive of activity. Today, it's all rather quiet, but inside the buildings is a time capsule of a bygone era, with exhibitions and old pumphouses to explore.

QUARRY BANK

Styal, Cheshire nationaltrust.org.uk

Quarry Bank and the wider Styal Estate offers a fascinating look back through time at some of the UK's most important industrial history. At its heart is a huge 18th-century red-brick cotton mill, sitting on the banks of the River Bollin, whose rushing waters powered the waterwheels on the factory's side. With connections to the Bridgewater Canal, cotton was shipped from Liverpool's bustling port and processed here by the workers employed by Samuel Greg, who lived in the grand house next door to the mill.

Beyond the mill lies a surprisingly green landscape – industrial infrastructure and natural woodland rarely go hand in hand, but here there are beautiful gardens with flowering rhododendrons and native trees towering as high as the mill itself. Amble around the mill yard with the dog to get a sense of the scale of the operation before heading into Styal village, where Greg's workers were housed in their own community. You can walk past their terraced houses and timber-framed cottages, taking turns to look after the dog as you explore inside some of the homes, and then wander on through the wider estate where more than 400 acres of pleasure grounds beckon for a light ramble.

Finish the day with a scone in the Garden Café, where there's water for the dog and plenty of hot tea for their owners.

MEOLS BEACH

Merseyside

Located on the northern edge of the Wirral Peninsula, Meols Beach is a huge expanse of soft yellow sand, ideal for games of fetch or long walks along the coast. Head east from here and you'll find yourself in North Wirral Coastal Park, a huge green area of dunes and grass with a lighthouse and a smattering of golf clubs. **Make a night of it:** Bring your tent and make camp at Oakwood Farm Chester touring park, which has grass and hardstanding pitches for campers or those on wheels. oakwoodfarmchester .co.uk 🐕2 ⓔ 🅿 <£50

Parking: Meols Parade, CH47 7AU

TAKE IN A FILM AT DUCIE STREET WAREHOUSE

Manchester duciestreet.com

Nights out in Manchester needn't mean leaving the dog behind: Ducie Street Warehouse, a few minutes' walk from Manchester Piccadilly Station, is a brilliant dog-friendly dining and drinking space with its own pet-friendly cinema. Check the runtimes to find out which screenings are letting dogs in, pick up your popcorn and head in to enjoy a dog-friendly film on the big screen.

↓ A spaniel on Formby Beach

Make a night of it: Sleep it off upstairs at Native Manchester, where chic serviced apartments are a great place to base yourselves in the city centre. nativeplaces.com 2 ♟2-4 🗓 <£100

cosmopolitan weekend on the coast and stay at the Hope Street Hotel in the city's Georgian Quarter. hopestreethotel.co.uk 1 ♟ <£100

Parking: Lifeboat Road Car Park, L37 2EB

BEACH

FORMBY BEACH   150

Merseyside nationaltrust.org.uk

Just half an hour from Liverpool city centre, this is one of Britain's most exciting beaches. Don't expect watersports and donkey rides here – it's all about the natural world at Formby, as its grassy dune habitats harbour some intriguing species from sand lizards to natterjack toads. Come at low tide and you'll be able to explore a cargo shipwreck and look out for 10,000-year-old footprints that have been preserved in the sand.

Make a night of it: Make it a

PLACE

YORKSHIRE SCULPTURE PARK   151

West Bretton, West Yorkshire ysp.org.uk

It's rare that you can sit and admire a Joan Miró or a Henry Moore with the dog by your side, but Yorkshire Sculpture Park is a gallery of a different kind: it's 500 acres and almost entirely outside, meaning dogs can take in the culture alongside you. Despite sitting right next to Junction 38 of the M1 motorway, the park is a breath of fresh air and green grass, with hills and woodland and two large lakes, plus the River Dearne running right through it. There are towering sculptures by the likes of Antony Gormley and Ai Weiwei, and an ever-changing roster of new and emerging artists, too.

BEACH

LYTHAM ST ANNES BEACH

Lancashire

There's typical seaside fun to be had at Lytham St Annes, with donkeys for kids to ride, sandcastles begging to be built on its huge swathe of soft yellowish grains, and ice cream vans at the ready for sticky treats all round. Hire one of the beach huts from St Annes Beach Huts (stannesbeachhuts.co.uk) to make the most of your day, and grab lunch from the Beach Cafe (beachcafefylde.co.uk), where you can sit outside at AstroTurf-topped tables with the dog.

↓ Reflections of the clouds on Lytham St Anne's Beach

Make a night of it: Stay right across the road from the beach in 11 Sandbank Apartment, where there's a small enclosed garden for the dog and adventures on the sand minutes away. stannesbeachhuts.co.uk 🐾1 👤4+2 ♨ £200
Parking: Fairhaven Road Car Park, FY8 1NW

PLACE

SKIPTON CASTLE

Skipton, North Yorkshire
skiptoncastle.co.uk

Skipton's huge medieval castle is astonishingly well preserved, with its entire roof keeping its halls and quarters dry and a handful of rotund towers remarkably intact. Inside, you can explore medieval kitchens, charming Tudor courtyards and the grand banqueting hall – all with the dog by your side.

↓ The author and two terriers enjoying fly fishing on a drizzly day at the Coniston Hotel

GO FLY FISHING IN THE DALES

Skipton, North Yorkshire
theconistonhotel.com

Fly fishing is something of a passion for Roddy, one of the instructors at The Coniston Hotel. He – and many others who share the same penchant for flinging wire into water to trick a fish on to a hook – says he'd travel for miles for a good catch. But he doesn't have to, as his grandfather's estate at The Coniston Hotel has a sizeable lake right at its heart, ideal for days spent on the water waiting for a bite.

Here, dogs are very much part of the fabric of life, too – ask Roddy about his pack of hunting hounds, which he walks around the estate every morning – and so your dog is welcome to join you for their fly fishing experience. You'll start on the shore in the gardens of the main house, where you'll learn the technique of swinging the rod, before picking your colourful, feathery bait and boarding the row boat.

With the dog on board – and possibly Roddy's little terrier, too – you'll row out into the middle of the lake, where you'll cast your line and drift amid the handsome Yorkshire Dales scenery until a trout takes your bait. Usually, you can take it back to the hotel and have it made up for dinner by the chef, but even if you don't catch a thing, there's something deeply meditative about the action of fly fishing, so it's a grand day out all round.

Make a night of it: Stay overnight at The Coniston Hotel itself, which has dog-friendly rooms with direct access to the lawns outside. There are excellent morning walks to be had around the lake, more dog-friendly activities such as clay pigeon shooting, and dogs can dine with you in the excellent restaurant. theconistonhotel.com 🐾2 🐕 ❄ 🅿 <£200

MOTHER SHIPTON'S CAVE & PETRIFYING WELL

Knaresborough, North Yorkshire
mothershipton.co.uk

Legend has it that Ursula Sontheil, who later became known as Mother Shipton, was born in a Knaresborough cave in 1488. She spent the first few years of her life there before her mother was carted off to a nunnery by a clergyman, and Ursula was taken in by a kind, Christian family. She grew up an outcast, taunted and teased by local children and adults alike, and so later in life she returned to the cave where she had once been happy with her mum, and began to study the surrounding forest and flowers, making herbal remedies.

Locals saw her as a witch – a label that was only amplified when she began having premonitions that, in many cases, came true. She foresaw the demise of Mary, Queen of Scots, predicted the defeat of the Spanish Armada, and even had visions of the Great Fire of London. Her story is now told within the leafy parkland around the cave, where you can walk with the dog on a lead to learn about her prophecies. Also within the forest, don't miss a visit to the Petrifying Well, one of the oldest tourist hotspots in the country, where visitors have been coming for centuries to see objects turned to stone within its mineral-rich waters. There's a museum with objects, donated by celebrities, that have been petrified in the well, and you can even buy a small, petrified teddy bear – which went from soft toy to solid object in just five months – in the gift shop.

BECK HALL

Malham, North Yorkshire
www.sawdays.co.uk/beck-hall

The leafy gardens at Beck Hall are a blissful little spot for afternoon teas or al fresco lunches, and the dog will love sniffing around the flowers and shrubs or paddling in the trickling beck that meanders alongside the property. Bedrooms here are a cosy, contemporary affair with the occasional four-poster bed and wallpaper printed with deer and birds of prey.

Dinner here – where the dog is welcome – is crafted by head chef Louise Kinsella, whose menu is inspired by the Hall's former owner and explorer Mr Hardacre and includes Spanish influences and Moroccan spices.

Where to walk: No trip to Malham is complete without a trip to Malham Cove, a curved cliff face that rises 80 metres above the Pennine Way around

1.5km from the hotel's front door. There are some excellent local walks in the Malhamdale brochure (available throughout the village), too.

WHAT'S NEARBY?
Try your hand at fly fishing with the dog at The Coniston Hotel estate (see page 123), a 15-minute drive south, or head into Skipton to explore a wonderfully preserved medieval castle (see page 122).

Need to know: Dogs are allowed everywhere in the hotel, including in the restaurant, and you'll be given a ground-floor room with close access to outside where possible. There are biscuits available at all times should good dogs need rewarding, and bowls filled with water in public areas. If allowed, they'll even be treated to a sausage at breakfast. Refrigerated food storage is available for those who need it, too.

↓ Port Erin Beach

MEET THE CREATURES LIVING IN THE ISLE OF MAN

Port Erin, Isle of Man
shonaboattrips.wixsite.com/calftrips

The Isle of Man is a haven for wildlife on both land and in the sea, and the best way to see much of it is on one of the wildlife cruises with Shona Boat Trips. The cruises leave from Port Erin daily throughout summer, heading south towards the Calf of Man, an island surrounded by dramatic rock formations and home to seals and seabirds. You might spot dolphins and sharks too.
Make a night of it: The Falcon's Nest Hotel in the heart of Port Erin is a lovely Victorian seafront stay. thenest.im

🐕1 🐾 <£100

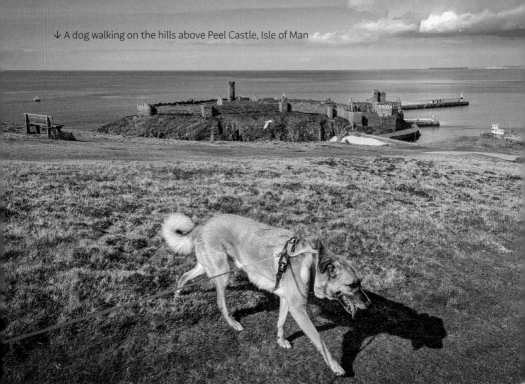

↓ A dog walking on the hills above Peel Castle, Isle of Man

NIARBYL TO PEEL COASTAL PATH

158

Isle of Man

START POINT: IM5 3BR
DISTANCE/TIME: 20km/6 hrs there and back

The Raad ny Foillan, or 'Way of the Gull', is the Isle of Man's coastal path, which tracks along the island's often dramatic cliffs and on to its various sandy and pebble beaches for almost 160km. One of the more enchanting sections of it is between Niarbyl Bay on the south-west coast up to the delightful town of Peel, 10km away.

You'll leave the car at the beach car park and start on the road, heading inland and then northwards from Dalby village before switching back towards the coast when the footpath turns seawards. From here on out it's all coconut-scented gorse in spring and wildflowers in summer, and panoramic ocean views. Looking south, the undulating green hills that stop abruptly at the seaside spread outwards, while to the north, Peel's hilltop Monument is your goal. Ever-present on the horizon ahead, it gets ever closer as you dip in and out of glens and on to pebble beaches along the coastline, willing you to keep going. Keep going you should, indeed, but not before you take in the scenery – on a sunny day, the waters below are brilliant, bright blues and greens, clear as the day.

Wildlife on this walk is plentiful (as is livestock): you might see hen harriers hunting in the sky, various gulls gliding below the cliffs and plenty of rabbits scuttling about in the undergrowth. Look out at sea for a hint of dolphins.

The final leg of the outward journey is up and over Peel Hill, which reveals the bustling little town spread out below, with its spectacularly tempting white-sand beach, just as you come over the brow. Head down towards Peel Castle (a dog-friendly attraction well worth exploring; manxnationalheritage.im) and let the dog run off-lead on the small Fenella Beach.

The return route is exactly the same, so head into town to refuel before making your way back. Alternatively, book a cab or catch the number 4 bus back to Niarbyl.

WHAT'S FOR LUNCH?
After a day spent on the coast, a little seafood shouldn't be missed, so head to The Boatyard (theboatyardpeel.com) in Peel town for Manx queenies (small scallops), local crab or fillet of whatever fish is freshest on the day.

Need to know: The coast path runs quite close to the edge of the cliffs at times so dogs with little sense of their surroundings are best kept on leads. There are a few stiles along the route, but all should be doable by dogs used to ascending stairs. Livestock is abundant here so keep your dog under close control at all times.

STAY

RIVERDALE RURAL HOLIDAYS

West Tanfield, North Yorkshire
riverdaleruralholidays.com

Set on the banks of the rocky River Ure, where herons and kingfishers hunt for their breakfast each day, the shepherd's huts at Riverdale Rural Holidays are something special. It's all quaint

farmhouse style inside with pretty printed wallpapers and a Shaker kitchen, but it's outside where the real pleasure begins. Each hut has a small, enclosed garden (1-metre-high wooden fencing), with a fire pit and loungers, plus decking with an outdoor kitchen and – the highlight – twin bathtubs overlooking the river.

Where to walk: There's a 30-minute walk from the site along the River Ure to the excellent Bull Inn (thebullwesttanfield.co.uk) in West Tanfield, or you could head south along the river for a couple of hours and divert into Grewelthorpe for lunch at The Crown Inn (01765 658210).

↓ Arty posing on the bed at Riverdale Rural Holidays

SILECROFT BEACH

Cumbria

The Lake District National Park isn't all about lakes and fells – there's a coastline here too, and Silecroft Beach is one of the best dog-friendly stretches of shingle you'll find. Black Combe Fell looms over the more-than 8km-long beach, and it's backed by a golf club for those inclined to tee off.

Make a night of it: The Old Kings Head, a 15-minute drive away, is a lovely pub to spend the night in south Cumbria. oldkings.co.uk 🐕1+ ⓔ <£100

Parking: Shore Meadow, LA18 4NY

GLEN WYLLIN BEACH

Isle of Man

The Isle of Man's most popular beaches have summer restrictions, but this one is dog-friendly year-round and at low tide has a wonderful expanse of sand and pebbles. It's one of the quietest year-round, too. Look out for oystercatchers on the shoreline and gulls nesting in the clay cliffs, and if you're there early in the morning you might even spot a hedgehog or two on the sand. The beach is wheelchair accessible via a ramp at low tide; at high tide, you have to walk along the coast path to reach the sand.

Where to stay: Right behind the beach is Glen Wyllin campsite, where grassy pitches are set along a babbling brook that leads down to the sea. glenwyllincampsite.co.uk 🐕2+ ⓔ <£50

Parking: IM6 1AL

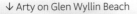

↓ Arty on Glen Wyllin Beach

↓ A spaniel on the grounds of A Cottage in the Clouds

STAY

THE COTTAGE IN THE CLOUDS

Lake District National Park, Cumbria www.canopyandstars.co.uk/ cottageintheclouds

If it's the simple life you're after, the Cottage in the Clouds is an idyllic and remote hideaway. Sitting 200 metres above Coniston Water, surrounded by grazing pasture spliced by drystone walls and often shrouded in cloud and mist, the house is entirely off-grid. This means chilly days are spent tending the log fires and boiling the kettle on a gas stove for warming cups of tea, and there's a wood-burning range for rustling up dinner using local produce. The cottage's owners, John and Maria, run the conservation-focused Nibthwaite Grange Farm, ethically rearing their own native animals for meat, dairy, soap and wool, and you can pre-order a selection of goods to keep you going for your stay.

Where to walk: Footpaths lead in all directions from the cottage, so there's ample walking right on your doorstep. Head north or east and you'll find yourselves in Grizedale Forest, where there are several waymarked trails across the Furness Fells.

> **WHAT'S NEARBY?**
> Just a 15-minute drive down the hillside takes you to Brantwood (brantwood.org.uk), a dog-friendly garden with a tempting tearoom, while a further 10-minute drive to the other side of Coniston Water means you can ride the National Trust's traditional steam gondola (nationaltrust.org.uk).

Need to know: This cottage is within a working farm estate, so be mindful of cattle and grazing sheep; the garden has drystone walls but it's not entirely enclosed so keep dogs under close control.

NORTHWEST ENGLAND & THE ISLE OF MAN

RIDE THE RAVENGLASS AND ESKDALE RAILWAY

Cumbria ravenglass-railway.co.uk

On the edge of the Lake District National Park, sandwiched on the coast between the Irish Sea and the fells of Cumbria, Ravenglass is a pretty spectacular location as it is. Exploring it on foot might feel like the obvious thing to do – there's plenty of exceptional walking here – but going by rail on the Ravenglass and Eskdale Railway has a special kind of appeal.

Opened in the 1870s, it was the first public narrow-gauge railway in the country and is now one of the longest-surviving, too. Departing from the main station at Ravenglass, it travels 11km inland to Dalegarth, passing the coastal estuary and trundling through native woodland that's home to red squirrels and buzzards. You could hop off for a wander along one of the request stops – buy the guide by Alfred Wainwright from the gift shop before you board – or just head directly to Dalegarth for a tea stop at the dog-friendly cafe.

Make a night of it: You needn't go far to find accommodation here, as located at Ravenglass terminus is a pair of lovingly restored Pullman coaches made up as self-catering accommodation. Each has a fenced garden out the front and an enclosed patio area out the back, a tiny but well-equipped kitchen and great views of the steam engines that pass by on the adjacent platform. ravenglass-railway.co.uk 🐕2 👥4 ☀ ♨ <£200

GET AROUND BY BOAT ON WINDERMERE

Windermere, Cumbria
windermere-lakecruises.co.uk

Seeing the Lakes from the high fells above is truly spectacular, but there's lots to be said for a sedate trip on the water itself, too. The boats that traverse the surface of Windermere – England's largest lake – are not only a lovely way to enjoy the scenery, but they're also one of the most efficient ways to get around the region. Hop on board in Ambleside or Bowness and they'll take you down to Lakeside at the southern tip, with a commentary about the waterside woodlands along the way, where it's then a 30-minute walk to the Lakeland Motor Museum (lakelandmotormuseum.co.uk), another top dog-friendly attraction and a welcome diversion from the rain when the weather's not on your side.

Make a night of it: Rothay Manor Hotel in Ambleside loves your dog almost as much as you do, and their leafy gardens are an ideal place to enjoy afternoon tea in the sun. rothaymanor .co.uk 🐕2 ♨ <£300

↑ A collie on the top of Coniston Old Man

WALK

CONISTON OLD MAN 165

Cumbria

START POINT: ///thrusters.secondly.stilted
DISTANCE/TIME: circular 10km/3.5 hrs

Your thighs won't thank you for tackling this walk but your heart – and eyes – will. The Old Man of Coniston is one of the Lake District's most favoured fells and the views from the 802-metre-high top are spellbinding. From the car park, you're in for a relentless climb to the summit but it's well worth it – once there, you'll look out at Dow Crag to the west and to the north see the peaks of Scafell Pike, Skiddaw Little Man, Broad Crag and Harter Fell. The return route goes down a steep zigzagging path with yet more gorgeous views of the handsome Low Water mountain lake.

WHAT'S FOR LUNCH?
Head into the village and make for The Coniston Inn (inncollectiongroup.com), where dogs get biscuits and you can order a proper pub lunch.

Need to know: Dogs can be off-lead but with steep climbs and stones underfoot it could be safer to keep them on. Directions available from lakeswalks.co.uk.

BEACH

ST BEES BEACH 166

Cumbria

Birdwatchers will want to beeline for St Bees, where there's an RSPB nature reserve on the headland above where fulmars, kittiwakes and guillemots can be seen in the skies. The beach has a shingle slope that leads down to soft sand that's almost always accessible, aside from at the highest tide times. A small tearoom doesn't allow dogs but offers takeaway sausage baps or scones with jam.

Make a night of it: Spend the night in a bell tent on the grounds of the majestic Muncaster Castle. muncaster.co.uk

Parking: Beach Road, Saint Bees CA27 0EY

STAY

ANOTHER PLACE

167

Ullswater, Cumbria www.sawdays.co.uk/another-place-the-lake

Sitting on a gentle grassy slope above the deep, dark waters of Ullswater lake, Another Place is not just another place to stay. The main house and a modern building next door house the guest rooms, many of which enjoy lake views, but for dog owners something even more special awaits: a small flock of luxury shepherd's huts sits just a few steps away, each with lake views of their own, plus patios complete with fire pit and dining table.

Ask for hut 46 and you'll have the most mesmerising view to gaze at from the patio or the rolltop copper tub inside: Hallin Fell, Bonscale Pike and Arthur's Pike all loom above on the opposite lakeshore, while right next to your hut is an enormous pink rhododendron that, when in flower, is abuzz with pollinating bees.

Lunches should be taken outside – when the weather permits – at the Glasshouse pizza restaurant, while dinners with the dog can be had in the Living Space restaurant in the main house. For something fancier, leave the dog in the hut and have a feast at Rampsbeck Restaurant, where local fish and lamb are the highlights when in season.

Kids will love the indoor heated pool, and dogs can roam free throughout the grounds.

Where to walk: In the porch of Another Place you'll find an array of colourful wellies to borrow for walking the dog when the weather's a little wet – and let's face it, the Lakes knows how to do a soggy day or two – and maps to take away so you can walk safely on the local trails. A 90-minute loop from the hotel takes you up the hill and on to the Ullswater Way, conveniently passing by the Brackenrigg Inn (brackenrigginn.co.uk) towards the end – a pint of their best bitter is a must. Other walks nearby include Whinlatter Forest (see page 134) and the 950-metre-high Helvellyn, best explored via Striding Edge.

Need to know: Beds and bowls are provided for dogs and there are waste bins throughout the site. The surrounding fields have livestock so keep dogs under control. The front desk will provide a monitoring system if you'd like to leave the dog in your room while you dine.

WHAT'S NEARBY?
The town of Pooley Bridge is a delightful day out – try the desserts at Granny Dowbekin's Tea Room and Gardens (grannydowbekins .co.uk) – and from there you can take the Ullswater Steamers (ullswater-steamers.co.uk) across the lake; hop off at Howtown and walk the Ullswater Way back to the town. A 30-minute drive west takes you to Keswick, where a surprisingly engaging museum on pencils is a dog-friendly highlight (see page 134) and plenty of pubs, restaurants and shops welcome dogs, too.

↓ The deep, dark waters of Ullswater Lake

↓ Arty on the WOW Trail at Whinlatter Forest

PLACE

DERWENT PENCIL MUSEUM

168

Keswick, Cumbria derwentart.com

Few probably imagined the production of pencils could be made interesting, but at Derwent Art's pencil museum, where the ubiquitous drawing pencils have been made for almost two centuries, you'll find yourself engrossed. On arrival, you'll be given a quiz to fill out as you wander through its small but engaging exhibition, and there's a prize at the end for all correct answers. There's geology, politics, spies and royal titbits here, as well as the world's largest pencil and tiny graphite sculptures on the tips of pencils. A delightful, rain-friendly diversion.

WALK

THE WOW TRAIL AT WHINLATTER FOREST

169

Cumbria forestryengland.uk

START POINT: Whinlatter Visitor Centre, CA12 5TW
DISTANCE/TIME: circular 7.5km/2–3 hrs

Runners, mountain bikers and walkers all flock to Whinlatter Forest, where more than 1,200 hectares of wooded trails and open fells are ripe for exploring. The coniferous and oak trees here were planted in the 1920s, meaning some have been standing for over 100 years, but it's not all about the old at Whinlatter, as in 2023 a brand-new trail was created offering a new perspective on the plantation and its surroundings. The WOW Trail is far more than just a walk, though. Starting from the visitor centre, you'll walk up to a viewpoint that has 270-degree views over Bassenthwaite Lake and the Skiddaw massif. You might spot ospreys soaring in the skies here if you come in spring or summer, and in winter the mountains are often cloaked in snow.

Along the route, which meanders through the forest for 7.5km, you'll find information boards that tell the tale of the plantation's management, its dedicated volunteers and the wildlife that thrives here, and be able to stop off at wildlife hides (no dogs inside) and at a collection of forest-bathing loungers that encourage you to lie back, look up to the woodland canopy and take in the peace of your surroundings. If you're a keen stargazer, do the trail twice – once in daytime and again at night, when the starry sky looks spectacular from the comfort of one of their forest-bathing benches.

Need to know: Waymarkers make this route easy to follow. Dogs can be off-lead but must be kept under control. The trail is accessible for Trampers, which can be hired at the visitor centre, and pushchairs, too.

WALK

COW GREEN TRAIL

County Durham

START POINT: Cow Green Reservoir Car Park, DL12 0HX
DISTANCE / TIME: circular 12km/5 hrs or 4km/1.5 hrs each way

Right at the heart of the North Pennines is Cow Green Reservoir, which sits within some of the most fascinating geological formations in Britain, including the enormous Whin Sill – a dark layer of rock that stretches as far as the Northumberland coast. From the car park, this walk can either be a 12km circular hike to Cauldron Snout, with a steep scramble down the other side and along minor roads back to the car park, or you can avoid the scramble with a 4km walk each way, enjoying excellent views over the reservoir.

Need to know: Download directions and geological descriptions at nationaltrail.co.uk.

↓ Cauldron Snout Waterfall on the Cow Green Trail

Fishguard

180

Pembrokeshire Coast
National Park

185
184
183
182

177
176
174
173

SOUTH WALES

PLACE

ST FAGANS NATIONAL MUSEUM OF HISTORY

171

Cardiff museum.wales

Kids will love exploring the historic buildings that line the footpaths at St Fagans, an outdoor museum on the edge of Cardiff. See traditional farm cottages, a clog-making workshop, an old village stores, former mills and even a drystone pigsty – each lifted brick-by-brick and reconstructed on this vast site. Dogs can't go inside the historic buildings, but if you travel as a group you can take it in turns.

↑ Arty at St Fagans museum, Cardiff

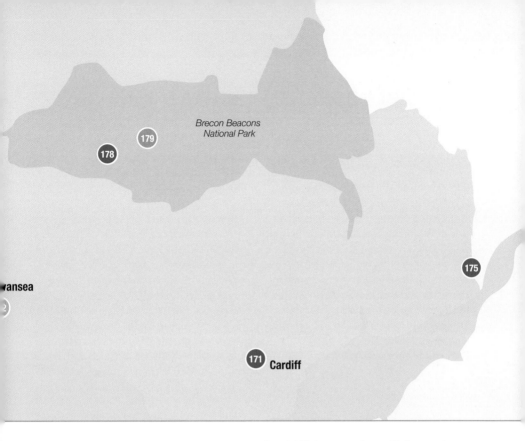

Brecon Beacons
National Park

179

178

175

ansea

171 Cardiff

MUMBLES BEACH

172

Swansea

Great days out can be had on Mumbles Beach, a sand-and-pebble dog-friendly stretch that yawns across Swansea Bay for 2.7km from West Cross down to Mumbles Pier (mumbles-pier.co.uk). There are cafes and bars all along this stretch, but the highlight of it all is that Victorian pier at its far southern tip. One of the few privately owned piers left in Britain, it has a classic amusements arcade (small dogs allowed inside if carried) and juts out more than 200 metres into the sea, where a working lifeboat station occupies the end.

The old lifeboat station still sits north of the pier and it was from here that the Mumbles lifeboat disaster began: a crew who were sent to rescue a German ship that had run aground capsized and were rescued by the lighthouse keeper's daughters, Jessie Ace and Margaret Wright. A blue plaque dedicated to their heroic efforts is located at the top of the pier.

The pier has two fishing platforms, so hire fishing rods from the pier's Beach Hut Cafe and try your hand at catching bass, mackerel, pollack or whiting. Or nip into the gift shop and grab a tub of dog-friendly ice cream to keep the dog happy while you build sandcastles on the beach. **Make a night of it:** The Oyster House is a lovely pet-friendly pub with rooms right on the promenade by the beach. oysterhousemumbles.com **Parking:** SA3 4EN for the pier end or SA3 4EL for the middle of the beach

RHOSSILI BAY 173

The Gower Peninsula

Bring your body boards and get your wetsuits on – Rhossili Bay is all about the surf. Sitting on the western edge of the Gower Peninsula, this utterly spellbinding beach has 5km of soft golden sand for dogs to run around on in the shadow of Worm's Head while you mess around in the waves that roll in from the Atlantic. **Make a night of it:** Book into the 17th-century Kings Head in Llangennith. kingsheadgower.co.uk **Parking:** Worm's Head Car Park, SA3 1PR

↓ One man and his dog look over Worm's Head at Rhossili Bay

BROAD HAVEN SOUTH BEACH 174

Pembrokeshire

Broad Haven Beach enjoys a pleasing expanse of soft sand that's neither yellow nor white – if it were a Farrow & Ball paint it would likely be called Morning Fawn or something equally fanciful. It's backed by dunes packed with dry shrubs and grasses, and out to sea is a brilliant view of the harsh crag that is Church Rock, an outcrop just 500 metres from the shore that resembles a church with a pointed spire. All of this makes it one of Pembrokeshire's most enticing beaches.

While you can park up just south of the beach and easily walk through the dunes and on to the sand, a far more enjoyable

↓ The ruins of Chepstow Castle

way to reach this 300-metre-wide cove is from the village of Bosherston. From the National Trust car park next door to the St Michael and All Angels church, you can walk along the shoreline of the Bosherston Lily Ponds. These winsome lakes were created more than 200 years ago as a feature for the Stackpole Estate, and today they thrive with otters, kingfishers and herons – and water lilies, of course. The trail from the car park crosses a pair of bridges and eventually leads down on to the beach, where you can throw the ball for the dog or laze about on the sand.

Make a night of it: The National Trust's Stackpole Quay cottages are right on the coast path and just a 5km walk from Broad Haven South via the sheltered Barafundle Bay. nationaltrust.org.uk

🐕2 👤3 ☀ ⊞ £200

Parking: SA71 5DR for direct beach access or SA71 5DH for the Bosherston Lily Ponds walk

PLACE

CHEPSTOW CASTLE

 175

Chepstow, Monmouthshire
cadw.gov.wales

Presiding over the River Wye on a precipitous limestone cliff, Chepstow Castle has 900 years of fascinating history within its enormous, iron-plated doors – which just happen to be the oldest castle doors in Europe. The castle's construction began in 1067 and over the centuries, numerous wealthy earls from both Wales and England had their own stamps put upon it, raising its walls and building towers and extra defences to keep their riches safe from intruders. The dog can join you on all ground-floor areas of the castle inside and out, where you can see weaponry and artefacts from throughout its history.

COOK YOUR-SELF LUNCH ON A COASTAL FORAGING EXPEDITION

Pembrokeshire
blackrockoutdoorcompany.co.uk

The Pembrokeshire coastline is a thriving habitat for fascinating flora and fauna – some of which can make a fine foraged lunch in the right hands. Join Dan Moar on his coastal foraging excursions along the southern beaches of the Pembrokeshire National Park and you can help him cook up a storm using seaweed, razor clams, mussels and cockles all found on your walk along the beaches.

Make a night of it: Lay your heads down at foodie-focused Penally Abbey. sawdays.co.uk 🐾1 ⛽ <£200

WOODLAND WALK, PEMBREY COUNTRY PARK & BEACH

177

Carmarthenshire
pembreycountrypark.wales

START POINT: Car Park 1, SA16 0EJ
DISTANCE/TIME: circular 3km/1 hr

Whether it's too hot for sun-exposed walks or it's drizzly and you want to wander somewhere sheltered, Pembrey Country Park offers fantastic woodland walks. This particular trail starts amid a plantation of slender Corsican pine trees along the coast, which give the forest a most Mediterranean feel on a sunny day, before heading inland to the main woodland. You'll amble beneath willow, hazel, sweet chestnut and lime trees, and be able to spot rare butterflies in the clearings, including dingy skippers and small blues.

Birdlife abounds here, with sparrowhawks hunting year-round and wood warblers and goldcrests flitting about in summer. Hiding beneath the ground are badger setts and fox dens.

> **WHAT'S FOR LUNCH?**
> The park's own cafe, Yr Orsaf (yrorsaf.cymru/en/), is a smashing stop for fry-ups, sandwiches, jacket potatoes and moreish lasagne.

Need to know: Dogs can be off-lead throughout the park and on the beach here. The trail is waymarked with green signs and directions can be downloaded from pembreycountrypark.wales. There's also a dry ski slope, kids' play area and miniature railway within the park and a Caravan & Motorhome Club campsite (caravanclub.co.uk).

DAN-YR-OGOF, THE NATIONAL SHOWCAVES CENTRE FOR WALES

178

Abercraf, Brecon Beacons National Park showcaves.co.uk

Bannau Brycheiniog or the Brecon Beacons is well known for its towering hills and mountains, but what lies beneath this undulating landscape is equally exciting. Two brave – or perhaps stupid – farmers, Tommy and Jeff Morgan, discovered this cave complex in 1912 when in search of the source of a spout of water they found coming from a limestone rock. What they happened upon stunned them – an underground lake with narrow passages turning off in all directions and a waterfall. They spent weeks coming in and out of the caves, mapping out its system and creating safe methods for finding their way back, and then their cunning nose for business led to the first tourist activity here: they began to charge people for guided tours of the underground caverns. Visitors were told to be prepared to get wet – they would be wading up to their knees in places.

Today, thanks to another novice caver named Eileen Davies, who managed to get through the 'long crawl' section for the first time in the 1960s, there are now 16km of explored passageways in this system and a handful of cavernous hollows that can be explored by the public – and you needn't even get your feet wet. Descend the steps into the cave system and see the caverns lit up in glorious drama with their stalactites and stalagmites, dog by your side, then explore the above-ground dinosaur park with life-sized models of millennia-old creatures.

WALK

FAN NEDD

179

Brecon Beacons National Park

START POINT: Maen Llla Standing Stone, LD3 8SU
DISTANCE/TIME: circular 5.8km/2 hrs

This walk is a great year-round summit in the Brecon Beacons that's unlikely to see the same hordes of walkers as its more popular neighbours. Starting from a likely Neolithic or Bronze Age standing stone, you will follow the road before hopping over a stile to bear west and start your

↓ A view of Fan Nedd mountain, Brecon Beacons National Park

ascent (dogs that can't manage stiles can walk along the road on the lead).

It's a fairly kind, gradual climb to the stone cairn, which is 20 metres or so below the official trig point on the mountain's 663-metre-high summit. On a clear day, you can see right across the western Brecon Beacons, or look east to Pen y Fan and Corn Du. You'll descend on the other side of the mountain before switching back to the start point along the Cambrian Way.

> **WHAT'S FOR LUNCH?**
> Refuel at the not-so new The New Inn (waterfallways.co.uk) in Ystradfellte, a 10-minute drive away. There's even a fire for the dog to warm up next to.

Need to know: Directions can be downloaded from wildtrailswales.com or on the OS Maps app (explore.osmaps.com).

SAIL WITH SEALS AROUND RAMSEY ISLAND

(180)

Pembrokeshire ramseyisland.co.uk

Sitting less than a kilometre off the south-west tip of Pembrokeshire, Ramsey Island is home to myriad exciting animals. Seals live here year-round, flopping about on beaches and rocky outcrops. But it's summertime that brings the best wildlife: between March and July, you'll spot Manx shearwaters coming in and out of their underground nests in rabbit burrows, guillemots flinging themselves off precarious cliff edges in search of supper, and little black choughs with their bright orange beaks flitting about the caves.

With so much rare and endangered wildlife, dogs aren't allowed on Ramsey Island, but they can join you in the zodiacs that race out and around the island for a water-bound perspective. Voyages of Discovery run regular hour-long tours from St Justinians Lifeboat Station near St Davids, which pass alongside The Bitches, a set of rocks and tidal race that often creates substantial waves (wear waterproofs!), and around the island. Keep an eye out for porpoises and dolphins in the water as you cruise and look up to see if any peregrine falcons are joining you on the voyage – they love to hunt over Ramsey's grassy top.

Make a night of it: Bring your tent and pitch up at Lleithyr Farm Holiday Park, which is just a few kilometres' walk into St Davids and a short drive from St Justinians. lleithyrfarm.co.uk 🐕2+ ☀ £50

single-room cabin with its mezzanine and veranda. There's a composting toilet – it's an off-grid escape, this one – and a gas-powered camping shower, and a selection of paraffin lights to cast a warm glow come night-time. Cook dinner on the open fire pit or drive out to the icing-pink Cottage Inn (**facebook.com/ thecottageinnpentrefelin**) nearby.
Where to walk: You're on the edge of the Brecon Beacons here, so tackle some of the National Park's many hills or mountains – Pen y Fan being the highest. For a quiet hike, try the 6km Fan Nedd circular (see page 141).

> **WHAT'S NEARBY?**
> One of Wales's most impressive castles is a 20-minute drive from The Log House Studio, perched on a limestone crag with glorious views over the surrounding green fields. Further into the Brecon Beacons National Park (around an hour from the cabin) is the National Showcaves Centre for Wales (see page 140), where you can drift into spectacularly lit cathedral-like caverns with the dog.

STAY

THE LOG HOUSE STUDIO (181)

Llandeilo, Carmarthenshire
www.canopyandstars.co.uk/loghouse

If communing in nature in your own woodland clearing isn't enough, this gorgeous little wood cabin sits on stilts like some kind of fairy house in the forest. Inside it's all woven Aztec-style rugs and colourful printed fabrics on the two beds and sofa, and there are hand-painted artworks adorning the walls created by the owner himself. Tim and his terrier, Charlie Brown, will greet you here and show you around the

Need to know: There's a kennels next door so if your dog is reactive it's best to book elsewhere.

↑ A dog paddling in a stream

LAMMAS ECO VILLAGE

Glandwr, Pembrokeshire
lammas.org.uk

Set across the hillsides deep in the Pembrokeshire countryside, Lammas Eco Village – named after the pagan harvest festival – is a tranquil, off-grid, working community. Its residents, a mix of families, couples and solo dwellers, are each responsible for their own smallholdings, where they grow food, farm animals such as chickens, cows and pigs, and manage a small woodland area for fire fuel. If it sounds like the good life, it can be far from it – and you'll learn all about it if you join a weekly tour with one of the residents.

All tours begin at the community hub, a large turf-roofed building clad with timber that wouldn't be out of place in Tolkien's fictional Hobbiton. Here, you'll learn how the village came to fruition after several years of battling with planning committees, and how volunteers came to help build the timber-framed hub to create a heart for the community. There's a small pond where toads and frogs thrive, alongside kingfishers and even the occasional otter, and once you've visited the communal areas you'll get to see one of the nine plots that make up the various smallholdings. There are cabin-style homes – hand-built by their owners – and houses that look as if they've been dug out from the hills and engulfed by pasture. Whoever leads your tour will regale you with stories of living off the land, learning the hard way and offer tips on everything from solar panel installation to growing your own lunch.

Make a night of it: The charming Ty Nodyn (see page 148) is a mere 30-minute drive from the Eco Village and offers its own little slice of the good life.

FOEL DRYGARN HILLFORT

Pembrokeshire

START POINT: ///giants.composed. handbags
DISTANCE/TIME: circular 4km/1 hr 30 min

A short but punishing climb, which begins as a gradual ascent amid grazing moorland and ends with a rocky scramble, takes you to the top of Foel Drygarn hillfort. Its original, Iron Age structure is visible in two rings of rocks that ensconce a trio of astonishingly large Bronze Age burial cairns. Find yourself alone up here and it can feel eerie and empowering all at once. The views are brilliant on a clear day when you can see out to the ocean at Newport and across the Preseli Hills – like you're on top of the world, or at least the top of Pembrokeshire. But the rocky cairns are a grounding sight, likely constructed more

↑ Arty atop Foel Drygarn hillfort

↓ The rocks of Foel Drygarn hillfort

than 4,000 years ago as a permanent memorial for our ancestors.

Once you've spent some time on the peak, a path snakes down the south-western side of the hillfort amid lunging rocky outcrops and back down on to the moorland. Head south-east until you hit the fence line and then switch back to return to the beginning, following the boundary of the grazing pasture.

> **WHAT'S FOR LUNCH?**
> Bring a packed lunch to munch on top of the hillfort so you can linger a little longer for those sweeping views.

Need to know: There are sheep grazing across the land here so dogs must be kept on leads; there are also a few sheer drops at the top, so be wary. The landscape is relatively easy to navigate without guidance but the OS map app (explore.osmaps.com) has a few options for routes across the hillfort and beyond.

STAY

BRECHFA FOREST BARNS

Llanllwni, Carmarthenshire
brechfaforestbarns.co.uk

Brechfa Forest is magical. Dense woodland, packed with ancient ferns and towering Douglas firs, is clad with a carpet of rich green moss, while conifer plantations line the footpaths and wispy lichen hangs off spindly branches – a sure sign that the air here is refreshingly pure. It's the sort of place that sets childish imaginations alight with thoughts of fairies and forest monsters and promises plenty of intriguing sniffs for the dog on your daily walks. All this, and lots more, is ripe for exploration from the cosy, quaint cottages at Brechfa Forest Barns.

But it's not all about location, location, location, here. The barns – lovingly run by dog-loving Nikki and Jay Channon and their two beagles, Oscar and Alfie – are a destination in themselves, for both dogs and humans. Pets are genuinely welcomed here, with no rules about who can go on the furniture, no limit to the size, age or number of dogs you can bring along, and no worries about escape artists thanks to the fully fenced-in gardens. There's even an enclosed sensory paddock artfully named Scentral Bark with toys, sandpits, agility equipment, trampolines and paddling pools for running off that excess energy.

There's a snug barbecue hut for hire where you can grill your dinner on open flames in the middle of the table without concern for the weather, and you can even pre-order frozen meals so you needn't spend too much time in the kitchen. Almost everything has been thought of here, making it a truly relaxing place for a break with the dog.

Where to walk: Beyond the Brechfa Forest Barns site lies a vast ancient woodland with waymarked trails and plenty of adventure for the dog. The Riverside Walk is just 1.8km and follows the gorgeous River Gorlech, while the 9km Forest Garden Walk is a half-day walk through redwood and eucalyptus forest.

> **WHAT'S NEARBY?**
> Within an hour's drive of Brechfa Forest Barns lies a coastline with ample dog-friendly beaches, from Llansteffan – which also has a dog-friendly castle – to the sweeping sands of Cefn Sidan Sands on the edge of Pembrey Country Park (see page 140).

Need to know: Dogs can go everywhere on site except inside the barbecue hut (there are recommended dog sitters should your pet prefer not to be left alone). If your dog sleeps on the bed with you, you must bring your own bedding.

↓ Let the outside in at Ffynone Bach

↓ Ffynone Bach is all about getting immersed in nature

STAY

FFYNONE BACH

Newchapel, Pembrokeshire
www.canopyandstars.co.uk/ffynonebach

Small but tall and certainly beguiling, Ffynone Bach is a one-of-a-kind cabin in the woods. It's all about nature immersion here – a huge central window brings the outside in, flooding this tiny off-grid house with light, while all around are native hedgerows, small woodland copses and farm fields. Come night-time, solar panels provide electricity for low-key lighting, but it's all about sitting outside by the fire pit, taking in the night's sky and listening out for hooting owls on the hunt.

Days can be spent soaking in the wood-fired hot tub, with a rinse off in the outdoor shower, and for colder days a log burner will keep the hut warm.

Where to walk: A footpath leads directly from the house down the hill into Penrhiw (30 mins), where the highly popular Nag's Head (nagsheadabercych.co.uk) is well worth a dinner out.

> **WHAT'S NEARBY?**
> The Norman Cilgerran Castle (cadw.gov.wales) is a 15-minute drive and dogs are welcome to mooch with you around ground-floor areas.

Need to know: There's not a huge amount of signal here so be prepared to go offline. The area isn't entirely enclosed, so dogs prone to roaming will need a longline and camping tie-out.

MID WALES

201
200 **Aberystwyth**
199

193 194
192
191
187
186

STAY

TY NODYN, NANTGWYNFAEN ORGANIC FARM

186

Panteg Cross, Ceredigion
canopyandstars.co.uk

Tucked away on a hillside in the idyllic Ceredigion countryside, with rolling farm fields and forest on its doorstep, Ty Nodyn is a unique little escape from everyday life. The cottage, which sits within an old farmyard barn on the Nantgwynfaen Organic Farm run by owners Amanda and Ken, is quirky to say the least. A pair of pianos make up the bed head and foot, there are guitars hung from the walls and record sleeves and comics pasted as wallpaper – look a little closer at those walls, too, and you might even find a few family photos pasted on to album covers.

A bare concrete floor and kitchen built with corrugated iron bring a cool industrial feel, but that's immediately offset by cosy Persian-style rugs and homely wood cladding on the far wall. It sounds like a clash of crazy design, but in reality it works like a charm – and the wood burner works to heat the whole place up, even in the depths of winter.

Outside your front door is a communal garden used by the owners and other guests – kids will love the metal slide that deposits them at the bottom of the lawn's slope – and beyond there are

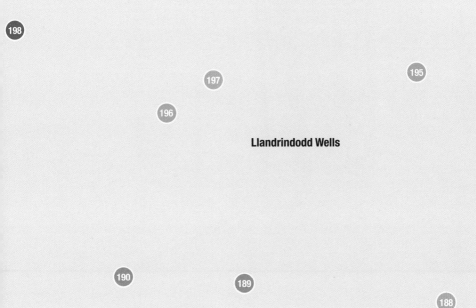

198

197

195

196

Llandrindodd Wells

190

189

188

Hay on Wye

footpaths across the fields for walking. Next door to Ty Nodyn is the farm's own honesty shop, and it's not just a few eggs and some jam. You can get everything you need here, from ingredients to bake bread and cupboard essentials to their own homemade sausages; there are lots of vegetarian and vegan options, too.

Where to walk: Head west to the coast path and wander in either direction from Aberporth. For a more challenging walk, head into the Preseli Hills where you could scale the likes of Foel Drygarn (see page 144).

Need to know: Dogs need to be kept under control or on the lead around the site as there are open camping pitches in the vicinity, too, but one of the best things about staying here is that there's almost always a spare empty field on the farm for you to use to exercise the dog. Bowls and towels for the dogs are provided.

WHAT'S NEARBY?
For days out, take a tour of the Lammas Eco Village (see page 144) with one of its inspiring residents, or hit the beach – Cilborth (see page 153) and New Quay (see page 154) are both excellent stretches of sand.

↓ The front terrace at Ty Nodyn

↓ The view from Pantechnicon Powys

STAY

IRMA'S COTTAGE

187

Llandysul, Ceredigion

There are many faces to this little cottage in the Ceredigion countryside: the original house was a tiny dwelling with charming stonework and a chunky brick fireplace, before it was all spruced up with new rustic plaster and fresh white paint in the 1970s. Later, a resident carpenter created the wooden mezzanine and clever switch-back stairs in the 1980s, and a small glass extension on its side was added in the 21st century, giving it an extra living space that lets the outside world in.

And the outside world is glorious here. Expect to watch birds flitting about in the tree branches right outside the cottage, and you can drink it all in with a bottle of something by the firepit on the slopes just above the house.

Where to walk: There's livestock all over this area of Wales, so head to the coast for walks with the dog. Try Cilborth (see page 153) and New Quay (see page 154), where they are welcome year-round. An excellent coast path walk can be had at Cwm Tydu (see page 153).

> **WHAT'S NEARBY?**
> Neighbouring the cottage is a whisky distillery and creamery where you can pick up a dram and wedge for lunch. Further afield, see how the residents of low-impact Lammas Eco Village (see page 144) live in their self-built homes.

Need to know: There's no Wi-Fi here, so come for offline breaks. Expect to see livestock in the fields surrounding the cottage, so keep the dog on a lead when outside; there's an outdoor tap for washing muddy paws, too.

CANOE THE WYE'S WINDING WATERS (188)

Hay-on-Wye, Powys canoehire.co.uk

The town of Hay-on-Wye is probably most famous for its myriad bookshops – many of which are dog-friendly – and annual literature festival, when bright minds and big thinkers come together to discuss novels, non-fiction and even kids' books over the course of ten days. But when the town isn't filled with word nerds, it's the river that becomes its focal point. Join the 'Hay Navy', as locals call it, and take to the water on one of the canoes for hire. From here, you can paddle eastwards on the winding Wye towards Hereford in England, spending an entire day on the water amid tranquil countryside, ending in Byecross.

You'll pass through Whitney-on-Wye, where a stop for lunch at a local pub wouldn't go amiss, and you might spot kingfishers and herons on the riverbanks, or maybe even an otter slipping below the surface in search of food.

Make a night of it: Book into one of the luxurious pods or lodges at Cynefin Retreats, just a five-minute drive from Hay, where floor-to-ceiling windows keep that immersion in nature going and the dog gets biscuits on arrival. pawsandstay.co.uk

PANTECHNICON POWYS (189)

Cefnperfedd Uchaf, Powys canopyandstars.co.uk

It's almost impossible to not have a sound night's sleep here, as this converted removals van is set within a vast lavender farm. The sweet, floral scent of lavender – which is often used in sleep mists to aid a good night's rest – will fill the air when their rows of purple crops are in bloom in the height of summer.

↑ The interior of Lofftwen Longhouse

The van itself is almost unrecognisable on the inside, with timber-lined walls, a kitchenette and even a small outside deck for al fresco breakfasts in the sun.

Beyond your front door lie rolling green hills, and at the bottom of the steps to the van is your own private wild swimming pond – perfect for refreshing summer dips or bracing winter swims.
Where to walk: Several footpaths lead from the farm and into the surrounding hills, so you'll never be lost for somewhere to walk. Alternatively, drive into Builth Wells and follow the bends of the River Wye as far as you fancy before turning back.
Need to know: Dogs must be kept under control or on the lead around the farm.

WHAT'S NEARBY?
For a little retail therapy, don't miss the farm's own shop, where you can buy lavender soaps, scrubs, lip balms and foot cream. In the little town of Builth Wells you'll find a chip shop and several pubs – the fry-ups at The Fountain Inn (fountaininnbuilthwells.co.uk) are great – and for a special Sunday lunch drive the half hour to The Felin Fach Griffin (eatdrinksleep.ltd.uk).

LOFFTWEN LONGHOUSE

Llanwrtyd Wells, Powys
canopyandstars.co.uk

Lofftwen Longhouse might sound like some sort of Viking abode, but really it's all very Welsh. Deep in the Powys countryside, this small but beautifully formed farmhouse dates back to the 1600s and has lots of original features, including flagstone flooring and exposed timber beams. Here, you're surrounded by 320 acres of farmland that's being used as a rewilding project. On local walks you might see weasels, pine marten and stoats, or even otters slinking around the River Irfon nearby.
Where to walk: You're in the Cambrian Mountains here so there's no excuse for avoiding a hill climb. From the farm, a footpath leads down to the riverside and along, where over the bridge several

↓ The rolling hills of Mid Wales as seen from Lofftwen Longhouse

WHAT'S NEARBY?

Stargazers will love watching the sky move from the outdoor patio at the cottage, but for the darkest skies you should drive out to the Llyn Brianne dam and reservoir, where there's very little light pollution. Dinners out should be had at The Drovers Rest Riverside Restaurant (food-food-food.co.uk), where local goat's cheese, venison, pork and salmon are on the menu.

other paths climb up into the steep hill west of the village. Alternatively, you could take on part of the Heart of Wales Line trail, which connects Craven Arms in Shropshire to Llanelli on the south coast of Wales.

Need to know: There's no enclosed garden here and so it's best to keep dogs on a lead in case roaming farm animals are nearby.

BEACH

CILBORTH BEACH 191

Ceredigion

In Welsh folklore, it's said that a passing giant got toothache around the soft, sugary sands of Cilborth Beach. He was in so much pain, the legend goes, he yanked the tooth out and threw it on the ground, and now it lies immortalised as rock on the southern tip of the cove. Whether or not you believe it to be true, be sure to explore the rockpools around it, as you might find a few smaller creatures making homes amid the crags. Cilborth is accessible via Llangrannog Beach, which is also dog-friendly year-round.

Make a night of it: Ty Nodyn (see page

148) is a gorgeous little hideaway for a night near the Ceredigion coast.
Parking: Llangrannog, SA44 6SN

CWM SODEN BUTTERFLY WALK 192

Ceredigion

START POINT: SA44 6LQ
DISTANCE/TIME: circular 4.8km/4 hrs

The pearl-bordered fritillary butterfly is rarely seen in Wales these days, but one of the few places you might spot it is in Cwm Soden – a National Trust-managed valley that's rife with flowers and these little iridescent orange flittering insects. Starting at Cwm Tydu, where a sheltered little beach is a perfect picnic spot for after the walk, you'll track along the coast path north to the gorgeous Castell Bach, a beach with an Iron Age fort overlooking the sea on the cliffs. Footpaths then bear inland, plunging down into the valley, where myriad butterflies enjoy the warm conditions in July and August each year. Look out for the iridescent common blue butterfly fluttering amid the meadowsweet and purple orchids and keep an eye out for enormous gold-ringed dragonflies. The route then turns back southwards and joins the coastal path again to reach the car park.

WHAT'S FOR LUNCH?

Bring a picnic to enjoy on the beach or in the wildflower meadows.

Need to know: Dogs must be on the lead around cliff edges, livestock and ponies. They can run free on the beaches. Directions available at nationaltrust.org.uk.

NEW QUAY NORTH BEACH

Ceredigion

Sandy and dog-friendly year-round, New Quay North Beach sits on the edge of a lively little harbour town that was once a central part of the region's fishing industry. Today, it's a great place for watersports – try your hand at kayaking or paddleboarding – and wildlife lovers come here to look out for seals and dolphins. If you're serious about seeing some sea creatures, take the dolphin watching trips with SeaMor (see 194, right) that leave from New Quay.

Make a night of it: Irma's Cottage (see page 150) is a lovely spot to continue nature-watching.

Parking: SA45 9NW

↓ Water-Break-its-Neck waterfall in Radnor Forest

DOG-FRIENDLY DOLPHIN SPOTTING ON A SEAMOR CRUISE

Ceredigion seamor.org

All sorts of intriguing sea creatures lurk beneath the surface of Cardigan Bay, and on this cruise you're guaranteed to see something special. Accompanied by a marine biologist and knowledgeable skippers and crew, your vessel will speed out into the bay to a collection of lobster pots. Your guide will lift the pot from the water to see what's been caught – it could be anything from small sharks to eels to spider crabs and, of course, lobsters – and then you'll pass through the bay's dolphin hotspot in search of those silvery sea creatures. Few trips return to New Quay without a dolphin sighting.

Make a night of it: Irma's Cottage (see page 150) is a charming little escape at Llandysul.

↓ The Elan Valley reservoir

WALK

FISHPOOLS, RADNOR FOREST

195

Radnorshire

START POINT: Fishpools
Car Park, LD7 1PA
DISTANCE/TIME: circular
3.8km/2 hrs

Follow a forest road up on to the hills and enjoy a ramble along the footpaths of former royal hunting ground Radnor Forest, with views over Bleddfa village – where the last wild wolf in Wales is thought to have been killed – and the plunging valleys around Abbey Cwm Hir.

> **WHAT'S FOR LUNCH?**
> Get classic pub grub at the Severn Arms in Penybont (LD1 5UA; 01597 851224).

Need to know: The route is waymarked from the car park.

WALK

NANT Y GRO

196

The Elan Valley, Powys

START POINT: Elan Valley Visitor Centre, LD6 5HP
DISTANCE/TIME: 5.6km/2 hrs

The Elan Valley is home to more than 100 sq km of reservoirs and dams, all set within a typically green and undulating Welsh landscape. For views of both water and the infrastructure that keeps these important reserves safe, the Nant y Gro trail from the visitor centre is a brilliant dog walk. There are a few brutal climbs on this trail but your eyes will thank your burning thighs – expect glorious views of the Caban Coch reservoir and the Garreg Ddu viaduct beneath you.

> **WHAT'S FOR LUNCH?**
> Head into the visitor centre for lunch with the dog, and don't miss the fascinating exhibitions while you're there.

Keep a keen eye out for otters around the reservoir's edge, and if you're extremely lucky you might spot a pine marten skulking about the valley. The bog mosses, heather and cotton grasses are a popular spot for ground nesting birds such as the golden plover and dunlin, so dogs must be kept under control and should stick to the footpaths.

Need to know: Directions can be downloaded from **elanvalley.org.uk**.

MID WALES 155

SEE PANDEMONIUM IN THE SKIES AT THE RED KITE FEEDING CENTRE

197

Rhayader, Powys gigrin.uk

There is nothing quite like watching birds gather and bicker over a meal at the Red Kite Feeding Centre in Rhayader. This isn't a peaceful birdwatching experience, but instead a feathery brawl between different species – kites, crows and even buzzards. Red kites were, until the early 1990s, almost extinct in the UK, but a reintroduction programme has seen their numbers soar and it all began here, on the Powell's family farm, after a nifty working spaniel left its kills out for the birds to feed on. Kites flocked to the area for the carcasses and, with the help of the RSPB, the first ever red kite feeding station was born.

Today, it's a slick operation – five hides (four of which allow dogs) skirt the edge of a field where a mound of fresh meat is laid out in the middle to encourage the action. Not that any of the birds need much encouragement – they wait in the trees surrounding the farm, their dark figures silhouetted on the branches, knowing the food will arrive. But kites aren't the only birds here – the noisy local crows tend to be the first to gorge on the feast. There are jackdaws and ravens, too, all joining in to create a chaotic cacophony of calls that say 'Keep off, this is *my* dinner'. But it's the red kites whose calls are most distinctive: known as a mew but better described as a screech, their high-pitched whistle will stay with you long after you've left the farm.

There's a literal pecking order here, with younger kites waiting for their elder relatives to swoop down for first dibs, and by the end of the day, more than 500 red kites could have visited the station.

Make a night of it: Spend the night on a lavender farm at Pantechnicon Powys (see page 151), a 30-minute drive from the red kite feeding station, where you've even got your own private swimming pond.

HAFOD ESTATE

198

Pontrhydygroes, Ceredigion
nationaltrust.org.uk

For aimless wandering in an area so dressed the view around every corner is a picture-perfect landscape waiting to be photographed, painted or have poetry written about it, the Hafod Estate has few rivals. Artists and travellers have been visiting Hafod, the creation of landscaper Thomas Johnes, for centuries since its establishment in the 1700s, each of whom have come to be inspired by its rippling rivers that flow through gently sloping, wooded valleys and the waterfalls that

flow between its drops. There are follies, bridges and formal gardens to explore, and areas for the dog to run around off-lead when there's no livestock in sight.

ABERYSTWYTH CASTLE

Aberystwyth, Ceredigion

The medieval ruins of Aberystwyth Castle sit right on the town's seafront, defeated by nothing but 17th-century politics and the brutal weather fronts that have hit it over centuries – plus a few plucky locals who helped themselves to its stones when it was cast aside by Oliver Cromwell. Today, you can walk about its ruins before hopping down to the southern beach, where the dog can run off-lead all year round.

BEACH

TAN Y BWLCH BEACH

Aberystwyth, Ceredigion

With light grey pebbles and shingle and backed by hills covered with lush green grass, this beach just south of Aberystwyth looks like it could be straight from a brochure for Iceland or Greenland. Those verdant hills, though, are in fact home to an Iron Age hillfort, well worth climbing for spectacular views over the area and out to sea.

Make a night of it: Gwesty'r Marine Hotel & Spa in Aberystwyth town centre is a 20-minute walk from the beach. gwestymarinehotel.co.uk 🐾2 🐾 ≤£100
Parking: SY23 1BJ

BEACH

WALLOG BEACH

Ceredigion

This shingle beach is wonderfully quiet and has a little piece of industrial history – a disused lime kiln – on its shores, too. It's a 30-minute walk along the coast path to reach Wallog Beach from Clarach Beach to the south, but it's worth it to be the only person on the shoreline – not uncommon even in summer.

Make a night of it: Gwesty'r Marine Hotel & Spa is a short drive away in Aberystwyth. gwestymarinehotel.co.uk 🐾2 🐾 ≤£100
Parking: SY23 3DL

← The bridge to Aberystwyth Castle

NORTH WALES

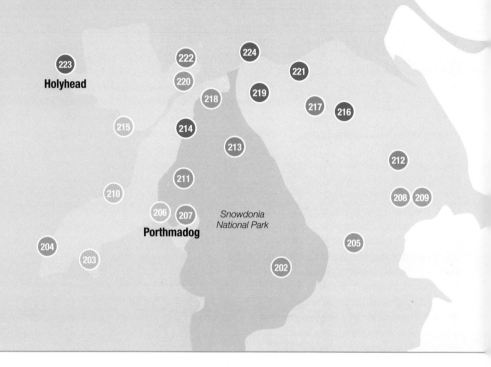

223
Holyhead

222
220
218
224
221
219
217
216
215
214
213
212
211
210
208 209
206 207
Snowdonia
National Park
Porthmadog
204
205
203
202

WALK

ARAN FAWDDWY AND GLASGWM

202

Snowdonia National Park

START POINT: ///domain.grounded.length
DISTANCE/TIME: circular 15km/6 hrs

While everyone else is queueing to reach the top of Snowdon or following the crowds up Cadair Idris, you should head to southern Snowdonia to scale its highest peak: Aran Fawddwy, which towers to 905 metres above sea level.

It's a challenging 6½-hour trek, starting from the valley of Cwm Cywarch and steeply climbing up to Drysgol (483 metres high) before reaching Aran Fawddwy's summit. If you're bringing lunch, have it here as on a clear day you'll enjoy spellbinding views across to the surrounding mountains as you munch on your sandwiches.

The route then descends to 600 metres or so to Waun Camddwr and then

WHAT'S FOR LUNCH?
Unsurprisingly, there are no pubs on this route, so either bring a picnic or drive south after your hike to Y Llew Coch pub (yllewcoch.com), where great local beers and mammoth portions await.

up 100 metres to Glasgwm, where there's a small lake and more brilliant views. The path then twists and bends to descend back into the valley where you began.
Need to know: The path can be boggy in places so you'll want good boots and gaiters; there are a couple of ladder stiles along the way, so it's best for small or agile dogs. Also be aware of free-roaming livestock. Directions can be found on alltrails.com.

BEACH

PORTH NEIGWL

 203

Gwynedd

Dog owners with a love of frothing surf should beeline for Porth Neigwl, also known as Hell's Mouth beach. Sitting on the Llŷn Peninsula and facing south-west, the Atlantic pulls no punches here with pounding waves that make for excellent body boarding or surfing.
Make a night of it: Spend the night at Y Granar Coch, a three-bed cottage just 20 minutes' drive from the beach. sawdays.co.uk
❄ ☀ ⠿ -£100
Parking: LL53 7LG

WALK

PORTHOR

 204

Aberdaron, Gwynedd

START POINT: LL53 8LH
DISTANCE/TIME: circular 1.6km/1 hr

The Llŷn Peninsula is famous for its craggy coastline and this National Trust walk takes in one of its finest sections, featuring 2,000-year-old island fortresses and dolphin and seal hotspots.

> **WHAT'S FOR LUNCH?**
> Head to Caffi Porthor (facebook.com/ PorthorWhislingsands), which serves cakes and light lunches from spring through summer.

Need to know: Directions can be found on nationaltrust.org.uk. There's a dog ban on the beaches near here throughout summer.

→ A person hiking the trails of Snowdonia National Park

PISTYLL RHAEADR

Llanrhaeadr, Powys

START POINT: SY10 0BZ
DISTANCE/TIME: 1.3km/20 mins each way

Test your leg muscles on a steep but rewarding climb to the top of Pistyll Rhaeadr – Britain's highest single-drop waterfall at a neck-cricking 80 metres high. At the base of a waterfall, once you've marvelled at the rushing waters, take the track that heads off to the right through woodland. You're in for a brutal incline, but once at the top you can watch the waters disappear over the edge and beyond along the picturesque valley.

> **WHAT'S FOR LUNCH?**
> There's a tearoom at the base of the falls for ice creams, homemade lunches or warming hot chocolates in winter (**pistyllrhaeadr.co.uk**).

Need to know: Keep the dog on the lead if it's busy or near ledges. Directions can be found on **alltrails.com**.

TRAETH Y GREIGDDU (BLACK ROCK SANDS)

Gwynedd

There is no car park for Black Rock Sands because the beach itself is the car park – you can drive your vehicle right on to the sand here, giving you prime position for sunbathing, sandcastle building and swimming in the sea. This enormous expanse of yellow sand is backed by the mountains of Snowdonia National Park, while across the ocean lies the verdant island of Anglesey.

Make a night of it: Bring your tent or your own wheels and camp out right behind the beach at Black Rock Sands Touring and Camping Park. blackrocksandstouringandcamping park.com 🐕3+ 🛞 ☀️ £50 🚻

← Pistyll Rhaeadr waterfall   ↑ An empty Black Rock Sands

RIDE THE FFESTINIOG & WELSH HIGHLAND RAILWAYS

207

Porthmadog, Gwynedd
festrail.co.uk

Once upon a time, the railways around Snowdonia were powered by gravity on the way down the mountain and then were horse-drawn on the way back up. They didn't carry passengers but instead ferried slate from the mines down into Port Madoc, today's Porthmadog, which was then shipped all over the world. Today, fortunately, diesel and steam offer a more reliable form of power and instead of freight carriages, a fleet of lovingly restored Pullman carriages and more modern cars made right here in Porthmadog are a far more comfortable way to travel on the rails.

The railway has several different passenger routes, travelling up into the soggy, slate-covered surrounds of Blaenau Ffestiniog – one of the world's wettest towns – or into the pretty mountain village of Beddgelert, where a dog-themed walk awaits (see page 164). If you want heritage carriages, take the Tan-y-Bwlch line, which offers fantastic mountain-top views on clear days, or for a much longer experience, the Porthmadog–Caernarfon Harbourmaster is spectacular. It's a seven-hour return trip (including a break for a walk), travelling over the Aberglaslyn Pass, through Beddgelert, all the way up to the line's highest point, Y Copa, before trundling down to sea level again at Caernarfon.

Make a night of it: The effortlessly cool Rocks at Plas Curig (see page 166) is a brilliant base for Snowdonia adventures.

STEAM AHEAD ON THE LLANGOLLEN RAILWAY

208

Denbighshire llangollen-railway.co.uk

Laid over the top of the old Ruabon–Barmouth main line, which was operated by Great Western Railway but closed in the 1960s, the Llangollen Railway is a standard-gauge line running alongside the meandering River Dee. Its 16km of track were meticulously laid by a team of enthusiasts, who saw the potential for a spectacularly scenic rail line in this idyllic valley in the 1970s. Today, it runs between

↑ A view across the river to the Llangollen Railway

TAKE IT SLOW AT LLANGOLLEN WHARF

209

Denbighshire horsedrawnboats.co.uk

Sometimes the old ways are the best ways and this rings true at Llangollen Wharf, where horses have been towing barges along the canal for over a hundred years. With absolutely no emissions involved, these trips are a serene and sustainable way to explore the incredibly romantic, scenic Dee Valley.

Make a night of it: Go off-grid and keep it sustainable at Copse Camp (see page 164), just a 20-minute drive north.

Llangollen and Carrog stations, the latter of which has been beautifully restored to its fine 1950s looks, and its heritage carriages are a delightful blast from the past.

Bring the dog on board for a small fee and watch the Dee Valley AONB whizz by out of the window, with glimpses of the river, native woodland and the Clwydian Range beyond. You can hop on and off at its various station stops, such as Berwyn Station, which sits on a gorge and offers access to Horseshoe Falls, or at Glyndyfrdwy Station, where a tearoom awaits with sweet treats.

Make a night of it: Stay 20 minutes north within the AONB at Copse Camp (see page 164), where you'll sleep in an eccentric little treehouse in its own woodland and with a fantastic outdoor kitchen.

TRAETH YR EIFL

210

Gwynedd

This pebble beach on the north coast of the Llŷn Peninsula is all about drama: the hills of Yr Eifl rise steeply from the beach, reaching up to 560 metres above sea level. This means you're overlooked by towering, gnarly cliffs, which showcase the region's hardy granite rock.

Make a night of it: The three-bed Yr Granar Coch is a charming hideaway for any trip to the Llŷn Peninsula.
sawdays.co.uk 2 ♨ 4 ⌂ ❄ ☀ ⊞ £100
Parking: LL54 5NA

BEDDGELERT (211)

Snowdonia National Park

START POINT: Stryd Gwynant, Beddgelert LL55 4LY
DISTANCE/TIME: circular 1.6km/45 mins

The tragic tale of Beddgelert – a 13th-century prince's faithful hound who was wrongfully killed by his master after the heir to the throne was attacked by wolves – will tug on the heartstrings of any dog owner. On this flat, short but captivating walk on the outskirts of Beddgelert village, you'll pass by the dog's gravesite to pay your respects before returning along the river.

WHAT'S FOR LUNCH?
Hearty pub food at the Prince Llewelyn Hotel (princellewelyn.co.uk).

Need to know: Directions can be obtained at the visitor centre (LL55 4YD) or downloaded from nationaltrust.org.uk.

COPSE CAMP (212)

Denbighshire pawsandstay.co.uk

Outdoor living is the name of the game at Copse Camp. This small, enclosed woodland is entirely off-grid, created by Jenny and Margaret, who have lived in this remote area for more than 40 years. The pair have lovingly crafted a truly special campsite worthy of the Lost Boys in *Peter Pan*, with a cabin set within the treetops, a compost loo that comes with its own library, an outdoor kitchen, and a gypsy caravan that doubles as a dining area and a spare bedroom. The eccentric decor – think colourful knitted sleeves on the tree's branches, walls covered in *Beano* magazine pages – is a nod to their creativity, and outside you'll find decking for outdoor dining, handmade chairs and sofas around the camp fire, and a wood-fired hot tub.

← Arty on the trail in Beddgelert

The estate the copse is set within is a whole 300 acres, which you're welcome to explore with the dogs on a lead if you want a short walk. You might meet the Mangalica pigs roaming in the woods or see their friendly Valais Blacknose sheep. There's a welcome hamper with pâté and preserves, and a nearby farm shop to stock up on local produce.

Where to walk: The National Trust's Erddig Hall (nationaltrust.org.uk) has 1,200 acres of parkland for exploring with the dog, and they can even go off-lead in specified areas (look out for the signage). Walk around the remains of the Norman motte-and-bailey castle, a unique waterfall designed by landscape architect William Emes, and ample woodland for shade on sunny days.

There are also trails right from your woodland, here, with footpaths leading to the lovely village of Pen-y-Stryt or into Llandegla Forest.

Excellent dinners – and handmade pitchers full of beer – can be had at the Three Pigeons Inn (threepigeonsinn.co.uk), just a ten-minute drive from the camp.

↑ The interior of the treehouse at Copse Camp

Need to know: They'll always keep a field nearby free of livestock for exercising the dog; water bowls, towels and treats are provided. Note that the treehouse is accessed by a suspended bridge, so nervous dogs might not be confident crossing it. Copse Camp is set up for two people, but extra guests can be added at the time of booking for an additional fee.

WHAT'S NEARBY?

Just 12km south of Copse Camp is the River Dee and the Llangollen Canal, where you can wander along the towpath for miles in either direction, enjoy horse-drawn boat trips (see page 163), or watch the narrowboats cruising across the 18-arch Pontcysyllte Aqueduct. There's also a heritage railway with vintage carriages and steam locomotives for a trip back in time through the verdant Dee Valley.

THE ROCKS AT PLAS CURIG

Snowdonia National Park

therockshostel.com

Banish memories of dingy youth hostels with tatty dorm rooms and regrettable shared toilets: The Rocks Hostel is the antithesis of every grotty place you've stayed in. Its communal chill-out spaces are like homely, stylish living rooms and the big industrial-style kitchen is always kept sparkling no matter how many bacon sandwiches have been cooked that morning. There are private rooms as well as shared dorms with cosy bunks complete with bedding and blankets, and outside is a communal hot tub and fire pit overlooking the mountains beyond. On a clear day, you can sometimes see all the way out to Snowdon itself.

Where to walk: There are ample walking trails directly from the hostel's front door, with a beautiful footpath that takes in the twin lakes of Llynnau Mymbyr, just across the road. From

here, you can also scale the 872-metre-high peak of Moel Siabod, one of the most popular peaks in Snowdonia and the highest in the Moelwynion range.

Need to know: Owners Christian and Annie have their own dogs so there's lots of practical touches here – think poo bags and dog walking maps at reception, metal rings for tying up dogs at your table or by the porch outside while you're removing muddy boots. Bring dog beds and bowls with you.

↓ The Snowdon Massif reflected in a lake

WHAT'S NEARBY?

Caffi Siabod, a five-minute walk west, is the local hiker's and climber's favourite dining spot: you'll see scores of gear-clad adventurers fuelling up and picking up packed lunches here before setting off on hikes, and you must stop in for a hearty meal or coffee. Head west in the car to see the gushing Swallow Falls, then continue on to the town of Betws-y-Coed where there are excellent dog-friendly restaurants and shops.

NATIONAL SLATE MUSEUM

214

Llanberis, Snowdonia National Park museum.wales

Remnants of the slate industry in Snowdonia National Park are almost impossible to avoid – the dark grey rock that makes up so much of the mountain range here is all over the place: on rooftops, in drystone walls and in enormous slag heaps around the former mining centres. At the National Slate Museum you'll learn about the mines and quarries where thousands of men and women worked to extract the popular building material and see demonstrations of slate splitting. Step inside the former workshops and offices of the Dinorwig Quarry and see the vessels that used to carry the slate on the Llanberis railway.

TRAETH LLANDDWYN

215

Anglesey

Sitting on the south coast of Anglesey, Traeth Llanddwyn is one of the island's most spectacular stretches of seaside. Its soft, sugary golden sand is divine under foot – and paw – and the views out to Snowdonia from here are truly arresting as the dramatic peaks punctuate the horizon to the east. Between May and September, there's a dog ban at the western end of the beach, though there's plenty of space for everyone, but come in early spring, autumn or winter and you'll get to explore Ynys Llanddwyn – a tiny island connected by a sandbar.

You can walk all the way across to its southern tip, past a pair of Celtic crosses built in the late 19th and early 20th centuries, and to the Tŵr Mawr Lighthouse, which became a working lighthouse in 1846. For those months when the dog isn't allowed on the island, there's plenty more to explore behind the beach, as Newborough Forest – a Corsican pine plantation that was created in the 1950s to stabilise the dunes and provide local timber – has endless trails where the dog can run off-lead. Look out for red squirrels bouncing from tree to tree.

Make a night of it: A 30-minute drive from Traeth Llanddwyn is the small but swish seaside town of Rhosneigr, where Sandy Mount House is a chic seafront stay. sandymounthouse.co.uk

2 🏠 🐾 <£200

Parking: LL61 6SG

DENBIGH CASTLE

216

Denbigh, Denbighshire
cadw.gov.wales

The remains of Denbigh Castle might be a decaying ruin, but high-tech additions to its medieval ramparts are more than making up for it: as you enter the gatehouse to explore inside, you'll hear the clattering of the portcullis shutting behind you and the roar of horses' hooves on the ground. It's not real, of course, as it's just a recording, but it offers an immersive welcome into the world of 13th-century Wales. Amble with the dog on a lead beneath its towering curtain walls, peer into the 12-metre-deep well, and look out for the unique carved figures within its stonework.

TY TWT

217

Tresaith, Conwy County
www.pawsandstay.co.uk/ty-twt

This charming wood cabin is nothing short of idyllic. Set within its own exceptionally delightful enclosed garden, packed with bright flowers that give off sweet scents in spring, it has a small lawn with deck chairs, a patio with a barbecue and pizza oven, and a pergola for shelter on those especially sunny days – and it's all strategically placed to take in the wonderful valley views, where mist mingles in the morning before clearing to reveal a patchwork of green farmland.

Inside the cabin itself you'll find a welcome hamper of fresh orange juice, tomatoes from the garden and some essential snacks – usually Welsh cakes –

↓ In the garden at Ty Twt

to enjoy, as well as a brilliant homemade guide to the area. A large log burner will keep you warm whatever the weather, while the rocking chairs on the veranda are the best place to sip your morning tea or coffee. While away soggier days with the board games or a deck of cards provided and bring a pair of binoculars for wildlife spotting – there are owls, badgers and deer roaming the lands around here, as well as swallows that love to duck and dive around the cabin's gables.

Where to walk: There are trails that follow along the River Aled just a few minutes from your front porch here, some of which pass waterfalls. You're also just a 20-minute drive from the beach at Ty Twt, meaning if you head northwards in the car you can let the dog run around on the sand at Rhyl or Prestatyn beaches.

The impressive medieval fortress of Denbigh Castle (see page 169) is just a 20-minute drive east of the cottage, where dogs can explore all the ground-floor areas – indoors and out – while on the lead.

Need to know: The garden here is enclosed, but fencing and hedging

↑ Arty at the base of Aber Falls

WHAT'S NEARBY?
A 20-minute drive north is the wonderful ruins of Gwrych Castle – you might recognise it from the 2021 series of *I'm A Celebrity* – which was saved from ruin by an 11-year-old child and now stands wrapped in climbers and surrounded by thick woodland (see page 172). Around 45 minutes north is the Great Orme Mines, a truly astonishing piece of ancient history where you can walk the dog around 4,000-year-old copper mines (see page 173).

isn't always high enough to discourage jumpers from escaping. The cottage welcomes one large or two small dogs; you must bring your own beds and bowls for them.

WALK

ABER FALLS 218

Snowdonia National Park

START POINT: Aber Falls Car Park, LL33 0LP
DISTANCE/TIME: 6.5km/3 hrs

If you've spent any time in Wales and have frequented a local pub or bar, you'll likely have seen the elegant bottles of Aber Falls Gin on the shelves. The distillery is based near to the eponymous falls, though somewhat disappointingly it's only water cascading over the 37-metre drop here. Still, the walk up to the falls and back is a delightful diversion – and offers an excellent excuse to reward yourself with a gin and tonic afterwards.

It has a couple of short-but-sharp climbs but once those are out of the way it's a pleasant amble up a gradual incline, across grazing pasture for sheep and along the Anafon River. Look out for the

↑ Bodnant Garden is a fairy-tale place to explore

hydroelectric building near the beginning, which is utilising the power of the falls to generate electricity for the local community, and the ancient crumbling walls from Iron Age settlements that thrived here thousands of years ago.

The falls itself is spectacular – especially after ample rainfall – and with a bit of a breeze you'll feel the spray on your face as you gaze at it. You'll cross over the river and head back along this side, enjoying views all the way out to Anglesey on a clear day.

> **WHAT'S FOR LUNCH?**
> Head to the distillery, of course, and have a gin with cake or a sandwich at the visitor centre cafe (aberfallsdistillery.com).

Need to know: Route directions can be downloaded from visitsnowdonia.info. A shorter, easier pushchair-friendly trail is waymarked in green from the upper car park (follow the road over the bridge).

PLACE

BODNANT GARDEN

Tal-y-Cafn, Conwy County Borough nationaltrust.org.uk

Glassy lily ponds leading to fairy-tale follies, a spectacular laburnum arch and bridges over waterfalls are just some of the delightful features throughout the manicured gardens at Bodnant. Dogs are welcome to explore on leads throughout this brilliant 80-acre space at certain times of day depending on the month (check online for the latest information). It includes formal planted gardens and arboretums; come in spring to see splashes of pink and white within the stunning magnolia collection, as well as carpets of yellow where daffodils poke their heads through the lawns.

↓ Arty overlooking South Stack Lighthouse, Anglesey

SAIL AROUND PUFFIN ISLAND TO MEET THE BIRDS

220

Anglesey seacoastsafaris.co.uk

Ynys Seiriol, or Puffin Island, sits at the northern end of the Menai Strait, the body of water that separates Anglesey from mainland Wales. Out here, back in the 6th century, monks set up a monastic community, the remains of which can still be seen today. Today, it's a favourite nesting place for seabirds such as puffins, eider ducks, guillemots and cormorants and the guided boat trips there and back are a great way to see them between March and July.

Make a night of it: Stay close to nature and stay at Wonderfully Wild (see right).

GWRYCH CASTLE

221

Abergele, Conwy County Borough gwrychcastle.co.uk

Saved from total ruin by an 11-year-old boy in 1996 who was so saddened by its decay that he formed a preservation trust to restore it, Gwrych Castle is an enchanting 19th-century country house. Today, the house is a largely hollow husk of its former self, its vast towers and crenelated ramparts open to the elements and awash with greenery in all available crevices. Wandering around former staterooms and banquet halls with the dog on a lead is an eerie experience; don't miss the 52-step marble staircase, too, which is now engulfed in ferns and moss.

WONDERFULLY WILL 222

Beaumaris, Anglesey
canopyandstars.co.uk

Upcycled furniture and retro kitchen fittings make the interiors of the six safari tents at Wonderfully Wild feel like home, while outside there's a wide deck and wood-fired hot tub to enjoy – plus 200 acres of fields to walk the dog across. There are barbecues for hire and a cool box for your food and drinks, and day trips to nearby dog-friendly Lleiniog beach. **Where to walk:** Explore the coastal path that trims the Isle of Anglesey, or head to the National Trust's Plas Newydd (nationaltrust.org.uk) to wander among cypress trees where red squirrels bound between the branches.

SOUTH STACK CLIFFS & ELLIN'S TOWER 223

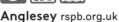

Anglesey rspb.org.uk

Come to South Stack at sunset for the best view of this much-photographed Anglesey icon. The white lighthouse and the island it sits on isn't accessible for dogs, but you can visit Ellin's Tower for a great view across to it. Trails lead up on to the craggy hills above for even better vantage points, and you'll spot guillemots, puffins and more in spring and summer.

GREAT ORME MINES 224

Y Gogarth Great Orme Country Park, Conwy County Borough
greatormemines.info

Mining has been big business in Wales over the last few centuries, but its mining heritage goes back way beyond the famous slate and coal mining areas further south. Here, at Great Orme, copper mining began as early as 4,000 years ago during the Bronze Age. Take the dog on a tour of its tunnels and delve into the site's history in the exhibitions.

↓ Arty pretending to be half-human on the boat trip to Puffin Island

SOUTHERN SCOTLAND

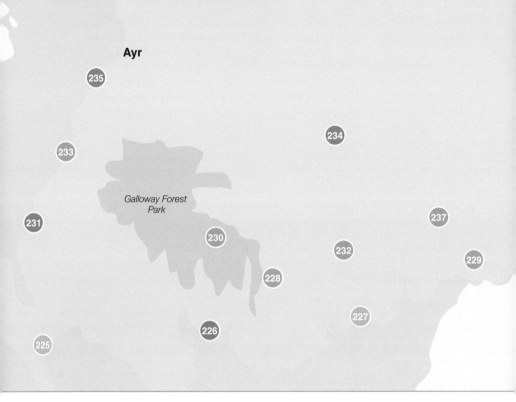

243

241

240 23

Peebles

Ayr

235

234

233

*Galloway Forest
Park*

231

237

230

232

229

228

227

226

225

BEACH

LUCE SANDS 225

Dumfries and Galloway

Almost 5km of beach stretches out into the ocean from the village of Sandhead when the tide's out, meaning there's ample space for dogs to race around after a frisbee or bound in and out of the ocean. Sandcastle construction is encouraged, and paddling in the shallow waters is essential. There are no facilities here, so bring your own picnic and a blanket for sitting on the sand and spend the afternoon watching the waves crash on the shoreline, with views of the Dumfries and Galloway coast ahead.
Make a night of it: The luxurious Glenapp Castle (see page 178) is a positively regal place to escape after a day on the beach.
Parking: DG9 9JA

LITTLE WILLOW

Kirkdale, Dumfries and Galloway

www.pawsandstay.co.uk/little-willow

This hand-built shepherd's hut – one of three on the same site – is all rustic charm inside, with untreated wooden walls and a lovely log burner for keeping warm come evening. But the draw here isn't the modern kitchen or plush leather sofa; instead, it's all about that view: set on a hill in the south of Dumfries and Galloway, this shepherd's hut overlooks the glimmering seas within Wigtown Bay. Sitting on the enclosed, south-facing decking with a sundowner in hand is the ultimate simple pleasure here.

Where to walk: The area surrounding the huts is rural, so walks along country lanes abound in the immediate vicinity. Further afield in Galloway Forest Park, you can take on the Bruce's Stone Trail at both Glen Trool (forestryandland.gov.scot) and Clatteringshaws (see page 177).

WHAT'S NEARBY?

You're just a 30-minute drive from the chaos of the Red Kite Centre at Bellymack Hill Farm (see page 176), where a feeding frenzy for the birds of prey takes place every day. Don't miss a day on Sandyhills Beach (see page 176) and head further afield (2 hrs by car) for a walk around the impressive, triangular Caerlaverock Castle (historicenvironment.scot).

Need to know: There's often livestock in the fields surrounding the site, but the decking is enclosed to keep the dog safe.

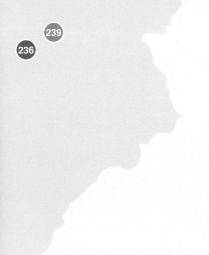

↓ A regal dog sits inside Little Willow

BEACH

SANDYHILLS BEACH

227

Dumfries and Galloway

At low tide, this beach is vast. Soft, silky sand is left soggy as the Atlantic retreats, its surface reflecting the low-lying hills that surround this protected cove. With a craggy coastline, there are caves to explore here and plenty of rockpools for seeking out marine life, while snacks can be bought at the tiny shop at the back of the beach.

Make a night of it: Book into a dog-friendly shepherd's hut at Little Willow on the 3 Little Huts site (see page 175), where the sea views are divine.

Parking: DG5 4NZ

↓ Sandyhills Beach

EXPERIENCE

WATCH THE KITES DESCEND AT BELLYMACK HILL FARM FEEDING STATION

228

Laurieston, Galloway Forest Park
bellymackhillfarm.co.uk

The skies above Galloway Forest Park are positively thriving with red kites, but to see them at their most impressive – and noisiest – head for the feeding station at Bellymack Hill Farm, where you can witness the scrimmaging clash that is dinner time for these magnificent birds of prey.

Make a night of it: Little Willow (see page 175) is a cosy shepherd's hut near the south coast just 20 minutes from the farm.

↓ A view across Clatteringshaws Loch

EXPERIENCE

SAMPLE SOME SPIRITS AT ANNANDALE DISTILLERY

Dumfries and Galloway
annandaledistillery.com

No trip to Scotland is complete without a whisky tasting, but lots of distilleries don't let dogs in. Fortunately, David and Theresa, custodians of the historic Annandale Distillery, are dog lovers themselves so you can come here for a flight of their fragrant drams – each a single cask, single malt whisky – in the cafe or shop. There's even a whisky afternoon tea if you're hungry, and dogs get water bowls and fuss on arrival.
Make a night of it: Just a short drive from Annandale, Trigony Hotel loves

dogs so much, they have their own house Doberman waiting to welcome you and the dog. sawdays.co.uk
 2+ ☀ ⚡ -£200

WALK

CLATTERING-SHAWS LOCH

Galloway Forest Park

START POINT: Clatteringshaws Visitor Centre, DG7 3SQ
DISTANCE/TIME: 8km/2 hrs

This walk is in two parts: the first follows a waymarked route to Bruce's Stone along the shore of Clatteringshaws Loch. The stone, it's said, is where Robert the Bruce rested before his victorious battle against the English in the early 14th century and it's one of two within this park connected to the King of Scots – the other is at Glentrool. You'll then head back to the

↓ Swans on the waters of Lochmaben

car park for the second part of the walk along an easy track up to the Benniguinea viewpoint (there's a stile with dog-friendly steps so only agile pets will enjoy this route), where you can sneak peeks at the loch below through the trees. The return is the same route, so take your time at the top to enjoy the view and look out for circling red kites or even osprey.

WHAT'S FOR LUNCH?
Clatteringshaws Visitor Centre has an excellent dog-friendly cafe (facebook.com/cafeatclatteringshaws), where soup and cheese scones are the best reward.

Need to know: The first half is waymarked; the second half is relatively easy to work out from the car park as a forest track leads up to the viewpoint, but directions can be downloaded from walkhighlands.co.uk.

STAY

GLENAPP CASTLE

Ballantrae, Ayrshire
glenappcastle.com

All turrets and crenelated towers, Glenapp Castle is a pretty spectacular place to retreat for the night in Ayrshire. Overlooking the coast, with views out to Ailsa Craig (see page 179) and the Isle of Arran in the north, the castle is in prime position for adventures on the west coast of southern Scotland – and its grounds feel as if they were made for well-to-do dogs, too. There are four dog-friendly bedrooms, each decorated in period style with plush patterned furnishings, with direct access to the outside gardens.

Where to walk: There are 110 acres of gardens for roaming at Glenapp, so there's very little need to venture beyond its borders – dogs can even enjoy a swim in the pond if so inclined. But don't miss out on the Ayrshire Coastal Path, which spans 161km north from here along sandy beaches and past dramatic sea-battered castles.

WHAT'S NEARBY?
It's a 20-minute drive to Girvan from here, where you can take boats out to the mystical Ailsa Craig for birdwatching and seal-spotting opportunities (see page 179), and one of the region's finest beaches is just 30 minutes south at Sands of Luce (see page 174).

Need to know: Dogs get beds, treats and bowls in the room. They can't join you in the main restaurant or drawing room, but everywhere else – including the Azalea restaurant in the glasshouse, where afternoon tea is the highlight – is fair game. You can leave them in the room if they're happy to relax while you take on the tennis courts, golf or hop on the hotel's own boat for a Hebridean sea safari, but the hotel will also arrange dog sitting if required.

CRUISE OUT TO AILSA CRAIG
233

Girvan, Ayrshire ailsacraig.org.uk

Visible from many beaches and harbours along the Ayrshire coast, Ailsa Craig is essentially a big old lump of granite in the shape of a Tunnock's teacake. It doesn't sound mightily exciting but take a boat trip out here with island expert Mark McCrindle and you'll find plenty of intrigue, from washed-up foghorns to the remains of a 16th-century castle. Plus – there are seabirds. Thousands of them. Puffins come to nest in spring until summer, alongside guillemots and squawking gannets. On a good day, you can land on the island (dogs on leads), and if the weather won't play ball, you'll get a view of the towering cliffs from the water below.

Make a night of it: Bed down in the plush Glenapp Castle (see opposite), just a 20-minute drive south.

↑ Ailsa Craig in the mist off the Ayrshire coast

WALK

LOCHMABEN
232

Dumfries and Galloway

START POINT: Castle Street Parking, Lochmaben, DG11 1LP
DISTANCE/TIME: circular 6km/2 hrs

Despite its small size, Lochmaben is blessed with three lovely lochs popular with locals for fishing and sailing. Walking around these lochs is equally enjoyable, though, and this route beginning from the town centre is a cracking exploration of all three. The trail takes in country lanes and easy-to-follow footpaths, and skirts alongside Mill Loch before returning into town.

> **WHAT'S FOR LUNCH?**
> There are a couple of cafes in Lochmaben for takeaways (not dog-friendly) but if you're craving a proper pub lunch, head to the creaky old Globe Inn (globeinndumfries.co.uk) just 15 minutes away by car in Dumfries. There's Robert Burns connections here and a very well stocked bar.

Need to know: Download the route from walkhighlands.co.uk.

DRUMLANRIG CASTLE AND GARDENS

234

Thornhill, Dumfries and Galloway drumlanrigcastle.co.uk

Day trips to Drumlanrig Castle and its gorgeous gardens are glorious, but staying overnight here is even better. There are both self-catering apartments and cottages, some with fully enclosed gardens, where once the day visitors have gone home you can enjoy the grounds of this magnificent stately home by yourself.

Where to walk: There are waymarked walks all over the estate right from your front door here: join the 2.5km Enchanted Forest trail (red) for an easy morning stroll alongside two lochs or take on the 4km Marr Burn route that follows the river.

→ The ruins of Dunure Castle
↓ The long driveway leading to Drumlanrig Castle

BRAE AT MOUNT FREEDOM 235

Donure, Ayrshire
www.canopyandstars.co.uk/brae

Three secluded cabins sit on this site and Brae is one of the most charming. Expect Alaskan wood cabin vibes, with wraparound verandas where rocking chairs await by the outdoor fireplace and plenty of pine inside where a modest kitchen and cosy living room make up the ground floor. The bedroom sits on the mezzanine within the steeply pitched roof, with a king-sized bed and small porthole-like windows offering a view on to the forested wilderness around you.

You'll find yourself somewhat off-grid here, with little phone signal and no Wi-Fi, so embrace the quietude and head outside, where there's a bathtub on the deck in which you should rightly spend

> **WHAT'S NEARBY?**
> The clifftop Culzean Castle (nts.org.uk) – a neoclassical Robert Adam construction – is a wonderful day out with walks amid follies and hidden beaches, while half an hour to the south is the harbour at Girvan where boats leave for the granite rock of Ailsa Craig (see page 179), where seabirds nest throughout summer.

hours watching the stars in the sky above and the ocean beyond.

Where to walk: Head down to the coast to walk along the coastal path, where you'll find the dramatic ruins of Dunure Castle on the Ayrshire Coastal Path. Inland, the trails at Galloway Forest Park – Clatteringshaws (see page 177) in particular – offer great hikes with loch views.

Need to know: There's no enclosed garden here but dogs can roam off-lead if kept under control.

ABBOTSFORD 236

Melrose, Scottish Borders
scottsabbotsford.com

If you recognise the name Abbotsford, it's because you might have seen it elsewhere. There are homes named Abbotsford all over the world, but this one sitting on the banks of the Tweed with its whispering grass pasture and fabulous gardens is the original. Abbotsford was, or is, one of the many masterpieces by Sir Walter Scott. While most of his works were written – either as poems or songs or short stories – this one was a physical representation of all the beauty he knew how to put into words. In short, this home in the Scottish Borders is simply idyllic.

It's also expansive. Surrounding the fine Scottish baronial mansion is a huge estate of 120 acres, running alongside the river with green fields where the dog can run free. There are waymarked walks you can follow, but you might prefer to aimlessly wander – no doubt as Scott would have done when seeking inspiration for his next work. Don't miss the sweet-smelling Regency Walled Garden, which is flushed with colour throughout the warmer months as countless flowers spring into life. While the dog can't visit inside the house itself, there's often a volunteer at the door who might be happy to keep an eye on well-behaved pets. Otherwise, take it in turns with others in your party to explore the interior, where you should look out for some really rather curious and gruesome gargoyles teetering on the ceiling.

← Steph Dyson walks Arty in the gardens at Abbotsford

TRAQUAIR HOUSE

Innerleithen, Scottish Borders
traquair.co.uk

The rather fortress-like home that is Traquair House lays claim to being the oldest inhabited home in Scotland. Still housing descendants of the Stuart family, who have lived here since the 1400s, it's a mighty mansion of turrets and tiny windows. While dogs can't go inside the house, they can explore the 4,500 acres of grounds with you, including the maze that was created using 1,500 trees, and nip in and out of the gift shops and cafe. Stop in to see potters creating delicate ceramics or artists making jewellery, and duck into the Traquair Brewery to buy a few bottles of their famous beers to take home.

KAILZIE GARDENS

Peebles, Scottish Borders
kailziegardens.com

Just outside the comely town of Peebles is Kailzie Gardens, where a riot of colourful flowers and regal old trees make for a pleasant day out. Drift beneath the laburnum arches in spring and enjoy the elegant rose gardens in summer. Reward yourselves with locally sourced lunch in the Courtyard Café.

THE POTTING SHED

Cowdenknowes, Scottish Borders
www.sawdays.co.uk/the-potting-shed

Tucked away within its own wildflower meadow, the Potting Shed was once a boiler room, where the heating system for nearby greenhouses chuntered away to keep the plants happy. It's come quite a long way from those days thanks to owners Luke and Kate Comins, who have redeemed its handsome brick walls and transformed its interiors to create a bonny wee space with a log burner, miniature Aga and modern kitchen for cooking up the eggs from the welcome hamper.

The dog will love roaming in the garden while you're sipping tea or wine on the patio furniture with a view of the River Leader beyond – true Borders bliss.

Where to walk: There are ample trails from the door – namely a heart-racing walk up Black Hill. You're a stone's throw from the Tweed here, so try the walk along the river path in Peebles (see page 184).

> **WHAT'S NEARBY?**
> The wonderful little town of Melrose is a short drive away from the Potting Shed, where you can explore the spectacular ruins of a Cistercian abbey, and a little further along the Tweed is Abbotsford, the former home of Sir Walter Scott (see opposite).

Need to know: The garden is fully enclosed but only by a metre-high fence, so jumpers might well find a way to escape. There's no livestock on site but there are free-range chickens so keep dogs under control at all times.

NEIDPATH CASTLE CIRCULAR

240

Scottish Borders

START POINT: Kingsmeadow Car Park, EH45 9EN
DISTANCE/TIME: circular 6km/2 hrs

Walking in Scotland needn't be all mountains and coastal drama. The River Tweed, which wends its way through the Scottish Borders and empties at Berwick at the border with England, has a kind of slow, subtle beauty to it. Its rocky waters are often visited by herons and kingfishers, and it passes through some of the Borders' most enchanting towns. This walk along the Tweed starts in Peebles, a well-to-do little town backed by forested hills, and it follows the river upstream past impressive houses and over footbridges across tributaries.

Once out of town, you'll find yourself in native woodland – oak and ash tower around you – and will eventually pass the lofty Neidpath Castle. Built in the 14th century, it has presided over these waters for centuries and today is a spectacular wedding venue. The walk continues upstream and over the undulating riverbank, then crosses the river over a pretty stone bridge. You'll get lovely views across the valley as you climb up into the woods before heading east again towards Peebles. The walk eventually rejoins the river with lovely views across to the town before finishing in the car park again.

WHAT'S FOR LUNCH?
The Park Hotel (parkpeebles.co.uk) has a vast beer garden for sunny days and a dog-friendly bar area for wet weather. Small plates and big burgers dominate the menu here and dogs always get a bowl of water.

Need to know: Dogs can be safely off-lead on much of this walk unless livestock is present. Directions can be downloaded from walkhighlands.co.uk.

↓ Neidpath Castle on the banks of the Tweed

↑ A view over Edinburgh from the Pentland Hills

STAY

MERKLANDS WOOD

(241)

Dolphinton, Scottish Borders
merklandswood.com

Around 30 minutes south of Edinburgh and set within a 20-acre woodland, this pair of lovely log cabins offer a fantastic break away from the city. It's fairly rustic inside, with pine-clad walls and antlers mounted above the beds, and outside is a beautiful deck with views over the forest and a hot tub for evening soaks. Best of all, the dogs get their own enclosed exercise field with agility equipment and balls to fetch, while humans get a fabulous welcome hamper with local gins and tonic.

Where to walk: You're on the edge of the Pentland Hills, where there are ample circular trails for long day hikes or short walks (pentlandhills.org).

PLACE

PAXTON HOUSE

(242)

Paxton, Scottish Borders
paxtonhouse.co.uk

As pink houses go, this one is pretty swish. Built from a rose-tinted sandstone and with neoclassical influences, it was the house of Patrick Home, who belonged to one of the wealthiest families in the Borders. His time here was short-lived, but his cousin, Ninian Home, later took on the house and filled it with his own lavish touches, which can be seen on a tour of its interior (no dogs, sadly). Beyond the symmetrical house, though, is a wonderful estate of woodland walks – ideal for those scorching days of summer – and flower gardens to explore. There are several waymarked walks, one of which crosses Britain's first ever suspension bridge, and the tearoom has a dog-friendly seating area indoors.

WILDERKIN CABIN

West Linton, Scottish Borders

www.pawsandstay.co.uk/wilderkin

Tucked away in a small, sheltered gully on the edge of the undulating Pentland Hills landscape, this little wood cabin is a divine retreat for dogs seeking solitude and a simple life. Here, you've got horses for neighbours (no pun intended) and further afield, rolling hills of sheep grazing make the outlook positively bucolic. All

worries melt away when there's a cup of tea to be had on the decking – best paired with the handmade chocolate left for you by owner Lotte.

Inside, you'll find sheepskin rug-clad chairs set around the huge, highly effective log burner and a small but well-stocked kitchen with a hob for cooking your morning eggs. The kitchen table enjoys prime position next to an enormous window with those dreamy Pentland views, and the king-sized bed sits on a platform at the end of the cabin, with skylights to gaze up at shooting stars.

While the cabin might seem remote – and it'll feel that way with no Wi-Fi and ropey phone signal – it still has the home comforts you'll want: a blissfully

WHAT'S NEARBY?
The city of Edinburgh is a mere 30-minute drive from the cabin, meaning you can enjoy buzzing city life by day before retreating to the silence by night. Edinburgh has myriad dog-friendly attractions, including the World

↓ Edinburgh as seen from the Dugald Stewart monument

warm shower will help you wind down after a long day's walking with the dog, and the record player has a stash of rocking albums next to it. There's a games box with plenty of two-player entertainment, too, so the lack of TV won't have you twiddling your thumbs come evening.

Where to walk: With the Pentlands on your doorstep, it'd be rude not to climb a hill or two. Download the trail map from pentlandhills.org and hit the footpaths that traverse the rippling green landscape from Carlops or Flotterstone. For something more sedate, the handsome, manicured Newhall Estate welcomes dog walkers across its 1,100 acres. Further afield, you might like to drive to Edinburgh to climb

of Illusions (camera-obscura.co.uk) and Summerhall's exhibition rooms (summerhall.co.uk). For dinners out, head to The Gordon Arms (thegordon.co.uk) in West Linton, which loves dogs and always has a coal fire going for extra cosiness.

the famous Arthur's Seat, or book into Unleashed Dog Parks' Midlothian private field (unleasheddogparks.co.uk) for an afternoon of agility.

Need to know: The composting toilet can get a bit stinky so squeamish travellers need not apply. There are no curtains on many of the windows, which may spook dogs as wildlife trots about outside overnight – which in turn may also spook humans! You'll want an eye mask for the summer months when the light lingers late into the night and appears early in the morning. There's no fully enclosed garden but your dog is welcome to roam off-lead as long as they're comfortable with the horses nearby; no bowls or beds are provided for the dog.

BEACH

EYEMOUTH BEACH

 244

Scottish Borders

Just across the border with England, Eyemouth is a pleasing little fishing town with its mariner roots in the 13th century, when smuggling was rife. It enjoyed a roaring haddock and herring trade in the 1800s, but today makes its money from tourists who come to enjoy its 500-metre-long sandy beach.

Make a night of it: Just a 30-minute drive south from Eyemouth is Cheviot Glamping, which has enclosed patios in its simple but smart Dog Houses (see page 115).

Parking: TD14 5EY

CENTRAL & NORTHEAST SCOTLAND

269

268 267 266

Aberdeen
265

264

Dundee

262
260

263

259 261

257 258 256

254 255 250 251 253

Loch Lomond and The Trossachs National Park

248 249 252

Edinburgh

247 246

Glasgow

245

STAY

THE WATERSIDE HOTEL (245)

West Kilbride, Ayrshire
watersideayrshire.com

Dusk ambles on the beach that skirts along the front of The Waterside are the highlight here: as the sun falls below the horizon casting hot colours across the sky, you can watch the light fade across Firth of Clyde and Isle of Arran beyond. The hotel is pretty special inside, too, though, with modern sea view bedrooms and an excellent dog-friendly restaurant

↓ The Ayrshire Coast Path runs 100 miles from Glenapp to Skelmorlie

serving Scottish classics such as cullen skink and Scotch beef shin.

Where to walk: The Ayrshire Coastal Path is on your doorstep here, so head out of the hotel and on to the beach and walk north or south for sweeping sea views in all directions.

BEACH

PORTOBELLO BEACH

Edinburgh

Edinburgh's suburbs tumble down all the way to the coastline overlooking the Firth of Forth, and Portobello Beach is the city's answer to Ipanema. There's a bustling boardwalk where locals come for running, skating or sipping coffee with a sea view, and a sandy beach split by wooden groynes where your pets can roam around the sand off-lead. It gets busy in summer, so come out of season for a more relaxing time, and don't miss a trip into Harry's Gourmet Treats on the

↓ Arty on Portobello Beach

high street, where you can buy freshly baked dog biscuits. Beach wheelchair hire is available from **beachwheelchairs.org**.

Make a night of it: Stay in the city centre at the chic Apartment on Cheyne Street (see below).

Parking: Westbank St, EH15 1DR

STAY

APARTMENT ON CHEYNE STREET

Edinburgh sawdays.co.uk

Edinburgh is a city full of lucky pups, not least because so many of its attractions are dog-friendly and there's plenty of exciting walking to be done. Bring your dog to the Scottish capital and live like a local in this chic city-centre apartment. Set within a townhouse on a tree-lined cobbled street, it's all calm neutrals and minimalist decor inside with bare floorboards and plaster-effect walls, plus there's a communal garden for morning loo trips with the dog. From here, it's just a 20-minute walk through the suburbs to

the city centre, conveniently past the Just Dogs pet shop on Deanhaugh Street.
Where to walk: A couple of streets away is Inverleith Park, a huge green space with cricket greens, allotments and a pond – and a morning coffee van – perfect for off-lead wanders and games of fetch. Head into the city centre to walk through Princes Street Gardens with views of Edinburgh Castle, or head down to Holyrood Park for big hikes up Arthur's Seat.

> **WHAT'S NEARBY?**
> As you're so close to the city centre, spend your days sightseeing on the Royal Mile and don't miss the statue of famous dog Greyfriars Bobby in Greyfriars Kirkyard. Nights out with the dog can be had in Edinburgh's New Town around Rose Street and Charlotte Square – try cocktails in Copper Blossom (copperblossom. com) or fine wines in Whighams Wine Cellars, where there's live music most nights (whighams.com).

Need to know: Nothing is provided here so you'll need to bring beds and bowls for the dog.

THE ANTONINE WALL TRAIL

North Lanarkshire

START POINT: Auchinstarry Marina, G65 9SG
DISTANCE/TIME: circular 10.4km/2.5 hrs

Part of the John Muir Way – a 215km hiking and cycling route across central Scotland between Helensburgh and Dunbar – this short but special hike is a fantastic way to combine history, nature and walking the dog. It starts in the town of Auchinstarry on the Forth & Clyde Canal, then quickly climbs on to the ancient Bar Hill Roman Fort, a UNESCO World Heritage Site. This is the highest point on the Antonine Wall, where the Romans held their northern frontier in central Scotland for hundreds of years. When you reach the top, you'll get spectacular views across the surrounding patchwork-green landscape and along the wall's earthworks, and be able to seek

↓ Arty posing outside Princes Street Gardens with Edinburgh Castle in the background

> **WHAT'S FOR LUNCH?**
> Big burgers, Scottish mussels and hearty breakfasts are served right on the pretty marina at The Boathouse (boathousekilsyth.co.uk).

out the remains of the headquarters building, bath house and east gate.

Heading along the wall, you'll reach Croy Hill, another Roman fort. Much of its remnants are long gone, but you can still see how they sculpted the landscape – much of it solid rock – to create their base. From here, you'll descend back down to the canal and head westwards along its northern towpath back into town for refuelling.

Need to know: This route is fully waymarked, but you can also download a map from johnmuirway.org. Dogs can be off-lead when under close control, but beware the route crosses a B-road twice.

EXPERIENCE

RIDE THE FALKIRK WHEEL

Falkirk scottishcanals.co.uk

This is no fairground wheel but instead an ingenious piece of engineering that connects the Forth & Clyde Canal with the Union Canal by carrying boats in its gondola up and down the 35 metres between the two waterways. Boat trips begin at the wheel, cruise along the Union Canal and through the brightly illuminated Roughcastle Tunnel before returning; a ride on the Falkirk Wheel can be quite the noisy affair, so dogs (and people) of a nervous nature might want to abstain.

Make a night of it: Stay in a unique pineapple-topped 18th-century summerhouse (see page right).

EXPERIENCE

SPOT SHIP-WRECKS AND SEABIRDS

Argyll and Bute boattripshb.com

The crew on *Jola Too*, a 12-passenger boat moored at Rhu Marina, love dogs so much they'll even provide refreshments for your pet alongside the Scottish tablet and local tea you can indulge in as you cruise. Many of their trips around the Clyde Estuary take in the fascinating sugar boat wreck, which now lies on its side in the middle of the estuary after it sank here in the 1970s. The two- and three-hour trips are great for dogs, as you'll have the opportunity to disembark and stretch your legs before the return leg.

Make a night of it: Stay 20 minutes north at The Inn on Loch Lomond for spectacular lochside walks on your doorstep. innonlochlomond.co.uk

STAY

THE PINEAPPLE

Dunmore, Falkirk
landmarktrust.org.uk

Just north of Falkirk and near the banks of the River Forth, this fruity summerhouse has an eccentric history. In the USA's state of Virginia, it's said sailors would place a pineapple on their gateposts to declare their return home from sea, and so when Lord Dunmore returned from his role as Governor of Virginia in the 18th century, he made sure the world knew it by constructing a stone pineapple right on top of his pavilion in the countryside of Falkirk.

Where to walk: There are ample trails from your front door here, with an excellent 90-minute walking route that takes in The Pineapple and Dunmore on walkhighlands.co.uk.

EXPERIENCE

TAKE A TOUR OF BASS ROCK

East Lothian seabird.org

Bass Rock should be as black as the night – it's rock made from the splutterings of a volcano that erupted more than 300 million years ago. Instead, this hulk of volcanic rock lying 5km from the North Berwick coast has a greyish sheen to its sides and a white top, thanks to the thousands of northern gannets that reside here between February and October. There can be over 150,000 of these boisterous birds in peak season, making it the largest gannet colony in the world.

Catamaran trips leaving from the Scottish Seabird Centre in North Berwick take you out on to the ocean passing by Craigleith, where around 15,000 puffins reside from March to July, and then on for a circumnavigation of Bass Rock, its noise – and smell – becoming ever clearer as you approach. You'll sail close to the island to gaze up at its towering cliffs, watching gannets perilously perched on tiny ledges where their nests are laid for new young to hatch – just watch out for guano falling from the skies as they circle and squawk overhead. On the way there and back, cast your eyes seawards and look out for dolphins and porpoises in the waters around you.

Make a night of it: Stay in the luxurious converted double-decker buses at The Bus Stop for an unusual night

away just 30 minutes' drive from North Berwick. thebusstop.scot 1+ 👤2-6 <£200

BROCK BOTHY 253

Clackmannanshire
canopyandstars.co.uk

If evenings spent with sundowners on the decking to the sound of dusk birdsong – binoculars at the ready for spotting woodpeckers or buzzards in the surrounding woodland – sound like your sort of getaway, then Brock is the perfect bothy for you. Somewhat stretching the definition of bothy – less of a farm labourer's hideout and more of a Scandi-meets-Scottish designer cabin on stilts with all the mod cons you could need – this is one of four little huts on the storied Brucefield Estate.

Each is equipped with an en suite and

↑ Brock Bothy through the trees

a huge double bed on a mezzanine, and the floor-to-ceiling windows invite you to sit and gaze for hours on end. There are clever little touches, such as the blinds that can be drawn from the top or bottom of the window for extra privacy, and the composting bin that helps keep waste to a minimum. There's heating and effective insulation for keeping cosy, and a log burner for extra ambience on colder evenings.

Where to walk: Don't miss an estate tour with the land manager, Graham, who will talk you through its history and show you where the red squirrels forage and walk you along the deer tracks (you might even see one or two as you roam). For a truly atmospheric ramble, head up to Dollar Glen, where trails lead up to a fairy-tale castle.

> **WHAT'S NEARBY?**
> The village of Dollar has some excellent restaurants, the highlight of which is The Forager (foragerpub.com), which allows dogs.

Need to know: The bed is accessed by a steep ladder so isn't suitable for anyone with mobility issues or a fear of heights. Dogs must be on a lead around the estate due to livestock.

↓ The guano-covered Bass Rock

CRARAE GARDEN

Inverary, Argyll and Bute nts.org.uk

Argyll is famous for its glorious garden trails, which you could turn into an entire day road trip (use gardens-of-argyll. co.uk to plan a route), but one of its most spectacular is Crarae – a Himalayan garden planted with species from Nepal, China and Tibet. Walk with the dog on a lead along its lush borders, through bamboo tunnels, past rocky gorges and trickling waterfalls, all planted and created by Lady Grace Campbell in 1912.

↑ Glenbranter waterfall near The Douglas Boathouse

THE DOUGLAS BOATHOUSE

Strathlachlan, Argyll and Bute
pawsandstay.co.uk

Studies have long shown that being near, on or in water can have a positive impact on our mental well-being, and so The Douglas Boathouse is the ideal place for a restorative break. Sitting right on the shores of Loch Fyne with a perfectly placed balcony in prime position for water watching, this old boathouse will draw you in immediately. It's all marine-themed inside, with nautical antiques and industrial-style boat lighting, and the cosy sofa points itself right at the main event: the shimmering sea loch outside.
Where to walk: There are walks along the loch's shoreline, but head inland to the waterfalls of Glenbranter (15 minutes by car) for a lovely waymarked 3.5km walk (follow the yellow markers) through woodland and to the Allt Robuic waterfalls. Alternatively, also from Glenbranter, you can head up to a viewpoint for a top-down view on the glen and the edge of Loch Eck.

> **WHAT'S NEARBY?**
> A 30-minute drive on to the northern edge of Loch Fyne brings you to Inverary, where the local jail is a dog-friendly museum (see page 196) and a little further south you can tour the only intact township left in Scotland at Auchindrain (see page 196).

Need to know: Dog bowls, blankets and sleeping mats are provided. There's no enclosed garden but plenty of greenery around for late-night loo trips.

↓ A dog poses on a rock during sunset by a loch in Scotland

WALK

BEN LOMOND 256

Loch Lomond & The Trossachs National Park

START POINT: Ben Lomond Car Park, G63 0AR

DISTANCE/TIME: 11km/5–6 hrs there and back

At 974 metres high, Ben Lomond towers above the eastern shores of Loch Lomond. This peak is the country's most southerly munro, which makes it a popular one – around 50,000 people climb it each year. But its rewards are so great, a few other hikers on the trail is no bother when you're faced with such exceptional views on a clear day.

There's a good, if occasionally rocky, path to follow here, which begins from the Ben Lomond car park at Rowardennan and climbs up through oak woodland to reveal captivating views of Loch Lomond very quickly. The views get better as you climb, and while tackling the zigzagging path to the conical summit, you'll be rewarded with vistas over the Trossachs, too. At the very top, expect to see as far as Ben Nevis to the north and Edinburgh Pentland Hills to the east, and the islands of Mull and Islay stranded out in the ocean when facing west.

Take the same route back down for an easy descent and to watch the loch disappear behind the trees as you get lower and lower.

> **WHAT'S FOR LUNCH?**
> It's either picnic time, or you drive south to Drymen and nip into Skoosh (facebook.com/SkooshDeli) for great fry-ups and warming homemade soups.

Need to know: Walking directions can be found on walkhighlands.co.uk, including an alternative, tougher return route.

AUCHINDRAIN HISTORIC TOWNSHIP

257

Auchindrain, Argyll and Bute
auchindrain.org.uk

In medieval Scotland, outside of the major cities, the country's population lived largely in small, intimate farming townships where the only food available was what was reared or grown by their own hand. But progression in farming practices brought a fight for more, better-utilised land, and so many townships were replaced with modern farms or, in the case of the Highland Clearances, the communities were driven out violently at the hands of landowners.

Today, Auchindrain is the only medieval township still standing in Scotland, and a mooch with the dog around its centuries-old buildings offers a fascinating and often affecting insight into Scottish life before the 1700s.

INVERARY JAIL

258

Inverary, Argyll and Bute
inverarayjail.co.uk

It has been well over 100 years since prisoners walked the halls of Inverary Jail, but their stories still haunt the cells here thanks to an absorbing and at times gruesome exhibition about life (and death) as a convict in Argyll's most prominent town.

LOCH ARKLET

259

Loch Lomond & The Trossachs National Park

With thousands of freshwater lochs across Scotland, there are a fair few inland beaches, too, and Loch Arklet has one of the quietest. There's a remote soft-sand beach next to the dam infrastructure at the western end of the beach, which even in the height of summer is often empty of other people. This is an idyllic spot for wild swimming in the loch, whose water temperatures are much more palatable than nearby Loch Lomond, and you'll have spectacular views of the Arrochar Alps in the distance.

Make a night of it: Inversnaid Bunkhouse is a rustic hikers' hostel inside an old chapel on the West Highland Way, just a 10-minute drive from the beach. inversnaid.com 🐕1 £100

Parking: There's a layby on the B829 at ///bypasses.heat.signature

ROOME BAY BEACH

260

Fife

Sitting just north of the charming fishing village of Crail, Roome Bay Beach is a wonderful sweep of sand and rocks, whose pools thrum with sea life when the tide's out. A disued paddling pool has been adopted by seabirds as a safe spot for a swim and a wash, and for families there's a playground on the sloped grassy area that backs the beach. It's a ten-minute walk into Crail village along the coast, so don't miss a stop in the harbour for a fresh local lobster lunch or crab roll at Reilly Shellfish (**01333 450476**).
Make a night of it: Reserve The Old Posthouse in Crail village and you'll be a short walk from this glorious beach.
crailposthouse.co.uk
Parking: Roomebay Crescent, KY10 3TT

↓ A soggy spaniel on the shores of Loch Lomond

THISTLE

261

Auchterarder, Perth and Kinross
www.canopyandstars.co.uk/thistle

It's just an hour from Edinburgh to Alexander House, where a handful of glamping options offer secluded breaks from the city. The most enchanting of these is Thistle, a chunky horsebox truck turned modern apartment inside, with a hot tub and brilliant views across the Scottish countryside. Beds and bowls are provided for the dog, and you can order in a hamper of local goodies to gorge on as you enjoy the scenery. On site, there are archery lessons and massages on offer, and beyond you'll find Loch Lomond & The Trossachs National Park.
Where to walk: The glorious Ochil Hills are on your doorstep here, so head into the hills to tackle the likes of the Glen Sherup horseshoe or to walk along Glen Devon Reservoir (see **walkhighlands.co.uk** for directions).

OLD COURSE, ST ANDREWS

262

St Andrews oldcoursehotel.co.uk

START POINT: KY16 9AB
DISTANCE/TIME: any

St Andrews' Old Course might be renowned as the 'home of golf' thanks to its centuries-old connections to the game, but once a week its players are banned and instead, locals bring their dogs to wander the fairways of this storied green. You can spend as much

↑ West Sands beach in St Andrews

or as little time on the 3km-long course as you like – a full circumnavigation would be around 8km – but don't miss a runabout on West Sands Beach while you're there.

WHAT'S FOR LUNCH?
When the weather's right, sit outside at the iconic Jigger Inn or, for inside dining, Hams Hame is a great grill restaurant (both oldcoursehotel.co.uk).

Need to know: While dogs can be off-lead here, try to avoid the pristine greens and bunkers.

THE FERRY WAITING ROOM 263

Balquhidder, Loch Lomond & The Trossachs National Park
canopyandstars.co.uk

Set within the woodland on the grounds of Monachyle Mhor Hotel, The Ferry Waiting Room is a truly unique place to kip for a night or two. And while the hotel might be all luxuries and tasting menus, this former Argyll and Bute council waiting room, which once served the Port Appin ferry, is anything but: beyond a bed with a duvet and a simplistic kitchen, you're very much back to basics here, so come prepared for late-night, torch-lit trips to the nearest loo.

The views from the end of your bed, however, more than make up for the minimalist lifestyle you'll lead in this two-room set-up – you'll sleep in The Ferry Waiting Room, while your rudimentary kitchen set-up (no fridge and no running water) is in a cabin across the decking. Leave the curtains open to wake up to hillside views, where pasture and pine forest tumble down to the Loch Voil, or sit at the kitchen table overlooking the bucolic scenery while you wait for the whistling kettle to boil.

Where to walk: You can walk along the relatively quiet road in either direction for lovely lochside strolling, or head up to Balquhidder's church and roam into the managed forest on the hillside. For more of a challenge, Ben More (1,174 metres) is a rewarding but steep hike.

WHAT'S NEARBY?
The hotel's sister cafe is just a 20-minute drive up the road and does great, casual comfort food. If you've got your own paddleboards, canoes or kayaks, Loch Voil is your oyster.

Need to know: The Ferry Waiting Room is sold as self-catering but you'll be hard-pressed to make much more than boiled eggs in its hob-only kitchen, as there's no running water (a vat of fresh water is provided) and very little room to manoeuvre. There's breakfast at the hotel for a rather princely sum, or you can drive up to Mhor 84, their sister cafe, for something more low-key. Bring your own bowls and bedding for the dog.

WATCH THE LIVELY STRATHMORE HIGHLAND GAMES

264

Glamis Castle, Angus
strathmorehighlandgames.co.uk

There is a no more Scottish event than the Highland Games, which take place every summer in towns and villages across Scotland to celebrate Scottish and

↓ The rustic interior of the Ferry Waiting Room kitchen

Celtic culture. Expect bagpipes, Highland dancing and kilts aplenty, alongside stiff competition for the best shot putt, hammer throw and caber toss. Within the grounds of the truly majestic Glamis Castle, the Strathmore Highland Games are a dog- and child-friendly event, with kids' games and ice creams to go round. **Make a night of it:** Book into the bougie Bruadar, a shepherd's hut set within its own spectacular glen just 25 minutes away by car. canopyandstars .co.uk 2 2 £200

WALK

OLD ABERDEEN AND THE BEACH 265

Aberdeen

START POINT: Aberdeen seafront, AB24 5NR
DISTANCE/TIME: circular 8km/3 hrs

Aberdeen's wide sandy beaches are a dog's dream and this walk starting from the coast of this North Sea-facing city offers an opportunity to let off some steam on the sand before heading inland to explore the university grounds. You'll walk all the way along the coast – note there are some dog-free areas of the beach – and along the esplanade as it curves around to the River Don estuary.

Head across the bridge and follow the river path inland for a while – its leafy banks are a welcome green sight – and then head south into Old Aberdeen. This is a largely university-owned quarter of the city and has some impressive architecture, built with local silvery granite. Expect behemoth cathedrals and Gothic university college buildings, with flourishing trees – which blossom beautifully in spring – manicured lawns and cobblestone streets making this

a quaint little utopia away from the concrete city centre.

When you reluctantly leave the handsome old quarter, you'll walk past the football stadium, then up and over Broad Hill and back down to the beach where you began.

> **WHAT'S FOR LUNCH?**
> Make like a student and head to Bobbin (crafted-social.co.uk), where there's international small plates, stone-baked pizza, wings, burgers and hot dogs on the menu and craft beer behind the bar.

Need to know: Much of this walk is along roads so dogs will need to be on leads for the most part. The best way to walk this route is to follow Google Maps and wander aimlessly a little in Old Aberdeen, but strict directions can be downloaded from walkhighlands.co.uk if you prefer.

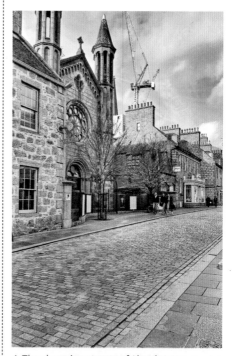

↑ The charming streets of Aberdeen

BEACH

CRUDEN BAY (266)

Aberdeenshire

On the Aberdeenshire coast lies Cruden Bay, an expansive sandy stretch of beach backed by a golf club and overlooked by the ruins of 16th-century Slains Castle to the north. This is a beach made for swimmers and an electronic notice board offers information about water quality to ensure safe paddling. **Make a night of it:** An hour's drive away is the unique and idiosyncratic two-storey bothy, Dairy at Denend (see page 202).

↑ Overlooking the beach at Cruden Bay

PLACE

FYVIE CASTLE (267)

Fyvie, Aberdeenshire nts.org.uk

Few castles in Scotland are quite as colossal as Fyvie. With several turrets perching atop tremendous towers and more than 50 windows just on its south facade, it really is something to behold. A fine example of Scottish baronial architecture, it has been standing here for some 800 years and while intruders were once locked up in dungeons and their wives blinded for their misdeeds, today visitors are welcomed with their dogs by the National Trust for Scotland.

You can amble with the dog on a lead around the vast estate, where you'll find a walled garden, a lake made in the 18th century, and a menagerie of wildlife, from red squirrels to darting swifts.

THE DAIRY AT DENEND

268

Newton of Begshill, Aberdeenshire

www.pawsandstay.co.uk/dairy-at-denend

A curious cabin with creative, thoughtful design is the best way to describe the Dairy at Denend, as every aspect of this self-catering accommodation is intriguing. Its exterior design is what will first catch your eye: what looks like two shipping containers, one plonked on top of the other with a perfectly curved edge, sit on a stilted deck in the middle of farm fields. A wood-burning hot tub and pizza oven will ensure you spend plenty of time outside, while inside it's a wildly colourful affair, with bright blue painted walls, red dressers and patterned curtains.

You've got tractor seats on top of milk churns instead of stools at the dining bar and old Kilner jars are used as lampshades. But perhaps the most enchanting thing is the views: endless fields yawn across the landscape outside the huge floor-to-ceiling windows.

Where to walk: If you're seeking some munros to bag, drive into the Cairngorms National Park to hike the likes of Cairngorm Mountain. For something less strenuous, try the short walk to Linn Falls from Charlestown of Aberlour.

WHAT'S NEARBY?
Sunnyside and Cullen have brilliant beaches for the dogs to run free on, while locally sourced lunches can be had at the Copper Dog (craigellachiehotel.com) in Craigellachie, a half-hour drive away.

Need to know: There's a pair of collies and livestock on site here so you might want to bring a longline for any free-roaming dogs on the deck. Dogs are allowed on the sofas when using the blankets provided. Bowls and spare leads are also supplied.

CABIN BY THE CASTLE

269

Duffus, Moray canopyandstars.co.uk

Surrounded by flat, endless farm fields in the Moray countryside on Scotland's north coast, this modest little cabin has a big, blockbuster view right from its porch and back garden: Duffus Castle. The 12th-century fortress started life as a motte-and-bailey residence for the Moray family and they lived there for half a millennium until it was abandoned in the 18th century. Today, its ruin sits atop a mound that rises up from the Laich of Moray and this cabin gives the best view of it.

If you can tear yourselves away from the windows, or the fire pit in the garden outside that overlooks the castle, you'll find a minimalist house with a cosy velvet blue sofa made for lazy nights in and a modern kitchen where your welcome hamper of local treats awaits. The dog will love roaming in the fully enclosed garden, while you can make use of the great board game collection or sit outside on the deck to watch the planes from the local RAF base practising their moves.

Where to walk: From the cabin, you have easy access to the footpaths that weave around Duffus Castle and the dog will love clambering on the ruin. Further afield, you can hike along the coastal path at Lossiemouth – head south-west along the beach and then cut inland through

the forest to walk back along the River Lossie for a lovely 6km stroll. For a more sheltered walk, head inland to Elgin, where there are waymarked walks in Quarrelwood forest (morayways.org.uk) of varying length.

↑ The view from the bed at the Cabin by the Castle

Don't miss a visit to Elgin Cathedral – a 13th-century church that has been in ruin since the Protestant Reformation of the 1500s. You can walk in and out of its lofty crumbling walls and explore the burial ground, where you will find the tallest gravestone in the country at 5 metres high.

Need to know: The garden is fully enclosed by a metre-high fence, so won't keep in dogs prone to jumping. Bowls are provided but you'll need to bring dog bedding.

> **WHAT'S NEARBY?**
> You're a short drive from some exceptional dog-friendly beaches here, so head north-west to Lossiemouth East Beach for off-lead adventures on sand and amid grassy dunes. The lovely coves around Hopeman village are smaller but still spectacular for a day on the sand, too, and there's a chippy 500 metres from the beach for fresh fish lunches.

THE CAIRNGORMS, HIGHLANDS AND ISLANDS

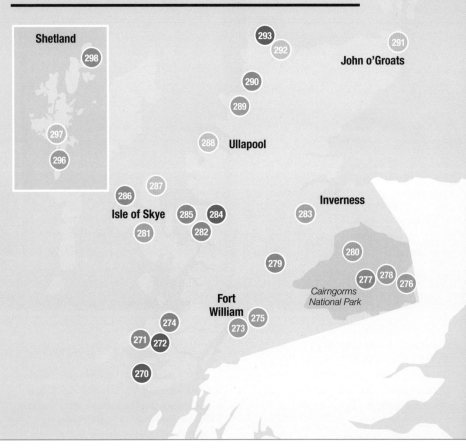

Shetland↑

Orkney
295
294

Shetland
298

293
292

291
John o'Groats

290

289

288 Ullapool

297
296

287
286
Isle of Skye
285 284
281 282

Inverness
283

280
277 278 276
279
Cairngorms
National Park

Fort
William
274
275
273
271 272

270

PLACE

ISLE OF IONA

270

Isle of Mull welcometoiona.com

Island life in Scotland has a certain appeal: it's slow, quiet and considered, and daily activities and movements are pleasingly dictated by tides and weather. You can enjoy a sense of all that on the Isle of Mull, of course, but to get a more remote and enchanting experience of life on a Scottish Island, a day trip to the Isle of Iona – accessible from Mull's ferry terminal at Fionnphort (calmac.co.uk) – is truly beguiling.

This 2.5km wide and 5km long island sits just off Mull's south-west coast and has a population of just 150 permanent residents. Life here is really rather different, with no supermarkets and not a single pub, and a reliance on the sometimes-undependable ferry service that connects with Mull. And yet there is a thriving community here, with a primary school and village hall, and a pair of hotels offering visitors the chance to stay overnight (St Columba, stcolumba-hotel.co.uk, is dog-friendly if you'd like to make a night of it).

In fact, there have been communities thriving on the Isle of Iona for centuries – most notably around the abbey founded by St Columba in the 6th century and the later Benedictine abbey. The ruins of monastic lives are evident across the island and you can walk off the ferry and directly into the past at the remains of the Augustinian nunnery, which dates from the 14th century. Look out for the beautiful carvings still present on many of the stones today, including the unusual 'sheela-na-gig', or 'Sheila of the Breasts', which depicts a naked woman with her legs apart supposedly used to ward off evil spirits.

Almost everywhere on the island is dog-friendly, including the delightful craft shop on Baile Mòr near the ferry terminal and the grounds of the abbey, and the island's size means it can be explored on foot in a day. You might want to wander up to Dùn Ì, a 100-metre-high hill with panoramic views over the island's northern half, or head south for a quieter hike across the golf course and then rocky moorland, ending at St Columba's Bay, where a white-sand beach is lapped by brilliantly clear waters. There are pristine white-sand beaches all around the island, which on a sunny day could easily be mistaken as Caribbean if it weren't for the icy waters around them – temperatures rarely reach above 14°C. Dogs will love paddling in the chilly seas and running across the beaches, which are all dog-friendly year-round, but they must be kept on leads around the livestock. A local fish dinner in the garden at Martyr's Bay Restaurant (www.martyrsbay.co.uk) by the port is an essential stop before heading back across the sea to Mull, too.

↓ Martyr's Bay on the Isle of Iona

STAY

TRESHNISH FARM

271

Calgary, Isle of Mull
www.sawdays.co.uk/treshnish-farm

Sitting on the north-west coast of the Isle of Mull with sea views and a bucolic surrounding, Treshnish Farm is as remote as it is idyllic. At over an hour's drive from Tobermory, you might often feel you've got the entire island to yourselves here – even in the height of summer. Although you're not alone, as owners Carolyne and Somerset live on site and manage their collection of traditional cottages themselves, as well as their small farm. Your dog won't be alone, either, as their three sheepdogs regularly roam the farm freely and will give you all a warm welcome.

The pair first found Treshnish in 1988 while on holiday and out hiking without a map. In a moment of curious coincidence, they remarked at how wonderful it would be to live somewhere like this, and now they know they were not wrong as they moved into the farm six years later. They spent the following years making their mark on the buildings and landscapes that surround Treshnish, and now there are nine different places to stay here, from a modest shepherd's hut on wheels overlooking the ocean to the single-storey Studio with its own enclosed garden. They have converted old tool sheds into romantic boltholes, built brand-new 'sitooteries' (outdoor seating areas) made from discarded windows, and done up traditional crofters' cottages to create

WHAT'S NEARBY?
Calgary Art in Nature (see opposite) has a gallery, woodland walk and cafe and is just a 10-minute drive from Treshnish, and Calgary Bay beach is nearby. If you want to escape some of the crowds at Calgary Bay, head south from Treshnish and take the 20-minute walk down to Tràigh na Cille, a black-sand beach that's great for a spot of open-water swimming.

their unique and eccentric collection. Each one feels homely in its own way, be it the presence of an oft-needed log burner or the careful selection of rugs and artworks to add colour and interest.

Outside the houses lies an environment that welcomes wildlife daily – be it otters, eagles or hen harriers – and several kilometres of craggy coastline to explore. And after dark, look up to see shooting stars or if you're lucky, the aurora borealis.

Where to walk: You can walk freely around the farm with the dog on a lead, but for a more involved hike try the Treshnish Headland route. The 11km walk takes around half a day, or a full day if you stop with a picnic lunch, and offers spectacular coastal views; use walkhighlands.co.uk for directions. Owners Carolyne and Somerset both have plenty of recommendations for local walks, too.

Need to know: There are cattle and sheep on site so dogs must be kept on leads unless in an enclosed private garden. There's no television and dubious phone signal so embrace the off-grid life and make use of the supplied board games.

CALGARY ART IN NATURE

272

Calgary, Isle of Mull calgary.co.uk

Sitting on the north coast of the Isle of Mull, this little complex of artist workshops, a gallery and cafe is a must-visit. A woodland sculpture trail is well worth exploring with the dog: you'll find ziplines to ride, swings to play on, towers to climb and bridges to walk across, as well as gorgeous views across the fields to the white sands of Calgary Bay (also dog-friendly year-round). Drift around the gallery, where local artists' works are on display, and enjoy a light lunch in the cafe, where organic Scottish produce is freshly prepared daily.

↓ Arty at Glencoe Lochan

WALK

GLENCOE LOCHAN

273

The Highlands

START POINT: PH49 4HT
DISTANCE/TIME: 1.6km–4.5km/
30 mins–1.5 hrs

Tucked away beside Glencoe village is this pretty little lochan with several trails through woodland and along the water that can be stitched together for a longer walk. Whichever you choose, don't miss heading up to the north-east end of the lochan for gorgeous views of the mountains beyond reflected in the water.

WHAT'S FOR LUNCH?
Glencoe Gathering at the Glencoe Inn (crearhotels.com) is a brilliant dog-friendly bistro just a 20-minute walk (or 5-minute drive) from the lochan.

STAY

MINGARY CASTLE

274

Kilchoan, The Highlands
mingarycastle.co.uk

Sitting on the south coast of the Ardnamurchan peninsula, which overlooks the northern coastline of the Isle of Mull, Mingary Castle is an intimate affair. Bring your dog and your appetite here, as this is more of a restaurant with rooms than a sprawling castle hotel and it has two AA rosettes to boot.

While the property's curtain wall is 13th-century, the interior rooms are within a Georgian extension and ooze antique style – think four-posters, dark wooden dressers and bold prints on the curtains and soft furnishings. Dinners are the highlight here, with carefully crafted tasting menus with Isle of Mull cheeses, hand-dived scallops and homemade sourdough, and wine pairings to make each different flavour sing.

Where to walk: The dog can run off-lead around the hotel's grounds as long as there's no livestock present, and there's a pebble beach across the fields on the coast.

> **WHAT'S NEARBY?**
> You can take a day trip to Mull from Kilchoan ferry terminal (calmac .co.uk), where Tobermory has a dog-friendly catch-and-release aquarium and a distillery where you can sample gins and whiskies in the dog-friendly shop. Time it for market day and you can get more exceptional local produce for your lunch.

Need to know: Dogs aren't allowed in the restaurant for dinner sadly, but they can be left in the room while you indulge or you may be able to eat in the lounge or bar area with them by your side. Breakfast can be taken in the bedroom if you prefer.

STEALL FALLS

The Highlands

START POINT: ///sweetened.commuting. fictional
DISTANCE/TIME: 3.5km/1.5 hrs there and back

With blockbuster-worthy views and a footpath that trails through woodland and a rocky gorge, this short route is easy to follow and offers a dog walk to remember. Park at the end of the road that cuts through Glen Nevis and head out on foot through a deciduous woodland where moss carpets the ground and rocky mountainsides poke through the trees. Once through the woodland, the glen opens up into

↓ A hiker beneath the mighty Steall Falls

meadows with a stream twisting across it, leading to the spectacular 105-metre-high falls surrounded by mountains. The return route is back the same way.

> **WHAT'S FOR LUNCH?**
> If the weather's good, have a picnic with views of the falls or sit in the garden at the Ben Nevis Inn (ben-nevis-inn.co.uk; no dogs inside). Fort William's The Grog and Gruel pub (grogandgruel.co.uk) is a great indoor option with real ales on draught.

Need to know: There are markers for this route but you can also get directions at walkhighlands.co.uk.

WALK

MOUNT KEEN FROM GLEN ESK (276)

Cairngorms National Park

START POINT: Invermark Car Park, DD9 7YZ
DISTANCE/TIME: 17.5km/5.5 hrs there and back

Away from the popular Cairngorm peaks, Mount Keen sits in the Aberdeenshire section of the national park and is the most easterly munro in Scotland. It presides over a vast moorland, rising 939 metres above sea level, and its name is taken from the original Gaelic, *monadh caoin*, which translates as 'smooth' or

> **WHAT'S FOR LUNCH?**
> You'll probably need a picnic for this hike. Or bring plenty of snacks and then drive 20 minutes south to Sinclair's Larder (facebook.com/SinclairsLarder/?locale=en_GB) in Edzell.

'pleasant hill'. And a pleasant hill it is – the walk from Glen Esk has excellent wide tracks and is relatively easy to follow without the need for a map and compass, and the climbing is rarely too strenuous.

Look out for red deer at the beginning of the walk through Glen Esk (dogs on leads here) and the Queen's Well, where Queen Victoria stopped off on a pony trek in the 19th century. Once at the top, you'll be able to look out across the near-endless moorland, and if there are no other hikers around, it can eerily feel like you're the only people in the world.
Need to know: There will likely be livestock along much of this route so dogs are best kept on leads.

STAY

THE FIFE ARMS (277)

Braemar, Cairngorms National Park thefifearms.com

At the heart of the village of Braemar sitting south-east of the Cairngorms Mountains, the Fife Arms is a Cairngorms institution. It was built for the well-to-do holidaymakers who came to the area after Queen Victoria's purchase of Balmoral in the 19th century and today the hotel has become a favourite for walkers, wedding parties and foodies seeking finer fare than the local pubs can provide. Its decor is nothing if not lavish, with tartan wallpaper, huge displays of fresh flowers and hand-painted murals on the ceilings, and there are hundreds of unusual artworks and antiques throughout the building and its bedrooms, including more than 100 pieces of taxidermy in just one corridor and more antlers than you'll care to count.

↑ Arty relaxing on a rock above Balmoral Castle

Where to walk: There are plenty of footpaths to follow around Braemar and along the river here, but head out to the Balmoral Estate for longer walks with brilliant castle views.

> **WHAT'S NEARBY?**
> Balmoral's gardens (balmoralcastle .com) are open to the public during selected summer months, while closer to home is Braemar Castle (braemarcastle.co.uk), which has been operated by the local community since 2007.

Need to know: Dogs can dine with you in The Flying Stag; dog-friendly rooms are all first-floor and come with a bowl, bed, treats and a turndown gift.

CREAG CHÒINNICH

278

Cairngorms National Park

START POINT: Balnellan Road Car Park, Braemar, AB35 5YE
DISTANCE/TIME: 2.5km/1 hr there and back

If you've got energy to burn and don't mind an uphill hike, there are wonderful views to be enjoyed from the top of this hill that sits above the village of Braemar within the Cairngorms National Park. The route begins in the centre of the village and heads east into the pine and fir woodland and is steep almost as soon as you're among the trees. After a few hundred metres, though, your rewards arrive in the form of views over the village and Dee Valley below.

> **WHAT'S FOR LUNCH?**
> Farquharson's Bar and Kitchen (facebook.com/farquharsons barandkitchen) welcomes dogs for hearty pub lunches.

Need to know: You'll need to cross the main road at the beginning of the walk to reach the footpath so keep dogs on leads to start with.

STAY

THE LOVAT HOTEL AND RESTAURANT

Fort Augustus, The Highlands
thelovat.com

Fine food, lochside adventures and your own private garden make The Lovat the best place to stay on the shores of Loch Ness. In the lively village of Fort Augustus, where the Caledonian Canal connects Loch Ness and Loch Oich with a series of five locks and a swing bridge, The Lovat is a supremely dog-friendly retreat. Its Garden Rooms are the dog-friendly bedrooms, which sit in their own block next door to the main building and have their own enclosed patios so you needn't worry about them escaping. There's a fully enclosed lawn outside the front of the hotel, too, where you can let them run around and enjoy games of fetch until dinnertime beckons.

The food really is the highlight here, with regularly changing tasting menus featuring foraged food from the surrounding hills and produce grown in their own garden. The dog can sit by your side as you sample fresh fish from the local lochs and Highland lamb from nearby farms, and at breakfast you can expect honey from their own beehive and Scottish smoked salmon. Even crockery is special here, with designer and handmade pieces that elevate the entire experience.

Bedrooms are simple and contemporary, with bright, fresh colours and bathtubs begging to be used for post-walk soaks, and the dog-friendly rooms are almost all accessible for wheelchair users. There's a well-stocked minibar in each room, too, so make the most of it as you sit on your private patio to watch the sunset paint pinks and purples across the sky in the evening.

Where to walk: There's a short walk down to the village's Loch Ness Viewpoint, which crosses the canal's

swing bridge and heads towards the loch's shoreline alongside moorings where boats bob about in the water. For something longer, though, tackle part of the Great Glen Way, which connects the village to Invermoriston – there's a 12km circular route on alltrails.com.

WHAT'S NEARBY?
There's plenty to do around Loch Ness, and Fort Augustus is a good base at the southern end of the water: head north to Drumnadrochit to climb aboard the Jacobite Cruises boats for tours of the lake (see page 216). On the opposite side of the loch, Dores Beach is a great place to let the dog paddle and don your own wetsuit if you're feeling brave, and south of this is the Falls of Foyers – a brilliant sight after heavy rains.

To the north, Abriachan Woods (abriachan.org.uk) has waymarked trails and areas where the dog can be off-lead when under control.

Need to know: There is a dog-friendly area in the bar of the restaurant, but dogs can be left in bedrooms should you wish to dine without them. Poo bags and bowls are provided for your pet in the bedroom.

EXPERIENCE

CANOE BENEATH MOUNTAINS ON LOCH MORLICH

280

Cairngorms National Park
lochmorlich.com

Few settings are as spectacular as Loch Morlich: sandwiched between the Glenmore Forest and the Cairngorm Mountains, this glassy loch with its yellow-sand beach is truly awe-inspiring – even when it gets a little crowded in summer. It's truly tranquil when you get out on the water, though. Hire a canoe from Loch Morlich Watersports right on the beach and you'll be able to take the dog out into the middle of the loch, away from the sandcastle-building throngs, for glorious views of those snow-capped mountains in the distance. Parking can be tricky, so arrive early if you've pre-booked or prepare to park on the road and walk to the loch.

Make a night of it: Craggan Mill is a luxurious six-bedroom home set inside a former corn mill with an enclosed garden and outdoor pizza oven.
caledonianescapes.co.uk

🐕2 👤16 🏠 ♨ <£400

← Canoes on the beach at Loch Morlich

EXPERIENCE

GO IN SEARCH OF EAGLES ON SKYE

281

Isle of Skye wildskyeboattrips.com

On the Isle of Skye's west coast lies the waters of Loch Harport, protected by a smattering of small islands and coastal headland. This sea loch has some spectacular scenery, with the Cuillin Ridge visible in the distance on a clear day. But it's not just fine views you'll come for, as here live not one, but two pairs of white-tailed eagles. They got here thanks to a reintroduction programme that began in 1975 on the Isle of Rum, around 25km south of Loch Harport. Since then, hundreds of pairs of breeding birds of prey have made the west coast of Scotland their home, and you can spot them and even feed them on boat trips with Wild Skye.

Boatowners and operators Kim and Stephen arrived in Skye by sea – they literally sailed from Devon to Portree in 2009 – and so are exceptional guides to navigating the salty waters of Loch Harport and beyond. Join their two-hour eagle trip and you'll get your own pair of binoculars, and Stephen, who has two degrees in wildlife photography and documentary making, will regale you with stories about the area and its feathered inhabitants before throwing out bait for the birds so you can watch them swoop down and snaffle their lunch.

Other trips involve mackerel fishing and possible minke whale and dolphin sightings. All trips require your own waterproofs as Skye's weather can be unpredictable.

Make a night of it: It's just a 45-minute drive to the lovely self-catering Near Byre (see page 219) from Carbost, where the boat trips depart from.

Where to walk: There's a short stroll starting behind the hotel that follows a track on a slope behind the main street with lovely views over the harbour, but for something a bit more substantial, allow 90 minutes at least for the out-and-back walk to the Scottish baronial-style Duncraig Castle. The trail is signposted, beginning up the hill from the Inn, and skirts around the loch's shoreline and through pine and fir woodland that battle for space with hundreds of rhododendrons.

> **WHAT'S NEARBY?**
> The main attraction in Plockton is Calum's Seal Trips (calums-sealtrips.com), which are free if you don't see a single seal on your journey, though that's an incredibly rare occurrence as Calum always knows where to find the cute sea creatures. Don't miss a trip to Coral Beach (a short walk over the rocks from a small car park near the airstrip), where the ground is made up of tiny shards of miniature coral and pretty shells of all colours.

Need to know: You'll need to bring your own bowls, towels and bedding here as there's nothing on offer for the dogs. They can dine with you in the bar area of the Inn.

↓ Pretty little Plockton

 STAY

PLOCKTON INN  282

Plockton, Wester Ross
plocktoninn.co.uk

You might first recognise Plockton's pretty seaside cottages from their role as Summerisle in the 1973 film *The Wicker Man*. Or perhaps as Lochdubh, the town where Hamish Macbeth, played by Robert Carlyle, lived in the eponymous TV series. Either way, there are no cheeky police officers and certainly no ritual burnings here, as Plockton is just a quiet little village on the shores of Loch Carron, with views of the hills around Stromeferry and Ardaneaskan. Base yourself at the Plockton Inn and you'll have delectably fresh seafood and a suntrap beer garden to enjoy, and easy access to this region's handsome, craggy coastline.

GO NESSIE-SPOTTING WITH JACOBITE CRUISES

Loch Ness, The Highlands
jacobite.co.uk

There's really only one way to explore Loch Ness fully and that's on the water. These cruises take in the loch's main sights and have excellent insightful commentary along the way. You'll cruise along the Caledonian Canal and on to the vast loch, then past the picturesque, crumbling ruins of Urquhart Castle. Look out for grand homes on the shoreline and undulating hills in the distance, all the while learning about how the legend of Nessie came to be, and how tales of the elusive monster are still puzzling scientists today.

Make a night of it: The Lovat (see page 212) is a superb dog-friendly hotel in Fort Augustus, a 30-minute drive south.

ATTADALE GARDENS

Strathcarron, Wester Ross
attadalegardens.com

Not all dogs want to climb mountains, so this pretty house and gardens on the edge of Loch Carron is a welcome change from the rugged, sometimes intimidating Highlands scenery. Come here for

↓ A labrador looking at the camera with Loch Ness in the background

↓ The house at Attadale Gardens

sedate strolls across manicured lawns, through sunken gardens, rhododendron groves and Japanese landscapes – all complemented by the presence of a Scottish baronial mansion and a collection of fine sculptures.

STAY

THE BIRDHOUSE

 285

Culduie, Wester Ross sawdays.co.uk

The Birdhouse isn't just in a spectacular location in its own right – sitting on a sloping hill overlooking the mountains of Raasay and Skye on the horizon – the drive to get here is equally incredible. Most who visit this tiny hamlet of Culduie, a few kilometres from the popular tourist town of Applecross, take the high road, quite literally, as you have to drive over one of the UK's most hair-raising mountain passes: the 626-metre-high Bealach na Bà.

Once you've scaled its scary heights and mastered those steep hairpin bends, The Birdhouse is the perfect place to decompress – especially as there's a pack of moreish cheese crackers and a bottle of fizz waiting for you in the fridge. The tiny house built in the back garden of the Shell Cottage B&B is so named for the song thrushes that reside in the trees behind, and you'll delight in hearing all manner of birdlife sitting out in the garden here, from cuckoos to gulls and more.

It's all rustic chic, with copper taps and wood cladding and lighting installations that look like buoys hanging by rope from the ceiling, and the fairy lights entwined with twigs above the bed head is a creative touch from owner Val's daughter. A small kitchen means you can make your own meals to enjoy out on the patio with views of the area's spectacular sunsets, or at the inside dining table where the

windows frame the Black Cuillins and Raasay's Dùn Caan peak in the distance.

The dog is welcome to roam in the enclosed garden as long as they're kept under control, but there's plenty more exploring to be done beyond The Birdhouse's confines.

Where to walk: The best walk from the doorstep is to the lovely pair of beaches just over the hill from Culduie, where when the tide's out there are rockpools filled with sea snails, crabs and even occasionally starfish; allow at least 90 minutes for the out-and-back walk. Head out the back of The Birdhouse's

> **WHAT'S NEARBY?**
> The popular coastal village of Applecross is home to the much-loved Applecross Inn (applecrossinn .co.uk), where locally farmed and caught produce stars on many of the plates coming from the bustling kitchen. There's also a beach at Applecross, which, at low tide, is a huge spread of soft golden sand.

garden, though, and you can roam on the hills above in any which way, getting an even better vantage point from which to watch the sunset over Skye beyond.

Need to know: Only one small Labrador-sized dog is allowed at The Birdhouse and they must be kept out of the bedroom. There are often livestock grazing around the village so dogs must be on leads or under control when off the property.

← The mountains on Raasay and Skye across the water from Culduie

NEAR BYRE

Balmaqueen, Isle of Skye
sawdays.co.uk

The Isle of Skye is known for its dramatic geology, spectacular sweeps of white sand and fiery sunsets that seem to go on forever, and thanks to its position on the north-west coast of the island, Near Byre is a special place to enjoy it all.

The converted barn has a real Scotland-meets-Scandinavia feel, with local artworks and original stone walls juxtaposed with contemporary wooden furniture and cool, calming blue colours. Evenings are best spent in front of the log burner or in the garden soaking up the views, perhaps spotting buzzards soaring in the skies, and days can be spent hiking in the local area or driving out to the island's best-loved sights. The dog will love sniffing about in the surrounding garden (not fully enclosed), and you might well meet owners Vicki and John and their caramel-coloured spaniel, Bramble, who will deliver a welcome pack of snacks and treats for your arrival.

Where to walk: There are ample walks from the door here – just ask your hosts for ideas – but the most astonishing scenery can be found further afield. The Fairy Pools is just under an hour's drive from Near Byre, offering a 2.5km there-and-back walk to an exceptionally blue pool fed by a small waterfall. Water-loving dogs (and humans) will enjoy a bracing dip, and you can wander further on to find more pools if you want a longer walk.

> **WHAT'S NEARBY?**
> Explore Dunvegan Castle (dunvegancastle.com) gardens, where the MacLeod clan have been in residence for upwards of 800 years, or take a boat trip to find wild white-tailed eagles (see page 214).

Need to know: Dogs stay free here and your hosts provide essentials like treats, poo bags, a bed, bowls and towels.

↓ The view from Near Byre

↑ The rocks of An Corran

BEACH

AN CORRAN 287

Isle of Skye

Skye has some spectacular stretches of white sand lapped by azure waters, but at An Corran, things are a little different. Don't expect fine grains of sand or picturesque dunes: this beach has a black shoreline and is strewn with rocky outcrops and loose black stones. It's hardly practical for sunbathing or sandcastle building, but it'll give history buffs something to write home about, as dinosaur footprints can be seen in some of the rocks here. They're best sought out during winter, when the wild weather washes the sand away to reveal the three-toed prints.

Make a night of it: Stay just an hour's drive away at Near Byre (see page 219).

Parking: IV51 9JT

BEACH

MELLON UDRIGLE BEACH 288

The Highlands

On a sunny day, Mellon Udrigle Beach is paradise in Scotland: fine white sands, grass-flecked dunes and waters so sparklingly clear it could be the Med. Its remote location, 4km from the A832, means it's quieter than many of the North Coast 500's favoured stretches of sand, too.

Make a night of it: There's a small campsite right next to the beach where dogs stay free, so hire a camper or bring your own tent. 2+ £50

Parking: IV22 2NT

LEITIR EASAIDH ALL-ABILITIES PATH

(289)

The Highlands

START POINT: Leitir Easaidh Car Park, A837
DISTANCE/TIME: circular 2.5km/45 mins

Whether you're a wheelchair user looking to get out into nature, parents pushing a pram or you simply want a walk that doesn't require a map and waterproof hiking boots, this trail that skirts alongside Loch Leitir Easaidh and Loch na h-Innse Fraoich on the Little Assynt Estate is the perfect choice.

Head through the gate from the car park and follow the flat, gravel path through a wild landscape of tall grasses, heather and low-lying trees – listen out for cuckoos in spring and look for pretty little chaffinches and wrens. All along the route, the Quinag mountain complex looms high above, either shrouded in dramatic cloud or silhouetted against a blue sky on clear days.

The route loops around at the end via a very low-level, small hill where you can get a view over the estate, and then returns the same way.

> **WHAT'S FOR LUNCH?**
> Bring a picnic to enjoy on one of the benches dotted around the trail here.

Need to know: There's no livestock but there are ground-nesting birds in summer, so dogs can be off-lead but must be kept under control. Try to keep them to the path to protect the fragile ecosystems that harbour so much of the wildlife here. There are two composting toilets along the route and a few rest areas for picnics.

↓ Arty surveying the landscape along the Leitir Easaidh All Abilities Path

KYLESKU HOTEL

(290)

Kylesku, Sunderland

kyleskuhotel.co.uk

Sitting right on the shore above Loch Gleann Dubh, Kylesku Hotel is a surprisingly serene place to stop on the UK's most popular road trip: the North Coast 500. Come here for a few nights and you'll find that once the day trippers and evening diners have moved on from this tiny fishing village, you'll have the dramatic lochside views all to yourself – aside from the other guests, of course (though with fewer than 20 rooms, it rarely feels overcrowded).

Here, you could sit in the bar and stare for hours at the scenery in the changing light, perhaps spotting an inquisitive seal swimming across the boat slipway or looking out for golden eagles or osprey in the sky above. Even in the driving rain, the loch and surrounding hills and mountains make a mesmerising sight. Pick up the bar's binoculars to look out for red deer on the distant slopes or come down early for breakfast in the hope of spotting a slinky otter in the water.

Bedrooms here are contemporary and cosy, with wooden furnishings and soft tartan throws, and some come with spectacular loch views. But the highlight at Kylesku really is the food: breakfast is a substantial Scottish feast – think black pudding and potato bread and local smoked trout on eggs – while lunch and dinner are dominated by seafood sold at market price. The chef cooks lobster to perfection, there are local mussels on offer farmed within sight of the hotel, and langoustines served grilled atop smoky steaks.

Where to walk: There are plenty of excellent walks nearby, and with Scotland's right to roam you could go almost anywhere. But for something simple with spectacular views on a clear day, head to the Leitir Easaidh all-abilities path at Little Assynt (see page 221), just a 30-minute drive south. Alternatively, there's a 6km coastal route in Scourie that starts at the beach and heads up the rocky coast and then inland past the primary school (beware of livestock).

For an excellent lunch, walk up through the livestock woodland behind the hotel and across the

← Arty enjoying sunset at Kylesku Hotel on the North Coast 500

↓ Sand and stones on Sinclairs Bay beach

bridge to the Surf & Turf food truck that overlooks the neighbouring Loch a' Chàirn Bhàin. There's lobster rolls and fish and chips on offer for the seafood lovers, while meat-eaters will relish the chance to try venison and Highland beef burgers.
Need to know: Dogs get treats, towels and a bowl mat in the room to keep the carpets clean, and there's a small

---

WHAT'S NEARBY?
The closest attraction well worth enjoying is right at the hotel's front door: North Coast Sea Tours (northcoastseatours.co.uk) run boat trips right from the slipway here out to the UK's highest waterfall, Eas a'Chual Aluinn. You'll cruise up to the falls, which crash 200 metres over a sheer drop, and then head back towards the hotel and beyond, beneath the impressive Kylesku Bridge to see a colony of grey seals. You might see sea eagles, golden eagles, dolphins, red stags on land, and otters, too.

---

enclosed woodland area (often with livestock grazing) behind the hotel for morning or evening toilet walks. Dogs are allowed in the bar area and honesty bar lounge to drink or dine with you, but not the main restaurant.

BEACH

SINCLAIRS BAY 291

The Highlands

Just north of Wick on the North Coast 500 driving route, this beach sits within a sheltered bay and is flanked by two 16th-century castles at each end. There's good surf for those with their own boards, and you'll often see seals and occasionally orcas from the sand.
Make a night of it: Stay in nearby Wick at Mackay's, where dogs can dine with you in the bar. mackayshotel.co.uk
🐕2 <£200
Parking: Noss Head Car Park, KW1 4QT

BEACH

CEANNABEINNE BEACH 292

The Highlands

If you're driving the North Coast 500 in either direction, Ceannabeinne Beach is an utterly irresistible stop. Its huge, flat surface of soft yellow sand – visible from the road – spreads out for hundreds of metres along the northern coast, and at low tide you can walk beyond the rocky outcrops that punctuate the sand to find yet more beach beyond them. The geology here is astonishing, as red cliffs are juxtaposed with dark black rocks that tower high above the sand, while the crystalline ocean beckons keen swimmers beyond. Adrenaline junkies should queue for the zipline that whisks adventurous visitors above the beach from one side of the bay to the other. **Make a night of it:** The Tongue Hotel loves dogs and is just less than an hour's drive from Ceannabeinne Beach. tonguehotel.co.uk

PLACE

SMOO CAVE 293

Durness, The Highlands

Located on the northern section of the North Coast 500, Smoo Cave has exciting history, fascinating geology and glittering pools within its cavernous confines.

↓ Arty trotting along the sand at Ceannabeinne Beach on the North Coast 500

Most impressive, though, is its towering entrance, which sits back from the sea shoreline within a sheltered gully and reaches 15 metres high and 40 metres wide. You'll walk along the clifftops from the car park and down a zigzagging staircase to reach its gaping entryway, and you can explore inside along walkways to get up close to its geological formations – largely made up of Durness limestone. Head across the covered walkway to see the Smoo burn, which flows into the cave through a sinkhole where daylight floods in and fills a pool beneath, and look out for information boards that chart the area's history.

It's thought that people have lived in and around this cave for upwards of 7,000 years, and Neolithic and Iron Age artefacts have been discovered during archaeological excavations. But most compelling was the Norse history: thanks to the discovery of nails and rivets from their ships, it's thought that there was a boatbuilding industry here around the 8th and 9th centuries. The cave, with its prime position at the shoreline, was also used by fishermen throughout the ages until the 18th century, and you'll spot a winch on the beach that would have been used to haul boats from the water and a small ruin that was used as storage.

↓ The gaping entrance to Smoo Cave

WAULKMILL BAY

294

Orkney

At low tide on the southern side of mainland Orkney, as the ocean retreats it reveals an enormous, golden sand beach flanked by sloping cliffs clad with heather that zings with purple flowers in late summer. On the exposed sea floor, shallow puddles of saltwater remain in places, hiding all sorts of intriguing creatures; seek out mussels clinging to rocks, clams buried in the tightly packed sands, and all manner of delicate and detailed shells. Best of all, the dog can run free on the 350-metre-deep and 300-metre-wide beach.

Make a night of it: The Murray Arms is just a 30-minute drive from Waulkmill Bay and is home to a fabulous seafood restaurant. themurrayarmshotel.com

🐾1 ≤£200

Parking: KW17 2RA

EXPERIENCE

GO HISTORY HOPPING IN ORKNEY

295

Mainland Orkney

historicenvironment.scot

Around 16km from mainland Scotland across the ferocious Pentland Firth, Orkney is an island of sparkling beaches, brilliant birdlife and some otherworldly geology. But while its natural wonders

will give you plenty to write home about, it's the man-made marvels that will have you most captivated. It was here, 6,000 years ago, that Britain's first farmers hit land, bringing with them cattle and livestock and building communities and societies that would – unbeknown to them – influence the rest of the British Isles. In various sites across mainland Orkney, now inscribed on the UNESCO World Heritage Site list, evidence of their civilisation can still be seen today.

Start your history-hopping adventure in the very centre of Orkney at the Ring of Brodgar, the UK's third-largest and one of the oldest stone circles. Around 60 stones once stood tall in this henge, built between 2600 and 2400 BCE on a heather-clad mound surrounded by a near perfectly circular ditch, and 36 of those still tower above the landscape today. Flanked by two lochs, Harray to the north-east and Stenness to the south-west, and surrounded by hills, the henge

is at the centre of a natural amphitheatre. There's little wonder, then, that this was thought to be the ceremonial centre for the Neolithic communities living here at the time – it would have been a spectacular location for burials, marriages and religious services.

Surrounding Brodgar are a handful of other intriguing sites: the mysterious mound of Salt Knowe, more standing stones at Stenness (accessible on foot from Brodgar), the Barnhouse Settlement village remains, and the astonishing chambered burial cairn of Maeshowe (dogs will have to wait in the car here). But the other crowning glory of Orkney's Neolithic history is a 15-minute drive west on the coast, overlooking Skaill Bay: the prehistoric village of Skara Brae.

Dogs can't go in the visitor centre here, but they can join you on the ancient site, where you can walk among the remains of homes built 5,000 years ago. There are stone beds and 'dressers' still visible in some of the structures, and each has its own hearth in the centre of the dwelling. You also get to explore the inside of Skaill House mansion with the dog, and then head down on to the beach below for a runabout on the bright-white sands.

The final stop on your tour of ancient Orkney should be the Broch of Gurness, the ruins of a tower and several dwellings surrounding it that are positively modern in comparison with Brodgar and Skara Brae. This was a thriving Iron Age community, perhaps one family or several, and you'll see kilns and water troughs built into the settlement alongside a tower that once rose 12 metres above the landscape to overlook the island of Rousay across the sea. **Make a night of it:** The aptly named Standing Stones Hotel is a great dog-friendly option for staying near Orkney's ancient sites. **thestandingstones.co.uk**

← The spectacular ruins of Skara Brae

ST NINIAN'S ISLE

296

Shetland

START POINT: ZE2 NJA
DISTANCE/TIME: 5km/1 hr 30 mins

Few walks have such a spectacular beginning as the coastal romp around St Ninian's Isle, a small, 72-hectare island in southern Shetland. Before you get on to the island, you first have to walk across a magnificent natural causeway made of fine, sugary sand, which connects the tiny isle to the mainland. Here, the dog can run free for a few minutes, perhaps launching itself in the sea or chasing a ball, before you put them on the lead and head up on to the island, where Shetland ponies and sheep roam, and the cliffs tower high above the ocean.

Navigate the island anticlockwise, heading north as soon as you're on the path, and you'll almost immediately come across the island's only building: a ruined 12th-century church, which sits on top of the remains of a much older church and an Iron Age settlement. It was here that the famous St Ninian's Isle treasure was found – a hoard of Pictish silver bowls, jewellery and weapons thought to date back as far as 750 CE, which was discovered by a schoolboy in the 1950s and now sits proudly displayed in the Museum of Scotland in Edinburgh.

> **WHAT'S FOR LUNCH?**
> There's nothing much around St Ninian's so bring a picnic, or head into the capital Lerwick (25 minutes by car) to scoff fresh local fish and moreish cauliflower 'wings' at The Dowry (thedowry.co.uk).

While settlements were indeed found here, the island has remained empty for centuries aside from the birds that nest here in summer. You'll see fulmars tucked away in the cliffs or soaring up and down with the thermals on the clifftops, and ground-nesting birds such as lapwings and skylarks live within its interior.

The views across the water to mainland Shetland are enrapturing, and on the western edge of St Ninian's lies a collection of dramatic sea stacks and the Selchie geo, a cleft in the island cut out by thousands of years of erosion. From here, if you could head westwards as the crow flies, the next bit of land you'd hit is Newfoundland and Labrador. The path heads south and returns to the car park along the beach again, where the dog can have one last hurrah off the lead before lunch.

↓ The author and her dog on St Ninian's Isle

Need to know: There's often livestock around the start point car park and on the Isle itself, and with steep drops from the clifftops, dogs are always best kept on leads.

↓ The author's weary walking boots on Minn Beach

BEACH

MINN BEACH 297

Shetland

Set on a sandy isthmus between two islands, connected to Shetland mainland by bridges, Minn Beach is a glorious dash of bright white sand lapped by sparklingly clear seas. Even on the sunniest summer day you could find yourself alone here – splendid isolation at its best.

Make a night of it: Book yourself in for a week at the Boatman's House on Unst (see page 230), accessible via the car ferries from the mainland and Yell.

Parking: ZE2 9LD

BOATMAN'S HOUSE

Unst, Shetland stay.shetland.org

When life gets too much and the world feels too busy, many retreat to the forest or the coast to find a calming sense of solitude. And when the forest or the coast aren't good enough, you can always retreat to Unst. This is the northernmost inhabited island in the UK – the only thing that stands in the sea between here and the North Pole is a few craggy rocks and the delightfully named Muckle Flugga Lighthouse – and with just 600 people residing on the island permanently, it's a spectacularly remote and isolated isle, perfect for getting away from it all. And the Boatman's House is a brilliant base for soaking up the quietude.

Set within the shore station for the Muckle Flugga Lighthouse, where lightkeepers and boatmen would live when off-duty in the times before automation, the Boatman's House has prime position on a steep, hilly promontory within Burrafirth Bay. Here, you can watch the waves roll in from the ocean over a bowl of cornflakes at the breakfast table or head into the garden with a pair of binoculars to keep an eye out for orcas or passing gannets. You might even spot an otter or

two slinking about on the boat slipway beneath the shore station.

The views and wildlife outside are indeed captivating, but inside, the quirky decor – think hand-drawn wallpaper, almost life-size sheep statues and handsome wooden carved gannets – is almost as charming and makes for a homely place to hole up in for a week or two with the dog.

Where to walk: By far the most exciting walk at this end of the island is the 8km trail in Hermaness Nature Reserve, which starts just a short stomp up the steep hill next to the shore station. From the car park, you can head across boardwalks laid out over the peaty bog towards the coastline, and then track along the clifftops to

scale Hermaness Hill. In spring and early summer, expect to see ground-nesting birds aplenty, including enormous great skuas (though beware their wrath when they're breeding – they're known to be somewhat antagonistic during the height of the season). Once at the coast, you might find a welcoming committee of puffins, fulmars and gannets, who nest in the nooks and crannies below or on the rocky outcrops at sea, and once you reach Hermaness Hill, you'll get excellent views out to Muckle Flugga Lighthouse. If you see nobody else on your walk, it's safe to assume that you may well be the northernmost human in the UK.

Need to know: The Boatman's House has a small enclosed patio, but down by the slipway opposite the Shorehaven Cottage is an enclosed paddock where the dog can run free.

Getting here: To reach Shetland, take a pet-friendly cabin with NorthLink (**northlinkferries.co.uk**) on the overnight ferry from Aberdeen, then drive north via two car ferries at either end of Yell to reach Unst. The drive takes approximately two hours, including ferries.

← Arty on a model Viking ship in Shetland

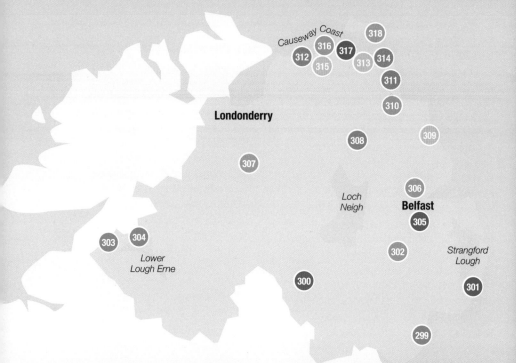

Causeway Coast

318
312 316 317
315 313 314
311
310

Londonderry

309
308
307

Loch
Neigh

306
Belfast
305

303 304
302
Strangford
Lough

Lower
Lough Erne

300

301

299

NORTHERN IRELAND

STAY

KRIBBEN COTTAGES

299

Annalong, County Down
kribbencottages.com

Just a few minutes' drive from the County Down coast, this little cul-de-sac of charming cottages is a brilliant base for those with both kids and dogs in their pack. All of the homes, sleeping between four and six people, are dog-friendly and while none have enclosed gardens, the communal gardens are large and there's a play area for the kids to entertain themselves on site.

Each home has its own secluded outdoor dining area and barbecue facilities, and from your doorstep you can hike up into the Mourne Mountains to bag peaks such as Rocky Mountain (404 metres) and Slieve Donard (850m). **Where to walk:** The Mourne Mountains are your oyster here, but if you don't fancy anything so strenuous you could head to the coast to walk on the Annalong Coastal Path. To the north, Donard Forest has lovely walking trails ideal for a little shade when the weather's too hot for the dog.

Need to know: You'll need to bring bowls and bedding for the dog. A longline might be useful if you're spending time

↓ The Mourne Mountains as seen from Dundrum Castle

outside and want the dog to have a little more freedom.

WHAT'S NEARBY?
A 20-minute drive north of the cottages is Newcastle's gorgeous Murlough Beach, where dogs are allowed to roam off the lead, all year round. There's a nature reserve behind the beach, too, where dogs should be kept on leads to protect the resident stoats and butterflies. In summer, don't miss a trip to the Carginagh Sunflower Fields (facebook.com/CarginaghSunflowerFields) to snap the family amid a sea of yellow.

PLACE

NAVAN CENTRE & FORT

Armagh, County Armagh
visitarmagh.com

Fans of Irish folklore will know Navan Fort, or Emain Macha, from its prominence in the Ulster Cycle tales. This more-than 2,000-year-old mound with its distinctive bank and ditch has featured in numerous stories over the centuries and is said to have been created by the ancient goddess of fertility, Macha, when she carved it out of the earth with her brooch and pin.

The site dates back to 95 BCE and has long been a place of ritual and tradition, though contrary to what its name suggests, it likely never served as a fort at all. Instead, in its early days it was inhabited by various communities, and later became a pagan temple made from wood and measuring around 45 metres wide. You can walk the dog along its banks and on to the mound to feel the presence of the ancestors who worshipped here long ago, or you can take a guided tour for a deeper understanding of its past.

Inside the visitor centre (the dog can't come inside but can wait in the car), you'll find exhibitions on the Ulster Cycle, displays with artefacts found on the site, and a dressing-up box for kids to have a little fun re-enacting Celtic life.

PLACE

CASTLE WARD

301

Strangford, County Down

nationaltrust.org.uk

If you were a fan of the popular HBO TV series *Game of Thrones*, you'll recognise several areas around the regal 18th-century mansion that is Castle Ward. Most notable is the Georgian farmyard, which starred as parts of Winterfell, home of the Stark family, but there are recognisable spots all over the leafy estate. There's plenty to please the non-set-jetters in your clan, too, as a riotously colourful sunken garden, miles of walking trails and a dog-friendly tearoom offer a fantastic day out with the dog – plus, there's an off-lead exercise field near the admissions hut so you can really tire them out.

WALK

ROYAL HILLSBOROUGH FOREST

302

County Down

START POINT: BT26 6AL
DISTANCE/TIME: circular 4km/1.25 hrs

Perched on the edge of Royal Hillsborough, a well-to-do town with a lively high street packed with independent shops and cafes, Hillsborough Forest is a 200-acre parkland with a lake and lots of waymarked trails. The lakeside trail follows the shoreline and then heads away into coniferous and broadleaf woodland, offering ample shade on sunny days. You'll spot enormous sculptures of foxes, rabbits and even a green interpretation of 'Big Foot' among the trees, and in winter waterfowl are to be found on the lake.

You can detour briefly to explore the grounds of Hillsborough Fort, a 17th-century construction built to protect the Carrickfergus–Dublin road, and stop to picnic on the benches by the lakeshore.

> **WHAT'S FOR LUNCH?**
> Keane's Deli (facebook.com/keanesdeli) is a short drive away in the town centre and has wheelchair access and a broccoli salad so moreish you'll be begging for the recipe.

Need to know: This is an exceptionally accessible walk: not only are the trails suitable for most wheelchairs, but they are waymarked well and the information board is written with braille for the visually impaired. Dogs can be off-lead but must be under close control, especially as it's popular with school trips.

KEENAGHAN COTTAGE

Belleek, County Fermanagh
keenaghancottage.com

Tucked away down a quiet road on the shores of tiny Keenaghan Lough, this modest thatched cottage is a gorgeous 18th-century sanctuary. Lovingly restored by its owners and decked out with all the mod cons you'd expect from any luxury holiday home, it's a charming space to spend a few days exploring County Fermanagh and neighbouring County Donegal.

There's an enclosed, wraparound garden for the dog to roam around, with plenty of perfectly placed seating for sundowners or al fresco breakfasts, and it even has a little pontoon from which you can launch your own paddleboards or kayaks, or simply have a swim in the lough.
Where to walk: You're just 15 minutes from the coast here, so head west to Bundoran to walk the dog on the beach and gaze out to Donegal Bay. To the east, Castle Caldwell Forest is an excellent shaded walking spot with plenty of marked trails.

> **WHAT'S NEARBY?**
> The little village of Belleek is famous the world over for its pottery – head to the shops to seek out a piece or two to bring home, then nip into the dog-friendly Black Cat Cove pub (blackcatcove.co.uk) for live music and a spot of lunch or dinner.

Need to know: Dogs must be kept out of the bedrooms and off the furniture. Bring your own bowls and dog bedding.

LUSTY BEG ISLAND RESORT

County Fermanagh
lustybegisland.com

If you've ever dreamed of being a castaway like Robinson Crusoe but without the shipwreck disaster and the cannibals – and perhaps with a few little luxuries thrown in – then Lusty Beg Island could be for you. This 75-acre island is an isle off another island, sitting in the cool waters of Lower Lough Erne. It's a five-minute car ferry ride from neighbouring Boa Island, which is connected to the mainland via a pair of bridges, and once you're here there's very little reason to leave. There's archery on site, kayaking from its shoreline, bikes for hire and RIB boat rides for thrill-seekers.

Fill up on hearty meals in The Lodge Bar and Restaurant and walk for hours with the dog in the gorgeous heritage woodland.
Where to walk: Beyond the island's own woodlands, you can head across the water on the car ferry and into County Donegal to follow the Lough Derg Pilgrim Path, a 12km hike along the shore of the lake. On the western shore of Lower Lough Erne you can visit Blackslee Waterfall, where a 6km walk will take you to its beautiful cascade.

> **WHAT'S NEARBY?**
> If you really feel the need to leave, head to the southern end of Lower Lough Erne and get out on the water on a hydrobike – dog included.

Need to know: Dogs must be on a lead around the accommodation and kept under control in the woodlands. You'll need to bring your own beds and bowls.

ST GEORGE'S MARKET

Belfast belfastcity.gov.uk

Belfast has had a Friday market for over 400 years and today, its vendors set up beneath the vaulted ceilings of the Victorian covered market hall in the city centre. You'll find everything from classic fruit and veg sellers to experts peddling antiques or new young bakers offering fresh cakes and cookies. The fishmongers and butchery stalls will be the biggest test of any dog's willpower, and on Saturdays, their noses will be set to sniff mode by a gloriously tempting array of food vendors selling Spanish tapas, Indian street snacks and traditional breakfast baps. Pick up a souvenir from one of the many craft stalls and sit down with a drink to enjoy a bit of live music.

CAVE HILL TRAIL, CAVE HILL COUNTRY PARK

Belfast

START POINT: Belfast Castle, BT15 5GR
DISTANCE/TIME: circular 7.2km/2 hrs

On the outskirts of Belfast lies a gorgeously green country park with some ancient ruins and – as the name suggests – cavernous grottos within its hills. Take the Cave Hill Trail, a somewhat strenuous walk with plenty of ascent, and you'll pass

> **WHAT'S FOR LUNCH?**
> Bring a picnic or after your walk, hop in the car and head up to The Crown & Shamrock Inn in Newtownabbey (facebook.com/crownandshamrock).

↓ Cave Hill Country Park

a series of caves thought to have once been mines. There's also an ancient fort up on the hill, but the highlight is the view over Belfast city.

Need to know: Dogs must be on leads. The walk is marked but you can get a map from belfasthills.org.

EXPERIENCE

GO TOTALLY WILD UNDER CANVAS

Gortin, County Tyrone
wildwithconsent.com

There's something addictive about wild camping. That wholesome feeling you get when waking up entirely surrounded by nature, without another soul in sight, is almost impossible to come by any other way. But strict laws in the UK forbid wild camping in most places outside Scotland, so there are a limited number of places where you can enjoy the freedom of pitching up wherever you like.

Fortunately, thanks to Wild With Consent, Sessile Oak Farm in County Tyrone is one of them, as they've teamed up with the landowner to allow intrepid campers to have the site all to themselves.

Bring your tent and pitch it among the deciduous woodland, where bluebells create a carpet of purple in spring and the Curraghbruck Hills spread out in the distance. You can walk the dog through the forest here, meaning there's little reason to leave beyond nipping into the dairy farm next door for homemade ice cream. You can try salmon fishing in the river to catch something for your supper, which you can cook on the raised fire pit as the dog roams free around the site.

The site sits within the Sperrin Mountains AONB, meaning there are hiking trails and mountain biking routes aplenty within a short drive, and if you bring a pair of binoculars you might spot red squirrels in the trees and sparrowhawks in the skies.

You're entirely off-grid here, so bring everything you need and, as with any wild camping spot, you must remember to leave no trace.

GALGORM

Galgorm, County Antrim

galgorm.com

If your dog prefers the finer things in life, Galgorm can deliver for both of you. This hotel is the height of Northern Irish luxury hospitality: there's a branded Bentley parked out the front at all times, the lobby is dripping with crystal chandeliers and ostentatious fresh floral displays, and the staff are often better dressed than their esteemed guests – most of whom will be wandering around in white robes at the end of each day, having spent several hours basking in various pools, saunas, steam rooms and hydrotherapy suites in the utterly expansive spa garden.

Once you get into the swing of life here – a hearty Irish breakfast in the morning, a stroll with the dog around the grounds or into town, and then a day in the spa before returning to one of the three restaurants for more indulgence at dinner – you'll no doubt resent having to return home to cook for yourself and make your own bed.

For dog owners, there are cottages on site, lodges and residences, but the best accommodation is in the shepherd's huts, though they're more like shepherd's chalets, as they have small kitchens, living areas and decking out the front complete with their own sunken hot tubs. You'll be greeted on arrival with a complimentary gin and tonic, a fridge of complimentary wine and beer, and a small pack of aperitivo snacks, and the dog will get its own bed and bowls to use throughout the stay. You can dine on the Ghillie's grill menu with the dog in McKendry's – a traditional Irish pub with hops draped above the bar and several cosy nooks and crannies to hide away in – or leave them in the room to sample the menus in the Italian bistro Fratelli's or afternoon tea in the pretty conservatory. Alternatively, you can request a transfer in that handsome Bentley outside to take you to town for dinners elsewhere.

Where to walk: You can play fetch with the dog along the riverside near the shepherd's huts, but for a longer walk, walk into town along the banks. It's a lovely, leafy stroll with a small woodland for them to explore and takes around an hour there and back. Alternatively, tackle the footpaths at Glenariff for something more substantial (see opposite).

WHAT'S NEARBY?
You're less than a 40-minute drive from the coast here, so head east to walk on the sands of Ballygally Beach (see below) or Ballycastle (see page 242) to the north.

Need to know: Dogs aren't allowed in the spa or any of the restaurants except the McKendry's pub. You can get takeaway pizza from Fratelli for a more relaxing dining experience in your shepherd's hut. Dogs can be left in the room should you wish to dine elsewhere or use the spa.

BALLYGALLY BEACH

discovernorthernireland.com

Along the east Antrim Coast and within the region's AONB, Ballygally Beach is a lovely place to spend a day on the sand. There's 300 metres of it, and between October and March the dog can enjoy off-lead walks (leads no more than 2 metres during the rest of the year). The highlight here is the spectacular coastal views, as dramatic headlands beyond rise up out of the ocean.

Make a night of it: Posh dogs should book into Galgorm Hotel & Spa (see opposite), which is just a 40-minute drive away.

Parking: BT40 2QQ

WALK

GLENARIFF WATERFALL AND SCENIC TRAILS

310

County Antrim

START POINT: BT44 0QX
DISTANCE/TIME: circular 3km/1 hr

Set within the Antrim Coast and Glens AONB, Glenariff Forest Park has plunging river valleys and glorious coastal views from its hilltops. This trail, beginning in the car park and immediately descending some steep steps into a verdant gorge, is a brilliant option for rainy days when you need a little shelter from the elements.

Down in the gorge, where boardwalks cling to the sides of the ravine, you'll find yourself surrounded by lush ferns, mosses and iridescent liverworts – it pays to look closely at the rocks and their foliage, as entire ecosystems can be seen clinging on. There are two waterfall viewpoints, where the river cascades over steep rocks and tumbles gradually down a rugged slope, and once you reach the bottom of the valley you'll cross the water at Ess-Na-Crub waterfall and follow forest tracks up to the car park again.

> **WHAT'S FOR LUNCH?**
> Around halfway you'll pass Laragh Lodge (**laraghlodge.co.uk**), a lovely riverside pub with great beers on tap and hearty food on offer. Just remember, you've got to climb a steep hill to get back.

Need to know: Dogs can be off-lead here but if yours is a swimmer, keep them out of the dangerous waters.

↓ Glenariff waterfall trail

MAGHERINTEMPLE LODGE 311

Ballycastle, County Antrim
irishlandmark.com

This little lodge near the Antrim coast is a small but handsome Scottish baronial home with a big historical connection. Built in 1874, it was owned by John Casement, whose son was Irish martyr Roger Casement, who was convicted of treason for supporting the independence movement and was executed in Pentonville Prison in 1916.

The turbulent and polarising political past is behind this home now, though, and today it's owned and run by the Irish Landmark Trust, who have restored its former style and created a pleasant little escape in the country. There are two bedrooms (the second has bunk beds only) and a well-equipped kitchen with old church pews to sit on by the back patio doors. You'll find it easy to switch off here, with no TV and no Wi-Fi, and just the sounds of the birds in the surrounding woodland and lambs in the fields to keep you company.

Where to walk: The lanes around the house are very quiet so you can walk out the front door and head in any direction for a short stroll. Longer walks can be had on the coast at Carrick-a-Rede (nationaltrust.org.uk) or Fair Head (see alltrails.com for directions).

WHAT'S NEARBY?

You're in prime position here for exploring the Antrim coast, as beaches like Ballycastle and Whiterocks (see page 242) are a short drive away. Head south and you can walk among the Dark Hedges, an avenue of 18th-century beech trees that were featured in and made famous by hit TV series *Game of Thrones*.

Need to know: The garden is enclosed on all but one side where a small gap in the hedge leads to the driveway. There's livestock nearby so keep your dog under close control at all times.

STAY

THE INN ON THE COAST

Portrush, County Antrim
innonthecoastportrush.com

You'll need to book ahead for this lovely little hotel in Portrush on the north Antrim coast as it's hugely popular with Northern Ireland's adventuring dogs. Its rooms are simple but functional, with plenty of space for the dog's bed on the floor. The real reason to come here though is that the staff simply love dogs – so much so, they'll likely greet your pet before they greet you. Dogs aren't just welcome but are actively encouraged, and they love mutts of all sizes – even your St Bernards and Great Danes.

The hotel is set back from the sea behind a golf course and is just a 25-minute walk into Portrush town centre, where beaches, cafes and restaurants are all tucked on to a small peninsula. **Where to walk:** Head across the street from the hotel and down Glen Road and you'll find yourself walking along the coast in no time. You can walk for miles here, all the way to Portstewart and back (7km) if you want to really stretch your legs.

> **WHAT'S NEARBY?**
> The Giant's Causeway Visitor Centre and tours are the main event in this area – and dogs can join you inside the exhibition there, too (see page 243).

Need to know: Dogs are welcome in the restaurant at the Inn on the Coast; they must not be left alone in the room.

BALLYCASTLE STRAND

County Antrim

Stretching across the north Antrim coast for over a kilometre, Ballycastle Strand is dog-friendly year-round and has lovely soft, yellow sand to stroll on. Let the dog run free here around the anglers who set up their rods on the beach and grab a morning coffee to sip on while you gaze out at Rathlin Island across the bay. Look a little further and on a clear day you can even see the Isle of Islay in Scotland.

Make a night of it: The Landmark Trust's Magherintemple Lodge (see page 240) is a charming place to stay just a five-minute drive from Ballycastle.

Parking: BT54 6QS

↓ Arty playing with a new friend on Ballycastle Strand

MARINE HOTEL BALLYCASTLE

Ballycastle, County Antrim
marinehotelballycastle.com

Right on the seafront in Ballycastle on the north coast of Northern Ireland, Marine Hotel has some of the best views in the country, with the rich blue ocean and the jutting cliffs of Antrim visible from some of its bedrooms and dining areas. Here, you'll sleep on king-sized beds, breathe the sea air from your balcony in the mornings, and eat your way through the excellent seafood on the menu at Marconi's Bistro downstairs. There's even a menu for the dog so they can have a treat, too.

Where to walk: Ballycastle Strand (see left) is a prime location for your morning strolls.

WHITEROCKS BEACH

County Antrim

Approach Whiterocks from the east and this beach will be completely irresistible, its vast stretch of bright white sand stretching out beneath the cliffs for what seems like miles. Between June and mid-September, you can't bring the dog down here, but come in spring, autumn or winter and the 3km of sands are all yours to run free on. Expect to see surfers in the sea when the waves are good, and anglers with their rods hoping for a catch. Don't miss mooching about the limestone rock formations at the eastern end of the beach.

Make a night of it: Stay in Portrush's Inn on the Coast (see page 241) for a reasonably-priced escape by the sea.

Parking: BT56 8NA

(see page 241)

WALK

THE GIANT'S CAUSEWAY RED TRAIL

316

County Antrim nationaltrust.org.uk

START POINT: Visitor Centre, BT57 8SU
DISTANCE/TIME: circular 4km/1.5 hrs

There are several legendary stories that chart the making of the Giant's Causeway. The most famous is of the giant himself, Finn McCool, who created the causeway to reach Scotland so he could battle his nemesis. After their fight, it's thought the Scottish giant destroyed the causeway, leaving just the relatively small cluster of hexagonal stacks you can see here today. An alternative version of this story sees Finn building the causeway for a Scottish love interest, but the construction is thwarted by his disgruntled grandmother, who uses magic to destroy it.

Of course, neither of these tales is true – the geology was formed by piping hot lava cooling quickly – but when you're standing on the geometric stones yourself, it's easy to see how the causeway inspired such folklore: it is a truly otherworldly, utterly uncanny sight. But it's also not the only incredible rock formation along this coastline, and this trail – the National Trust's red route – takes in a host of other fascinating geological sights.

It begins from the visitor centre and bears east, ascending on to the clifftops

↓ The cliffs at Whiterocks, near Portrush

coastal path – up to around 12 metres – and gradually get shorter as the causeway juts out into the sea, like some sort of hellish staircase leading to the netherworlds beneath the ocean.

Spend some time on the stones, clambering across them and looking out to sea, where on a clear day Scotland seems just a giant's hop away, before heading up the tarmac road back to the visitor centre.

> **WHAT'S FOR LUNCH?**
> The visitor centre has a dog-friendly cafe serving Irish stew and vegetarian pasties.

Need to know: With such steep cliffs, dogs must be kept on a lead along the trail, and especially on the Giant's Causeway itself. This area gets incredibly busy during summer and school holidays, so you'll need to book ahead to park at the visitor centre. Aim for an off-season visit if you can. This route is well waymarked but directions are available from the visitor centre.

↓ A seascape on Rathlin Island

almost immediately, affording excellent views of the craggy north Antrim coast. In spring and summer, bright yellow gorse and wildflowers line the footpath and birdsong from the ground-nesting birds in the nearby fields is a superb soundtrack. There are several viewpoints where you can stop and examine the coast – bring binoculars for even better views – and you'll walk across the headlands of Weir's Snout, Aird Snout and eventually down on to the shoreline via the Shepherd's Steps. There are 162 of them so you'll need good knees and a head for heights.

The trail continues east to the Amphitheatre, where the cliffs have worn away in a bowl shape, and it's down here you'll begin to see some of those iconic hexagonal rocks, like stacks of 50 pence pieces perfectly aligned along the coast. Erosion has caused the trail to fall apart around here, so you'll turn back at the Amphitheatre and then stick to the lower path along the shoreline towards the main event: the Giant's Causeway.

From afar, it just looks like a jumble of rocks jutting into the sea, but as you get closer and stand on the stones yourself, the uniformity of them is utterly stunning. They rise highest around the

TAKE A TOUR OF GIANT'S CAUSEWAY

County Antrim nationaltrust.org.uk

If you don't fancy walking down to the Causeway and you don't plan on a big cliff walk either, the tour from the visitor centre is an excellent option. There are buses to take you down and a guide will explain everything from how the rocks were formed to the myths and legends that surround them. In the visitor centre, you'll find an excellent exhibition that explores the geology, wildlife, history and the people the coastline has inspired over the centuries. The dog is allowed all over the site, including in the cafe.

Make a night of it: Magherintemple Gate Lodge (see page 240) is a lovely self-catering option for exploring the Causeway Coast.

RATHLIN ISLAND

County Antrim rathlin-ferry.com

From the shores of Ballycastle Strand (see page 242) you can see the L-shaped Rathlin Island, flung out to sea at 6.5km from the North Antrim coast. The low-lying isle stretches 6km from east to west and has a population of around 140 people. Hop on the ferry from Ballycastle and come here for a taste of remote, island life, where myths and legends intertwine with fascinating history, and a host of enchanting seabirds make their home each summer.

The island has been inhabited for thousands of years and, during the Neolithic period, it was thought to be a prolific producer of axe heads. It was one of the first places in Northern Ireland to be raided by Vikings, and it's said that in the 1300s, Robert the Bruce rested here, finding inspiration to continue his battles with a new army in Scotland after watching a spider fixing a hole in its web. It was after this that he regained his status as King of Scots.

Today, the island's most famous residents are the hundreds of puffins that make their home here from April through July. Head out to the RSPB's Rathlin West Light Seabird Centre (rspb.org.uk) to see them dodder about on the cliffsides, alongside pretty little guillemots and razorbills, before taking one of the many walking trails around this rugged part of the island.

Make a night of it: Rathlin Glamping Pods has one hut dedicated for dog-friendly stays, so book ahead to secure your spot right opposite a lovely beach. rathlinglamping.co.uk 🐕1 👤2 ☀ 🐾 <£100

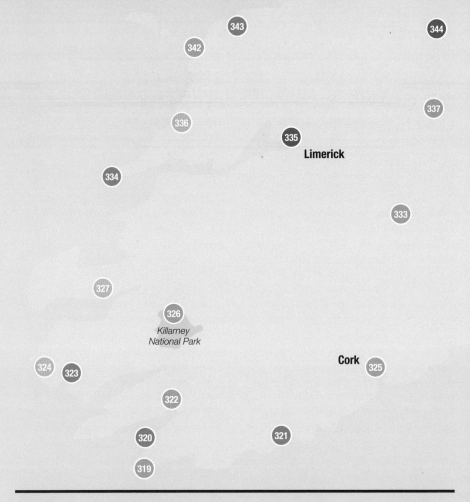

343
344
342
337
336
335
Limerick
334
333
327
326
Killarney National Park
324 323
322
Cork 325
320
321
319

SOUTHERN IRELAND

EXPERIENCE

PADDLE AROUND THE COAST OF COUNTY CORK

319

County Cork summersup.ie

Test out your balance – and the dog's – as you take to the waters around the edge of Ireland's Mizen Peninsula on a stand up paddleboard. The team at Summer SUP will teach you all you need to know, and you'll be gliding along the water, or perhaps taking an accidental dip, before you know it.

Make a night of it: Stay at the stunning Artists' Cottage (see opposite) on the Sheep's Head Peninsula.

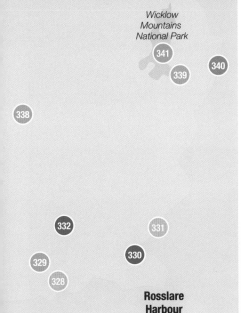

Wicklow
Mountains
National Park

341
339
340
338
332
331
329
330
328

**Rosslare
Harbour**

↓ The Mizen Head Peninsula

THE ARTISTS' COTTAGE & STUDIO

320

Bantry, County Cork www.sawdays
.co.uk/artists-cottage-studio

The Artists' Cottage and Studio is a
pair of old-fashioned farmhouses with
wood-burning stoves, an Aga and plenty
of mesmerising views out over the ocean
and to the knotty hills of the adjacent
Mizen Peninsula.

Just the drive to this former
farmhouse on the Sheep's Head
Peninsula is spectacular – think twisting
coastal road with views out to a frothing
sea below – but nothing quite beats
sitting on the garden bench, overlooking
the pool and the ocean beyond with
a cup of tea, or something stronger, in
hand while the dog sniffs about in the
beautiful, leafy garden.

↓ The lounge area at the Artists' Cottage and Studio

Where to walk: You might be tempted to head up on to the Sheep's Head Way here – a truly excellent hiking path that takes you all the way to the peninsula's end, where a lighthouse stands tall above the sea – but with so many sheep here, dogs have been banned from the trail. Instead, head down to the cove at Dunmanus Bay (a 25-minute walk from the house) to let the dog run off-lead on the pebbles. In low season, when the roads are quiet, walk along the coastal road towards the lighthouse for epic views.
Need to know: The garden is fairly well enclosed except for some shrubs at the back where determined dogs could get through; the main gate also has a gap at the bottom, which could cause a problem if you have a small dog.

> **WHAT'S NEARBY?**
> A 40-minute walk along the coastal road takes you to the lovely White House Cafe (<u>whitehousecafe.ie</u>), where sandwiches and cakes are served amid walls plastered with local art, while further along is the village of Kilcrohane, which has a few pubs and restaurants. The culinary highlight around here for dog owners is Arundel's by the Pier (<u>arundelsbythepier.com</u>), where local mussels will delight seafood fans.

STAY

DUNMORE HOUSE

Clonakilty, County Cork
<u>dunmorehousehotel.ie</u>

Sitting right atop the cliffs overlooking Ring Head in County Cork, Dunmore House is a charming family-run hotel. They play to their strengths here: the bedrooms have captivating ocean views, the outdoor terrace is idyllic for sundowners over the sea, and there's a fine-dining restaurant featuring local *fruits de mer*.

For the dog, there are intimate gardens to sniff around and a bar where they'll be welcomed with a bowl of water and, if they're good, a treat from the staff. It's here, among the leather sofas and wood-panelled walls, that you can enjoy

WHAT'S NEARBY?
Head 15 minutes south from the hotel along the quiet country lane and you'll find Duneen Bay tucked away beneath the cliffs, and further still is Long Strand Beach, where you'll also find the excellent Fish Basket restaurant (thefishbasket.ie).

an array of excellent dishes, too. Try the seafood platter for something really indulgent and save space for something sweet to finish.

Where to walk: Inchydoney island is temptingly just across the water from Dunmore and you can do a lovely hour-long stroll around its edges (see alltrails.com for directions). Clogheen Marsh Nature Reserve also has excellent walking trails.

Need to know: Dogs aren't allowed in the main restaurant at Dunmore but they're welcome everywhere else. There is no limit to the number of dogs allowed in each room, but you'll need to call ahead to check if you're bringing a pack.

TAKE THE BOAT TO GARNISH ISLAND

County Cork garinishisland.ie

Just over a kilometre off the coast of Glengarriff lies the meticulously groomed Garnish Island, just 500 metres wide and 400 metres long, ensconced in a sheltered inlet and surrounded by the hills of the mainland. The island had been largely ignored for centuries, aside from a 19th-century tower built there during the Napoleonic Wars, until it was bought by the Bryce family in the early 20th century. Today, their hard work alongside landscape architect Harold Ainsworth Peto has turned it into a gardener's paradise.

Board a ferry from Glengarriff to land here and you can walk around all of the gardens with the dog on a lead, admiring the sea views from its outer edges

↓ A dog walker on a beach on Inchydoney Island

and exploring all manner of follies and planted beds. There's classical Italianate architecture mixed in with manicured Arts and Crafts-style hedgerows, and a 'jungle' area with thick woodland where New Zealand ferns and rhododendron and Chinese *Schima khasiana* thrive.

A walled garden is home to heated glasshouses and potting sheds and is where potatoes, fruit and cut flowers once provided sustenance for the Bryce family, but today it's all about ornamental plants and you should explore all four corners of the walls, where unique and unusual structures mark the edges. Finally, don't miss a photo opportunity at the Grecian Temple, where a rotunda sits on a promontory and looks out over the sea and mountains beyond.

Make a night of it: The Artists' Cottage (see page 247) is just a 45-minute drive from Glengarriff.

↓ The gardens at Garnish Island

BUTLER ARMS HOTEL

Waterville, County Kerry
butlerarms.com

Sitting on the popular Ring of Kerry, the Butler Arms Hotel has prime position within one of its most spectacular bays. Dog-friendly rooms here are on the ground floor and each has its own little terrace so you've got direct access to the outside.

↓ A coastal view on the Ring of Kerry

Traditional decor and plush marble bathrooms make it feel luxurious, while dinners in the dog-friendly restaurant are all about local seafood, from oysters to mussels and smoked salmon.
Where to walk: You can wander on the lawns right along the seafront for a short morning or evening stroll, but longer walks can be had along the Kerry Way or on the Termons Ridge Loop (directions at alltrails.com).

BEACH

ST FINIAN'S BAY

324

County Kerry

Venture beyond the popular Ring of Kerry on to the Ring of Skellig and you'll find the coastline much quieter, and St Finian's is a special place to while away a few hours. This lovely sandy beach is small but still large enough for a game of fetch or a sandcastle-building contest – and you can do that all with views of the dramatic, jagged Skellig Islands in the distance.
Make a night of it: Book into the lovely Butler Arms (see opposite), which is just a 20-minute drive east.
Parking: ///feeding.grownups.sensing

EXPERIENCE

WALK IN THE FOOTSTEPS OF THE TITANIC'S LAST PASSENGERS

325

Cobh, County Cork titanic.ie

Almost everywhere you go in Ireland there's a *Titanic* story: a village resident worked on it, or perhaps a group of local lads had their part in building it. Cobh, pronounced 'cove', is no different. But this town's story goes a little deeper than most, as this was the final stop for the

Titanic before she left, never to return.

This little town on the south coast of Ireland was called Queenstown back then, a name that was given to it by Queen Victoria after she first set foot in Ireland through its port in 1849. The *Titanic* dropped anchor in its deep harbour on 11 April 1912 and some 123 passengers boarded its decks through the White Star Line building on the pretty, colourful waterfront that's made up of traditional British architecture you can still admire today.

On a tour of Cobh with local experts Michael and Pat, a passionate pair who met in the Irish Naval Defence Forces on Spike Island just across the water from Cobh, you'll discover not just the little connections to the cruise liner across the town, but also delve into the personal stories of some of those who boarded and disembarked here. The most exciting of these is that of Father Browne, who left the ship at Cobh to return home and whose photographs are now some of the few we have that show what life on board

the ship was like.

Make a night of it: The bright and breezy Emmet Hotel in Clonakilty has individually decorated boutique bedrooms and is just an hour from Cobh. emmethotel.com

 WALK

ROSS ISLAND 326

Killarney National Park

START POINT: Ross Castle, V93 V304
DISTANCE/TIME: circular 5.5km/1.5 hrs

Sitting on the edge of Lough Leane in Killarney National Park, the lush Ross Island is split from the mainland by a skinny channel and is connected to it by a pair of bridges, where this walk begins. You'll first be greeted on the island by a 15th-century castle, thought to have been built by Irish chieftain O'Donoghue

Mór. The tower is steeped in myth and legend – including one about its builder rising on horseback from the surrounding waters each May – and a prophecy once told it could only be conquered by a ship. This prophecy spurred its defenders on during Cromwell's 17th-century conquest, and it was the last place to succumb to his forces in Munster. As the prophecy predicted, it was finally taken by Cromwell when one of his generals guided a ship across the loch, causing its inhabitants to surrender.

Mooch around the castle and grab an ice cream or cake at the little food shack before you pick up the main trail, which leads southwards through a forest of handsome beech, sycamore and oak trees. Another dose of history is not far away from the start, as you'll pass an ancient copper mine when you swing westwards towards the other end of the island. The oldest operation of its kind in Ireland and thought to be one of the most sophisticated in north-west Europe, this mine is said to have been active as far back as 2400 BCE. Over the years, excavations have revealed its productive past, including a smelting camp, where the ore would have been moulded into tools. Later on, the Ross Island Company developed the mine and employed 500 workers to extract copper from the rocks here, though flooding from the nearby loch became an issue and it was eventually abandoned and left to submersion in 1828.

Every now and then, the woodland along the trail opens up to reveal gorgeous loch views and on a clear day you can see right across the water to 832-metre-high An Sliabh Corcra or the Purple Mountain. There are viewpoints to walk out to – most are on rougher ground so not suitable for wheelchairs or buggies – and the path eventually turns northwards towards Library Point, where you can trot around the headland and enjoy more views out towards Innisfallen Island and the mountains beyond. From here, you'll walk back the way you came for a kilometre and then bear left towards Ross Castle to return.

> ### WHAT'S FOR LUNCH?
> Post-walk pints and pizzas are best had at the Killarney Brewing Company's HQ (**killarneybrewing distilling.com**) in town, just a five-minute drive or 30-minute walk from the Ross Island car park.

Need to know: Dogs can be off-lead throughout the trail, though they're not allowed inside Ross Castle. The main trail is largely suitable for off-road wheelchairs and pushchairs except around the extra viewpoint trail.

↑ The author and Arty on Ross Island

INCH BEACH 327

County Kerry

Poking out from the Dingle Peninsula, Inch Beach is an unusual stretch of sand – and not just because its name suggests it is far smaller than it is (there's over 5km of beach here). Rather than hug the coastline, a soft, golden sand dune system has built up perpendicular to the southern edge of the Dingle Peninsula, sticking right out to protect the waters of Castlemaine Harbour.

You needn't worry about tired legs here, as you can drive right out on to the sand, making the beach accessible for all ages and abilities. Blue Flag rules in Ireland mean dogs must be kept on leads but get yourself a longline and they'll have a little more freedom as you explore.

Make a night of it: The homely Pax House in Dingle has one dog-friendly bedroom so book ahead to snap it up. pax-house.com 🐕1 <£200

Parking: on the beach

↓ A dog walker on Inch Beach

WOODSTOWN STRAND 328

County Waterford

Look out for low tide times in Woodstown Strand so you can make the most of this vast stretch of sandy beach on the estuary of the River Barrow. Dogs can run free here outside of the summer peak months (June through August), and kids will love picking oyster shells and razor clams off the sand.

Make a night of it: Book into one of the self-catering lodges on the grounds of Waterford Castle Resort, just a 30-minute drive away. waterfordcastleresort.com 🐕1 <£200

Parking: ///petals.residency.doorways

WALK AMONG THE ARTWORKS OF WATERFORD WALLS

(329)

Waterford, County Waterford
wallsproject.ie

The historic city of Waterford has intriguing tales from the past aplenty – the Vikings settled here and made it an important trading post over 1,000 years ago, after all. But it's the modern murals that will most likely catch your eye, splashed across some of the city's buildings like it's getting tarted up for a big night out.

The murals – part of the Waterford Walls project, which brings together international artists to paint the city in technicolour each summer – provide a dog walk with a difference: you can park along the waterfront and wander up into the centre via Bridge Street, where a block of apartments is awash with pink and purple as a flock of baby birds is depicted feeding from its mother, a creation by Hampshire-based Curtis Hylton. Opposite, a huge pink and purple flower by Sophie Mess complements the picture.

Elsewhere, you'll find a psychedelic stag by French artist Céz Art on The Glen, a pair of sloshing koi carp on O'Connell Street, where you can sit outside with a beer in hand from a nearby bar, and even a majestic golden retriever wearing a Shakespearean ruff around his neck. The dog is a depiction of Ned, trusted sidekick of the project's creator, Edel Tobin. Load the map from the Waterford Walls website and take yourselves on an artistic tour of this great city.

Make a night of it: The Strand Inn at Dunmore East, right on the south coast, has lovely dog-friendly bedrooms and brilliant fish and chips on the menu. thestrandinn.com

↘ Johnstown Castle from across the water

IRISH AGRICULTURAL MUSEUM & JOHNSTOWN CASTLE GARDENS

330

Murntown, County Wexford
johnstowncastle.ie

A stunning romantic, neo-Gothic 19th-century castle stands at the heart of Johnstown, where pristinely kept lawns, lakes and gardens make up a regal estate of 120 acres. A walk with the dog will reveal a prairie-planted walled garden with swishing grasses and fiery floral displays, and there are wildflower meadows dotted across the estate to encourage pollinators and butterflies to return. Bring a picnic and sit at the lakeside, where you can gaze at the reflection of the magnificent castle in the glassy water, and don't miss a peek inside the Irish Agricultural Museum on site.

beach wheelchair hire is free from Surf Shack Curracloe (+353 87 061 2125). **Make a night of it:** Wicklow Head Lighthouse (see page 263) is just an hour's drive from Curracloe. **Parking:** Y21 EH99

BEACH

CURRACLOE BEACH

331

County Wexford

On Ireland's east coast, just 15 minutes north of Wexford, Curracloe has some of the finest, softest sand in the country. From the car park, you can amble all the way down its more-than 5km of sand to Raven Point and then back through the nature reserve. Dogs must be on leads;

PLACE

DUNBRODY FAMINE SHIP

332

New Ross, County Wexford
dunbrody.com

It's thought that over the course of just ten years in the mid-1800s, more than 2 million Irish citizens emigrated from their homeland to the USA. Escaping the dreadful Great Famine, which decimated livelihoods and killed over

a million people after a disease ripped through the country's potato crops, they set sail in droves for a better life in the land of opportunity. It was from the historic medieval docks in New Ross that thousands of these hopefuls departed, and while today little is left of the original port infrastructure, a to-scale replica of the Dunbrody Famine Ship is permanently docked on the River Barrow in the centre of town.

Guided tours of the ship leave on the hour, beginning in a reconstruction of the ticket office, where you'll hand over your boarding pass to be allowed on to the ship outside. Lively guides and actors in period costume regale you with stories of life during the Famine, and when on board you'll see exactly what it was like for the 200 or more passengers who spent the eight weeks at sea to reach New York.

The *Dunbrody* was one of the more 'luxurious' so-called famine ships, as she started life as a cargo vessel formerly used for carting timber, cotton and sometimes guano from the Americas to Ireland. This meant the ceilings within the belly of the ship were high, offering more space than the average passenger vessel. This is where the luxury ended, though, as hundreds of people were crammed four or five to a bunk in its lower decks, with only 30 minutes each to utilise the upper, outdoor decks for cooking and fresh air. Rats, seasickness and disease were not uncommon within the ship's berths.

Back on dry land, after you've explored the ship in your own time, a final exhibition in the adjoining museum recounts the numerous famous faces whose descendants made the often perilous journey across the Atlantic, including John F. Kennedy. The former US president's great-grandfather sailed from New Ross in 1848; a statue now stands a few hundred metres along the river from the ship commemorating the town's most famous connection.

THE DOLMEN LOOP IN THE GLEN OF AHERLOW

333

County Tipperary

START POINT: Lisvarrinane village
DISTANCE / TIME: circular 11km/3.5 hrs

The gorgeous Glen of Aherlow, a valley sandwiched between the hill of Slievenamuck and the Galtee Mountains range, has several circular trails to follow, ranging from 30-minute strolls to four-hour romps. This trail, which takes you up the sloping sides of 369-metre-high Slievenamuck to enjoy grand views of

↓ The gorgeous Glen of Aherlow

the Galtees across the valley, has excellent scenery and some fascinating history to boot.

It begins in the village of Lisvarrinane and is waymarked with red arrows that'll guide you up the sloping hill, past a bench where you should stop to savour spectacular views, and to the top, where a passage tomb is marked by a tumble of grey, lichen-splattered stones. From the summit, you'll get near-panoramic vistas, spotting the more-than-700-metre-high Slievenamon to the east and the Slieve Felim Hills to the north.

The return is, pleasingly, mostly downhill and some of the mountain views slink away behind the horizon as you descend. The walk conveniently ends by passing the excellent Moroney's pub on the R663, so you can end with a pint of Guinness as your reward.

> **WHAT'S FOR LUNCH?**
> The swish Mikey Ryan's Bar & Kitchen (**mikeyryans.ie**) in Tipperary has dog-friendly tables outside (with parasols) and serves local blue cheese salads and a range of international dishes.

Need to know: There may be livestock so dogs must be under control with good recall or on a lead. Directions at **aherlow.com** or **discoverireland.ie**.

↓ The bridges of Ross near Loop Head

LOOP HEAD LIGHTKEEPER'S HOUSE

334

Kilbaha, County Clare
irishlandmark.com

The life of a lighthouse keeper wasn't always an easy one, but when you check into Loop Head's keeper's cottage you'll soon lose any sympathy for them: the views here, and the vast emptiness of the coast around you, is truly spectacular. The cottage, and its adjoining lighthouse, was built in the mid-19th century, though a lighthouse has been protecting County Clare's shores here since the 1600s. The cottage is decked out in period furniture, and the lighthouse still guides ships at sea today on a fully automated programme.

Where to walk: The best walk is on your doorstep around Loop Head itself – keep the dog on a lead, as the cliffs are high. Further north is the spectacular Bridges of Ross cliff walk, which has some of the region's most intriguing geological features.

↑ A stunning sunset in County Clare

BUNRATTY CASTLE & FOLK PARK

Bunratty, County Clare
bunrattycastle.ie

The history around Bunratty goes way back beyond the 15th-century castle that now stands on the grounds. Vikings once traded here, and three other castles have since stood on the spot where the crenelated towers now loom. It's an impressive and well-preserved structure, but the most extraordinary sights at Bunratty are the various historic homes and dwellings that surround the castle.

What looks like a small village of old, sometimes ramshackle houses is in fact a living history museum: each building within the Folk Park has been plucked stone-by-stone from its original spot somewhere in Ireland and rebuilt here to preserve its place in history. From quaint thatched cottages painted in yellow to striking blue fishermen's houses and regal pink farmhouses, there is a charming array of architecture from the ages here.

You can walk in and out of the homes with the dog by your side, and in each one you might find a costumed actor performing traditional crafts or doing baking displays. There's lots for kids to get involved with, including a small animal farm, where you can meet pygmy goats and handsome Highland cattle. Imaginations will be set alight on the Fairy Trail through the woodland, and there's always much delight at the counter of the traditional sweet shop, where you can buy a bag of penny sweets to chomp as you drift around – think rhubarb and custards, lemon bonbons and chocolate mice.

A reconstructed village street has several shops, including a working post office and traditional public house –

↓ The author and Arty at Bunratty Folk Park

↓ Arty plays with fellow Manchester Terrier Brannagh on Doughmore Beach

there's Guinness on offer and the dog's allowed in, too – and you must seek out the two resident Irish wolfhounds, Meabh and Saoirse, for a photo opportunity with your own dog. A playground will keep the kids busy, and if you're lucky you might find a folk musician performing an impromptu song or two in the street.

BEACH

DOUGHMORE BEACH

 336

County Clare

There's nothing quite like a large, flat stretch of sand to let the dog race around on and Doughmore has that in droves. Next door to the rather ugly Trump International Hotel, it's a spectacular 2.5km of golden sand with undulating grassy dunes at its back. It'll take a good 80 minutes to walk from the southern

end to the northern and back, and when the tide is out you'll have a vast expanse of excellent compacted sand to play fetch on. You might even catch a glimpse of local horse riders enjoying the sea air, too. **Make a night of it:** Stay by the sea at Loop Head Lighthouse (see page 259). **Parking:** ///stably.outings.leader

WALK

DEVIL'S BIT LOOP

337

County Tipperary

START POINT: Devil's Bit Car Park (///habitation.forgetting.aspiration)
DISTANCE / TIME: circular 5km/1.5 hrs

With a gentle 200 metres of ascent, this moderate hill walk is a wonderful way to get great views over County Tipperary without too much sweat. You'll follow forestry tracks and gravel footpaths up on to Devil's Bit hillside, and skirt around its edges through lush woodland. Where the trees have been cleared by forest management, you'll get glimpses of the emerald countryside around you, and if you're feeling adventurous you can scramble on to the Devil's Bit rockface at the peak for an even better vantage point.

> **WHAT'S FOR LUNCH?**
> In nearby Templemore, One19 Coffee House (**instagram.com/ one19coffeehouse**) does cracking cheese toasties and sausage rolls, and pup-cups for the dog.

Need to know: Dogs can be off-lead but must be under control and return when called; directions on **alltrails.com**.

TAKE THE KIDS ON AN ADVENTURE AT CASTLECOMER DISCOVERY PARK 338

Drumgoole, County Kilkenny
discoverypark.ie

A thrilling day out for families, this adventure park has everything from ziplining to climbing walls. With the dog on a lead, you can try archery, orienteering or even axe-throwing, and if one of your family is happy to stay on the shoreline, the rest can give raft-building a go and get to test their creations out on the water. For a more sedate afternoon, you might prefer to try canoeing on the lake, which is surrounded by 80 acres of leafy woodland. **Make a night of it:** Stay nearby at Croan Cottages where pets are welcome with their families on a smallholding in the Kilkenny countryside. croancottages .com 🐕2 👤4-6 £200

GET WILD FOR THE NIGHT 339

Rathdrum, County Wicklow
tipiadventures.ie

If you were lost in the forest and had to stay overnight, alone with nothing but the dog by your side, would you know what to do to survive? Few people do, but the intrepid team at Tipi Adventures Ireland are the experts in outdoor skills and in their own private woodland near

↑ The mountains around Rathdrum

Rathdrum village, they will show you the ropes – and the dog can come, too.

Their courses are paired with an overnight adventure in the woods: there are tipis and trekking tents for extra comfort, but the most exciting accommodation by far is up in the trees. Choose a hammock or a tree tent and you'll get to snooze up high with the birds, who will wake you with their dawn chorus in the morning.

By day, after a restful night in the forest, you can choose from a range of courses. You might want to try traditional crafts, such as spoon carving or building a bushcraft chair, which you'll then get to take home. Or you can opt for something more involved: the fundamental outdoor skills workshop is three hours of survival skill essentials, from fire starting to harvesting water safely and responsibly. Whatever you choose, you can spend the rest of your time there testing out your newfound skills, or simply soaking up the birdsong in the woods.

Make a night of it: Stay on site in one of their brilliant tipis or tents set up within the woods.

STAY

WICKLOW HEAD LIGHTHOUSE

340

Wicklow, County Wicklow
irishlandmark.com

Built in 1781, Wicklow Head's original tower has seen some drastic changes to lighthouse technology over the centuries. Its light source initially came from 20 animal-fat candles reflected in a huge mirror, though it never got to upgrade to something more sophisticated as in 1836, lightning struck, destroying its insides. The tower remained but a new lighthouse was built closer to the cliffs, and so this one lay derelict for centuries until the Irish Landmark Trust took it on for renovation in the 1990s.

Today, it has two double bedrooms with amazing sea views – it's surrounded by ocean on three sides – and a cosy living area for board game nights over a bottle or two. If you're making your morning coffee, just don't forget the milk, as it's a 106-stair climb to the kitchen!

Where to walk: The most arresting walk in the area is from the lighthouse to the cliffs and along the coast to the town of Wicklow, around 3km each way. You can let the dog off-lead in Murrough Park on the seafront in Wicklow town.

WHAT'S NEARBY?
For excellent meals and somewhere you can dine inside with the dog, The Brass Fox in Wicklow (wicklow.thebrassfox.ie) serves excellent burgers, pizzas and fish and chips.

Need to know: As you might expect, there's quite a winding staircase in the tower so you might well need a head for heights. The lighthouse doesn't have a secure garden but there is a large grassy area around it where you can let the dog off-lead as long as it's kept under control and away from the cliffs.

GLENDALOUGH MINERS' ROAD WALK

County Wicklow

START POINT: Glendalough Lower Car Park
DISTANCE/TIME: 6km/1.5 hrs

One of several trails around the Glendalough area, the Miners' Road is one of the easiest. It's a point-to-point trail that skirts along the northern edge of the lake on a wide forest track and has utterly enrapturing views across the lake and the steep, forested hillsides that surround it.

> **WHAT'S FOR LUNCH?**
> Sit outside at Casey's Bar & Bistro (glendaloughhotel.com) next door to the car park.

There is easy access to the water from this trail, meaning dogs that love to swim can enjoy a refreshing dip and a drink, and you'll find a 150-year-old ruined miners' village at the end, left over from the lead and zinc extraction operations, before you turn back towards the car park.
Need to know: The route is waymarked but trail guides are available at the visitor centre or online at glendalough.ie. The trail is largely paved or gravel so is suitable for robust buggies and wheelchairs.

CRUISE PAST THE MIGHTY CLIFFS OF MOHER

County Clare doolinferry.com

The vertiginous Cliffs of Moher are one of Ireland's most spectacular sights: layers of sandstone, siltstone and shale

↓ A hiker overlooks the Glendalough Valley in County Wicklow

are piled up high – sometimes over 200 metres – to create a vertical cliff face that looms large over a vast Atlantic Ocean. It looks downright dangerous to stand on top of, and yet you'll see thousands of seabirds nesting here for breeding season in spring and summer, perching precariously on the tiny ledges with vertical drops beneath them.

You can, of course, walk along the cliffs via the visitor centre (cliffsofmoher .ie), but a far more awe-inspiring view is to be had from below. Board the Doolin Ferry and you'll sail right out to the cliffs, spotting puffins, guillemots and auks in the sea around you. This vantage point really shows off the scale of these towering cliffs and dramatic sea stacks that jut out along the 4km of coast.

The boat has both indoor and outdoor areas, making this an all-weather activity, and there's a live commentary offering insight into the surrounding area. Even in the soggiest of conditions, the cliffs are a truly astonishing sight – just be sure to bring your sea legs if the wind is getting up.

Make a night of it: Stay at the other end of the County Clare coastline just over an hour away in Loop Head, where the lighthouse keeper's cottage is a lovely getaway (see page 259).

(see page 259)

STAY

WOOD SMOKE AT AILLWEE MOUNTAIN

Ballycahill, County Clare
www.sawdays.co.uk/woodsmokecottage

Hidden away inside a hazel woodland in northern County Clare, Wood Smoke is a gorgeous little cottage escape just a few kilometres from the coast. The house

---

is all swish modern design with plenty of homely touches, but the best bit is outside: a wood-fired hot tub and sauna await amid the woods to warm you up on those chilly Irish days.

Where to walk: Dogs can enjoy the sands of Bishop's Quarter Beach (just a few kilometres away) throughout the spring, autumn and winter, and before 11am and after 6pm in summer. For a longer walk, try the Cappanawalla Loop (directions on alltrails.com), which has excellent sea views.

PLACE

BIRR CASTLE DEMESNE

Birr, County Offaly birrcastle.com

A castle has stood on the ground here since the Anglo-Norman period, but over the centuries it was besieged, ruined and rebuilt several times. Today, the fortress is a dramatic Gothic creation sitting sandwiched between parkland to the west and the town of Birr to the east. The grounds here make for wonderful walking, but most intriguing is the enormous Leviathan of Parsonstown telescope plonked amid the lawns. Designed and built right here by the 3rd Earl of Rosse in the 1840s, it was the largest telescope of its time, utilising reflection to present the night's sky to lucky observers. Head into the Science Centre on the castle grounds to understand more about how it works (no dogs inside, sadly).

NORTH IRELAND

365

364

363

*Glenveagh
National Park*

362

361

*Ballintroy
& Wild Nephin
National Park*

360

*Lough
Conn*

359

358

Carrick-On-Sharron

357

356

355 354

353

352

*Lough
Mask*

*Lough
Ree*

351

*Lough
Corrib*

350

349

345

Aran Islands

PLACE

THE ARAN ISLANDS

345

County Galway <u>aranislandferries.com</u>

Flung off the west coast of Ireland around 13km from the County Galway coastline, the Aran Islands is a gloriously remote archipelago of three limestone isles, each with its own character and unique community who have, over the centuries, divided the land by an extensive network of criss-crossing drystone walls. Getting here is half the adventure – ferries depart and return to Rossaveel daily with

↑ The dramatic cliffs of the Aran Islands

Dublin

connecting shuttle buses from Galway city – and while it's less than an hour by boat, you'll feel a world away from the mainland once arriving at the largest island, Inis Mór.

It was here that the award-winning 2022 film *The Banshees of Inisherin* was filmed, and you can follow in the footsteps of Colin Farrell and Brendan Gleeson by hiring bikes – and dog buggies, if necessary – to explore the island (**aranislandsbikehire.com**). Cycle to Dún Aonghasa, a prehistoric hillfort on the edge of a 100-metre-high cliff that was built over 3,000 years ago; this is where Padraic and Dominic shared a drink on numerous occasions in the film. The nearby village of Gort na gCapall is where the crew constructed Padraic's cottage, too.

Elsewhere, you can walk the dog on the white sands of Kilmurvey Beach or stand on the rocks to gaze over the 'Wormhole', a naturally formed, rectangular pool within the rocks on the southern edge of the island. It might look like an inviting swimming pool, but the undercurrents here are strong so don't let the dog jump in – any diving here should be left to the professionals who come for the Red Bull Cliff Diving World Series.

ZANZIBAR LOCKE

Dublin lockeliving.com

Few dog-friendly hotels have as great a city-centre location as hipster Zanzibar Locke, which sits right on Dublin's River Liffey at Ha'penny Bridge. This means it's a short walk across the water to the famous cobbled lanes of Temple Bar, where you can sample the city's favourite drink – Guinness – outside various traditional pubs that ring loud with live music at weekends.

The hotel has its own excellent bar and restaurant, though, which is dog-friendly and serves breakfast baps with plenty of vegan options and hearty lunches, and bedrooms are more than just a place to sleep. This aparthotel comes into its own for dog owners, as many of the city's restaurants still don't allow pets inside, so with a small kitchenette at your disposal you can have the flexibility of cooking for yourselves whenever you fancy. Book one of the rooftop rooms and you'll even get an enclosed balcony for the dog to enjoy a little outside space.

Where to walk: A 30-minute stroll along the river brings you to Phoenix Park (phoenixpark.ie), where the dog is allowed to be off-lead throughout, though do beware of deer and keep them under close control. Look out for the towering Wellington Monument and an 18th-century magazine fort, and across the river from Phoenix Park you can walk through the Irish National War Memorial Gardens with the dog on the lead. Head east to the coast to enjoy Howth Cliff Walk for a longer stroll (see opposite).

WHAT'S NEARBY?
Beyond the pubs of Temple Bar lies the lovely Iveagh Gardens (iveaghgardens.ie), a 20-minute stroll from the hotel on the south side of the Liffey, where waterfalls and sculptures and planted beds make a wonderful place to wander.

← Arty on the bed at Locke Zanzibar in Dublin

Need to know: The hotel only allows dogs under 20kg; you'll need to bring all your own dog gear as no bowls or beds are provided for dogs. Dublin gets incredibly busy on weekends at all times of year, so this is a stay for confident dogs used to crowds.

BEACH

DOLLYMOUNT STRAND

Dublin

Sitting on Bull Island in Dublin Bay, this spectacular stretch of sand is a brilliant place to walk with the dog, as it stretches for a full 5km along the east coast. Dogs must be kept on a lead due to its status as a nature reserve for waders in winter; bring your binoculars and you might well spot peregrine falcons and short-eared owls year-round, too.

Make a night of it: Stay in the city at nearby Zanzibar Locke (see opposite).
Parking: On the road that runs along the southern end of the island

↓ Heather and wildflowers lighting up the coast path around Howth

WALK

HOWTH CLIFF WALK

Dublin

START POINT: Howth DART Station
DISTANCE/TIME: circular 6km/2 hrs

Just outside Dublin centre lies the small coastal village of Howth, which sits on a peninsula of the same name. From the train station, you can follow waymarkers for this walk up on to the clifftops, where you'll get views of an endless sea and Lambay Island in the distance. Once you spot the Baily Lighthouse on Howth Head you'll know you're over halfway, as this marks your return through the village to the station.

> **WHAT'S FOR LUNCH?**
> Seafood tapas at Octopussy on Howth Pier (octopussy.ie) – book ahead if it's sunny; this place gets full fast.

Need to know: There are green waymarkers for this route so you needn't follow a map, but directions can be found at sportireland.ie.

DÚN NA SÍ HERITAGE AND AMENITY PARK

Aghanargit, County Westmeath
dunnasi.ie

If you're having a hard time convincing the kids to come out for a walk with the dog, the Amenity Park at Dún na Sí might just tempt them out. This gorgeous public park was once just a grazing common, but today it has a thriving population of birds within its wetlands, wooden walkways over marshes, and sculptures made by local students created with recycled materials. There's a butterfly garden, bird hides and two brilliant playgrounds for kids of all ages. Pick up a light lunch or a cake and coffee for your afternoon adventures from the on-site cafe.

GLENGOWLA MINES

Glengowla, County Galway
glengowlamines.rezgo.com

Glengowla Mines is a somewhat misleading name, as there's as much above ground as there is underground here. Set within a working family farm, there is indeed a deep, dark mineral mine that was abandoned in 1865, which you can tour with a guide to see marble caves and fluorite and quartz deposits. Up above, you can watch traditional turf cutting and sheepdog herding demonstrations on the farm and enjoy a stroll along the old railway line that once connected the city of Galway to the west coast.

↓ A shaft entrance at Glengowla Mines

GLASSON LAKEHOUSE

351

Killinure, County Westmeath
glassonlakehouse.ie

Just a short hop off the M6 between Dublin and Galway, the luxurious Glasson Lakehouse sits prettily on the shores of Lough Ree. Surrounded by the lush green lawns of its own golf course and overlooking a tiny inlet just off the south-west section of the vast, 105 sq km lake, it's a supremely popular spot for Ireland's city-dwellers seeking a quiet escape from the chaos of the capital, and even well-heeled Belfast folk have been known to fly down in their helicopters and land right on the hotel's waterfront for a weekend away.

There's no shortage of things to do here, as the hotel has its own activity hub, where you can hire motorboats or canoes to get out on to Lough Ree – pack a picnic to make a day of it – and there's a spa for when you feel in need of a little rejuvenation. Kids will love the on-site playground, while dogs are welcomed almost everywhere, including by the pool and at the private-hire, wooden hot tubs, where they can snooze in a bed by your side while you enjoy a soak with a glass of something special.

The dog-friendly rooms are all on the ground floor and have their own patios, where you can sit on loungers when the sun's out and the dog can sniff about in the manicured hedgerows. When you check in, you'll get bowls and a rope toy or ball for the dog to keep them entertained.

For a more secluded and serene experience away from the main hotel, request The Cabin when you book and you'll get to stay in a stylish, standalone wood cabin next to the sheep paddock, which has a copper rolltop bath on the decking and a gorgeous wood burner in the living room.

Where to walk: Hop in the car and head five minutes north to Portlick Millennium Forest to follow a series of waymarked trails that will take you alongside Lough Ree, across farmland and past a private medieval castle. You could walk for just

WHAT'S NEARBY?
The attractive medieval town of Athlone is a 10-minute drive from Glasson and there are guided walking tours with local experts who have the lowdown on local folklore and famous residents (athloneguidedtours.ie). Further afield and great for families is the Dún na Sí Amenity and Heritage Park (see opposite), where there are wildlife hides, kids' playgrounds and sculptures dotted around.

half an hour or take on a 5km route that takes around 90 minutes, and the dog can be off-lead along the way.

Need to know: Dogs can be left in the room if you'd like to dine in the restaurant area or at Tom's Fish & Tackle bar; otherwise, the lobby is the dog-friendly eating area. Dogs shouldn't be walked across the golf course greens, but you can amble down the lawns that lead to the waterside pontoons for a quick morning wee walk.

STAY

LOUGH INAGH LODGE 352

Connemara, County Galway
loughinaghlodgehotel.ie

This former fishing lodge – built in the late 1800s and once part of the Martin Estate owned by politician Richard Martin, who was known for his love of animals – has been turned into a welcoming hotel where the dog can join you for long walks by the lake and relax in the bedroom while you dine on local mussels, oysters served with Guinness or duck breast from a nearby farm.

WHAT'S NEARBY?
A 15-minute drive from the lodge is Kylemore Abbey, where an order of Benedictine nuns live within a Gothic nunnery and handsome walled gardens make for a wonderful afternoon stroll (see opposite), and north of Lough Inagh you can take the dog on boat tours of stunning Killary Fjord (see opposite).

Décor throughout the hotel is of its time, with rich red fabrics and dark-stained furniture providing a period feel to the property, and your days can be spent exploring the Connemara countryside or out on the water with a rod and line, luring salmon, sea trout and grilse.

Where to walk: There are endless wonderful walks on the doorstep here: head to Connemara National Park, where walks range from a simple 1km nature trail in Ellis Wood to a 7km hike around Diamond Hill, which affords views of the undulating Twelve Bens. For a coastal jaunt, head out to Renvyle Beach, a 25-minute drive west, which has wonderful mountain views and brilliant white sands (see page 274).

Need to know: As with many hotels in Ireland, dogs aren't allowed in the restaurant so they'll need to stay in the room or car while you dine.

KYLEMORE ABBEY

Pollacappul, County Galway
kylemoreabbey.com

Sitting on the edge of Pollacappul Lough, its turrets reflected in the glassy waters, there's little wonder an order of Benedictine nuns chose Kylemore Castle, as it was called before 1920, to become their new monastic home. The castle was built in the 19th century as the not-so-modest home of Galway MP Mitchell Henry, but it was left empty much of the time after his wife died in 1875, and so while fleeing World War I in Belgium, a group of nuns founded their abbey here and it now sits in near-silence amid a thousand-acre estate.

A trot around its footpaths and trails will introduce you to some of the finest woodlands in Connemara – the name Kylemore is taken from the Irish 'Coill Mór', which means 'big wood', after all. The forest is so lush here it's classed as a coastal temperate rainforest, and native and non-native trees create a spectacular canopy to walk beneath. To see some of the finest specimens, follow the Tree Trail, which passes through an avenue of nine lanky pines standing to attention and explores woodlands with ash, horse chestnut, spruce and African blue Atlas cedar trees.

Closer to the abbey itself, a stroll around the Victorian walled garden is another delightful diversion. The 6-acre space has formal flower gardens, glasshouses, rockeries, lime kilns and herbaceous borders. There's a kitchen garden where you can see seasonal vegetables growing, and a fabulous fernery, all overlooked by the charming head gardener's home. Before you leave, don't miss an opportunity to stock up on local produce from the shop and cafe, where the head chef makes a luxuriously smooth ice cream.

CRUISE ALONG A GLORIOUS GLACIAL FJORD

County Galway killaryfjord.ie

There are just three glacial fjords in Ireland but none is as spectacular as Killary, a 16km ravine carved out by melting glaciers

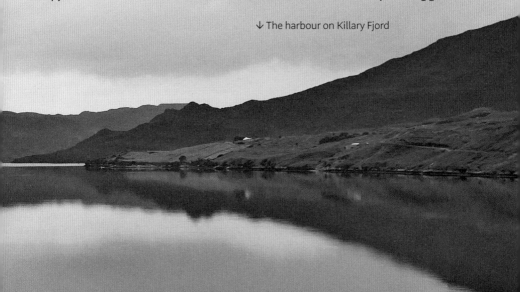

↓ The harbour on Killary Fjord

around 2 million years ago that now sits beneath the waters of the Atlantic Ocean. The fjord is surrounded by the dramatic peaks of the Twelve Bens and the Mweelrea Massif in County Mayo to the north, and the Maumturks Mountains rise above the land in County Galway to the south. On its shores lie abandoned famine villages that were left behind by hungry residents in the mid-1800s.

Join a Killary Fjord Boat Tours trip on the *Connemara Lady* and you'll see it all from the water, with an expert guide on board to talk you through the geology and Irish mythology, including the love triangle legend of Diarmuid and Grainne. You might spot dolphins in the water and seals on the shoreline, while occasionally otters can be seen scuttling along the rocks.

On board, you can enjoy a pint of Guinness and a bowl of local mussels in the restaurant as you sail past the ropes where they're grown, and you'll spot salmon leaping from their circular farms in the sea.

Make a night of it: Stay inland at Lough Inagh Lodge (see page 272), where more watery adventures await.

BEACH

RENVYLE BEACH

County Galway

A striking crescent of white sand split in two by a rocky outcrop, Renvyle Beach is a north-facing stretch with crystalline waters and spectacular views of Mweelrea Mountain and the islands of Inishturk and Clare. There are no facilities here, so bring your own picnic and enjoy this gorgeous, quiet stretch on the Galway coast.

Make a night of it: Stay inland at Lough Inagh Lodge (see page 272) just 20 minutes away.

Parking: At the end of Tully Beg road, which leads to the beach

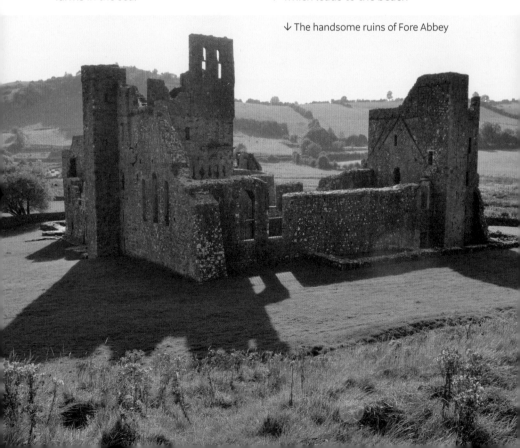

↓ The handsome ruins of Fore Abbey

FORE ABBEY

356

Fore, County Westmeath

heritageireland.ie

Few places in Ireland are as atmospheric as Fore Abbey, a towering grey ruin amid a bright green landscape of lush grass and wooded hills – especially when it's a little drizzly and grey outside. As you wander in and out of the remains of the old abbey, which was founded in the 7th century by St Féchín, it's hard to imagine that it once bustled with 300 monks as its peak. Spend an hour or so here with the dog, soaking up its tranquil spirit.

TULLYNALLY CASTLE

357

Castlepollard, County Westmeath tullynallycastle.ie

This immense castle started life as a simple, square plantation house built by Henry Pakenham in the 1730s. But several owners and a couple of centuries later and today it's a warren of grand staterooms, great halls and Victorian kitchens. Come here with the dog and you can walk around the forest glades and formal gardens, which date back over 200 years but have been updated by current owner Thomas Pakenham and his late wife, Valerie. Look out for the llamas in the paddock by the castle, and don't miss climbing up to the top of the viewing mound to look over the bucolic estate.

↓ Boats bobbing on the River Shannon

TAKE A SELF-DRIVE CRUISE ON THE RIVER SHANNON

358

County Leitrim emeraldstar.ie

The River Shannon is Ireland's longest waterway, stretching all the way from County Cavan and draining into the Atlantic at Limerick, 260km to the south. It has long been one of the most important rivers in Ireland, connecting the west coast to the city of Dublin via the Grand Canal, and it was used for transporting the country's biggest export, Guinness, among other things. The river is a haven for wildlife with wetlands and marshes surrounding its banks, and wends its way through villages, towns and cities such as medieval Athlone and charming Drumod before it widens out in sections to feed vast lakes, including the enormous Lough Ree.

Exploring the river by boat is by far one of the greatest pleasures in Ireland: cruising on its quiet stretches between towns, watching kingfishers and herons feeding on its bountiful fish, and stopping for a swim in the lakes makes for a wonderful week away in one of Emerald Star's cruisers. The vessels come in varying sizes, from nippy little three-berths to party boats that sleep ten people and come with top-deck barbecues and sunbeds on the bow.

Boat hire is from Carrick-on-Shannon, a lively little town in County Leitrim, and from here you can head north towards Lough Key, where moorings are available at the verdant Forest Park (see below). Alternatively, head southwards and you'll find yourselves in the handsome village of Drumod, where dog-friendly pubs and wonderful riverside walks abound. Kids will love taking charge at the automated lock system on the Shannon, and dogs will enjoy plenty of towpath strolls when they're not snoozing on deck.

DRUMMANS ISLAND TRAIL

359

County Roscommon

START POINT: F52 PY66
DISTANCE/TIME: circular 1.5km/1 hr

The Drummans Island Trail is one of many in Lough Key Forest Park, a beautiful 19th-century park and forest with a smattering of adventurous activities on offer for families, from kayaking to orienteering to climbing and a few indoor activities, too. It starts by tracing along the lakeside from the car park and then into the forest, where huge broadleaf trees and conifers provide a welcome canopy when the sun is shining.

You'll walk through the awe-inspiring Red Cedar Grove, where the trees can tower up to 60 metres above you, and then pass over the quirky 19th-century 'fairy bridge', which looks as if the stone has been carved into unusual curvy shapes. The limestone was, in fact, quarried from the lake, so its curvature is thanks to the flow of the water rather than any man-made endeavour. Once across the bridge, you're on Drummans Island, where you'll walk along the shoreline again – look out for kingfishers and moorhens on the water. You will

then turn inland through the Bog Garden, which is made traversable by wooden boardwalks, and head back over the bridge and along the trail once again.

> **WHAT'S FOR LUNCH?**
> You can sit outside at the on-site cafe or bring a picnic to enjoy on the benches by the lake.

Need to know: The site is privately owned and run so there's a small fee to get in (contactless payment available); dogs must be on a lead throughout the forest park.

↓ Arty on the Drummans Island Trail

THE LETTER-HEAD LOOP, WILD NEPHIN NATIONAL PARK

360

Wild Nephin National Park
nationalparks.ie

START POINT: Letterkeen Trailhead
(///befriend.rhythms.rhythms)
DISTANCE/TIME: 12km/3 hrs

There's over 150 sq km of wilderness to explore in Wild Nephin National Park, which spreads itself across the west coast of County Mayo in a landscape of mountains, alpine heathland and lakes, and it is home to one of the few preserved active blanket bogs in Western Europe. This trail loops around a small 200-metre-high hill in the southern side of the national park and you'll walk through thick forestry, over boardwalks on bogs and along riverbanks, with beautiful views throughout. At its highest point, the trail reaches 311 metres and there are expansive views of the surrounding hills and mountains, including of Nephin Beg's 681-metre-high peak. Once beyond this, you'll find it's a pleasant downhill walk back to the car park on the second half of the hike.

WHAT'S FOR LUNCH?
This is a wild and remote area so you'll need to bring a picnic if you want to eat during your hike. Otherwise, hearty meals can be had at Cobbler's Bar & Courtyard (wyatthotel.com) in Westport, a 30-minute drive south of the trailhead.

Need to know: The route is waymarked by purple arrows, but some waymarkers may be missing. To be safe, download directions from alltrails.com. It can be boggy so good boots are necessary. Dogs must be kept on a lead at all times.

PORTBEG HOLIDAY HOMES

361

Bundoran, County Donegal
portbegholidayhomes.com

Set along the Wild Atlantic Way on the west coast of Ireland, this collection of modern seaside holiday homes in Bundoran make a budget beach break. The Marine View townhouses are the most dog-friendly, sleeping up to six

↑ A dog enjoying the beach along the Wild Atlantic Way

with their own enclosed gardens, and you can walk from here to the soft yellow sands of little Bundoran Beach or vast Tullan Strand for seaside fun.

Where to walk: The Rougey Cliff Walk, between Bundoran Beach and Tullan Strand, is a glorious stroll and can be made circular by heading back along Tullan Strand Road.

PLACE

BE AWED BY THE SLIABH LIAG CLIFFS

County Donegal
atlanticcoastalcruises.com

Killybegs Harbour and the wider Donegal Bay is a stunning part of Ireland's

↑ The drama of the Sliabh Liag cliffs

coastline, pockmarked with tiny inlets and flanked by a pair of lighthouses that have kept mariners safe for well over 100 years. The highlight on an Atlantic Coastal Cruises trip, though, is the geology: the Sliabh Liag cliffs, towering up to 600 metres above the ocean, are some of the highest in Europe and are always an arresting sight when seen from below, while across the bay you'll pass the otherworldly rock formation of Benbulbin in County Sligo's Dartry Mountains.

Look out for dolphins breaching in the waters beneath the cliffs, or see seals lolling about on the rocks. Basking sharks are regular visitors to these waters, too, and seabirds such as gannets and kittiwakes abound in the cliffs' crevices, nesting throughout summer.

Make a night of it: It's less than an hour's drive to the lovely Lusty Beg Island Resort (see page 235) in Northern Ireland.

THE GLEN TRAIL

Glenveagh National Park

nationalparks.ie

START POINT: Glenveagh Castle
DISTANCE/TIME: 16km/4 hrs there and back

It's near impossible to get lost on this lovely long walk through the middle of Glenveagh National Park, as it follows a largely straight bridle path alongside Lough Veagh, the largest lake in this 16,000-hectare national park.

The trail affords glorious views of the lake and its surrounding mountains and passes through a number of abandoned settlements left behind as residents sought fortune elsewhere.

Bring your binoculars to look out for the park's feathery predators: peregrines, sparrowhawks, kestrels, merlin and even golden eagles could be spotted. And look out for red deer and Irish hare as you walk, especially on the mountainsides across the water from the bridle path. If you're incredibly lucky, you might even spot an elusive otter.

At the southern end of the lake you'll continue to follow the Owenacoo River and the terrain begins to gently ascend for the last few kilometres. You can turn back at any time, but if you go all the way to the end, you'll find the path meets the R254.

WHAT'S FOR LUNCH?

There's a cafe in the visitor centre, though the dog isn't allowed inside so you'll need to get takeaway to eat outdoors, or you can enjoy homemade cakes and scones from the tearoom at the castle (outside only for dogs).

Need to know: The Trail Walker Bus connects the national park visitor centre and car park to the beginning of the bridle path trail at the castle; if you prefer to walk the extra section, it's an added 2km each way. Dogs must be kept on leads throughout the national park.

WHAT'S FOR LUNCH?
There's a small cafe in the car park, but for something more substantial, bring a picnic and choose a bench along the route.

WALK

ARDS FOREST PARK LOOP

County Donegal

START POINT: F92 PK3V
DISTANCE/TIME: 5.5km/1.5 hrs

There are several different trails to follow in Ards Forest Park, including an all-abilities path that means wheelchair users and those with pushchairs can get out and enjoy the woodland. This walk

encompasses the best bits of the forest park, though, with beaches, sand dunes, bogs and forest tracks all in one hike.
Need to know: The park is owned by Coillte so there's a small entry charge per car but contactless payment is available, and it does mean there's a great kids' playground on-site. Get directions on alltrails.com; dogs must be on a lead according to Coillte rules.

BEACH

MARBLE HILL STRAND

County Donegal

One of the northernmost beaches in Ireland, Marble Hill is a sublime stretch of white sand that, at low tide, seems to go on forever before you reach the shoreline. It's about 300 metres deep and a kilometre wide, and is a fantastic family-friendly beach with calm water for swimming and occasionally good surf for those with boards and wetsuits. Get coffee, cake and ice cream from Shack Coffee (facebook.com/ShackCoffee.ie) and look out for the sauna trailer that occasionally sets up on the adjacent road.
Make a night of it: Stay in the unique railway carriages, glamping tents or converted boats at Corcreggan Mill. corcreggan.com 🐕1 🚻 <£100
Parking: Marble Hill Court

← A lough in Glenveagh National Park

INDEX OF PLACES

H

I

J

K

L

M

N

PICTURE CREDITS

All photos belong to the author with the exception of:

CANOPY AND STARS 89, 104, 106, 129, 142–3, 143 bottom, 146, 147, 149, 150, 151, 152, 169, 193 top, 199, 203

GETTY 10, 17, 19, 20–1, 22, 24–5, 28, 29, 31, 33, 34–5, 36, 38, 40–1, 42, 43, 47, 49, 50, 51, 52–3, 60, 62–3, 65, 71, 77, 78–9, 80, 83, 85, 86–7, 90, 91, 92, 93, 95, 99, 100, 100, 101, 102, 105, 107, 109, 110–11, 121, 122, 131, 135, 138, 139, 141, 154, 155, 156–7, 159, 160, 161, 162–3, 166–7, 171, 176, 177, 178–9, 179 bottom, 180–1, 180 bottom, 184, 185, 186–7, 188–9, 192–3, 194, 195, 196–7, 198, 200, 201, 205, 209, 212–13, 214–15, 215 bottom, 216, 220, 223, 225 bottom, 233, 236, 237, 239, 240, 241, 243, 244–5, 247, 249, 250, 251, 252, 254–5, 256–7, 258, 259 top, 259 bottom, 262–3, 264, 267, 269, 270, 272–3, 274, 275, 276, 278, 279, 280–1, 288

MATT LAWRENCE PHOTOGRAPHY 69

PAWS AND STAY 27, 32, 57, 58 top, 58 bottom, 75, 76, 165, 175

SAWDAYS 54, 118, 132–3, 206, 207, 218 top, 218 bottom, 219, 248

This book has been produced in association with:

Sawday's

www.sawdays.co.uk
Sawday's have been personally inspecting and recommending characterful hotels, inns, B&Bs and self-catering places across the UK and Europe for more than 25 years.

CANOPY & STARS

www.canopyandstars.co.uk
Canopy & Stars, Sawday's younger sibling, takes things outside, going in search of treehouses, cabins and yurts that give guests space to live a life more wild.

paws & stay

www.pawsandstay.co.uk
Paws & Stay is the puppy of the family, created in 2021 as the UK's only dog-first travel website, to help people find places where both they and their dogs would be warmly welcomed.